EQUIPPED FOR THE END-TIMES

TEN VITAL PRINCIPLES FOR HIGH IMPACT LEADERSHIP

DR. AL NUCCIARONE

ISBN 978-965-7542-89-7

Editing and Lay-out:
Billie Nucciarone, Petra van der Zande, Tsur Tsina Publications, Jerusalem, Israel.

Photo Credits: Cover picture: Free Bible Images www.freebibleimages.org Internet, Nucciarone family private pictures, Petra van der Zande

Order information:
https://www.lulu.com/en/us/shop/dr-albert-nucciarone/equipped-for-the-end-times/paperback/product-6kryp5.html?page=1&pageSize=4
https://www.lulu.com/spotlight/tsura

www.tsurtsinapublications.com

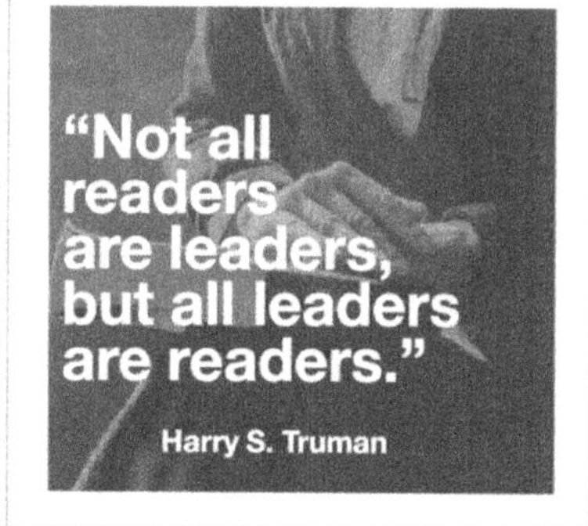

DEDICATION

I would like to dedicate this book to four people who have greatly impacted my life.

Dr. **Billy Graham** is my spiritual father.
On June 25, 1970 I went to his crusade at Shea Stadium in New York. No one invited me, I just read about it in the newspaper. It was a divine appointment. I heard the Gospel from this great man and put my trust in Christ. Dr. Graham is now with the Lord. He said, "If people tell you I died, don't believe it. I just changed addresses." I praise God for the legacy he has left for many generations.

Dr. **Luis Palau**, another great evangelist, is known as the Billy Graham of South America.
I have met him on several occasions in the States and in Europe. When I was at Dallas Seminary, a group of six students got together with him and we prayed for four hours. He was the main speaker at the mission's conference that year, and it was there that I committed my life to serve the Lord overseas. In a book written about his life, it says that when his father died, his mother constantly encouraged her children to "preach the Gospel and plant churches." That was his mission.
My wife and I had a chance to visit with him and pray with him in August of 2019. I invited him to Israel for a tour and he really wanted to come, but he never made it. A few months ago, he went to be with His Lord. He went to a better place.

> "I am sure of this, that He who started
> a good work in you will carry it on to
> completion until the day of Christ Jesus."
>
> Philippians 1:6 Holman

Korky Davey I consider to be the foremost street preacher in the world.

The staff evangelist for Open Air Campaigners has trained Christian workers all over the world. I first met him in Milan, Italy where he taught our workers on how to use the sketch-board to communicate the Gospel. When we moved to Vienna, I invited Korky to come and train local believers to reach out in the open air. What an impact he has had. His vision, enthusiasm, and love for the Gospel are infectious.

Irene Levi - I consider her to be the greatest saint in Jerusalem.

She has lived in Israel for more than 70 years. She was a teacher, a Hebrew scholar, a lover of the church and a lover of Jews and Arabs. At the age of 101, she continues to praise the Lord. She is my example and my spiritual mother.

FOREWORD

Solomon said. "And furthermore, my son, be admonished: of making many books there is no end; and much study is a weariness of flesh" (Ecclesiastes 12:12). That is true of most books, but the Bible is a book you can never get tired of reading or studying. God has preserved His Word. One of my dreams in life was to write a book. Now I have written four. I have enjoyed doing it. I find it exciting to share with others what God has taught me. It also helps to exercise my own mind.

In writing books, I have been guided by great people and great concepts. Professor Hendricks at Dallas Seminary encouraged us to write books and to write them in simple terms so that teenagers can understand. He was a master communicator. The founder of Reader's Digest was an impatient reader. He wanted to start a publication that had concise, simple, and picturesque articles.

When a series of *Idiot Guides* or *Books for Dummies* came out - like *The Complete Idiots Guide for the Middle East Conflict* - I knew those were the kind of books I needed to read. These illustrated books are written with simplicity and humor. Humor is a way to communicate truth while bringing down walls of defense. Aristotle said, "*Man does not think without an image or a picture.*"

Educating the mind without educating the heart is no education at all.

—Aristotle

This book, as well as my other books, was done in collaboration with our church's media director, Petra Van der Zande, an accomplished writer, editor, and publisher. I basically write the book, my wife, Billie, edits it, and Petra does the rest. We share the same philosophy:
We want our books to be easy to read, well structured, and well-illustrated.
If you are looking for a scholarly treatise, you will not find it here.
Our goal is that the book be Biblically based and speak to the mind in understandable concepts and to the heart to encourage us to keep loving and serving the Lord.

Dr. Albert Nucciarone
Jerusalem, June 2021

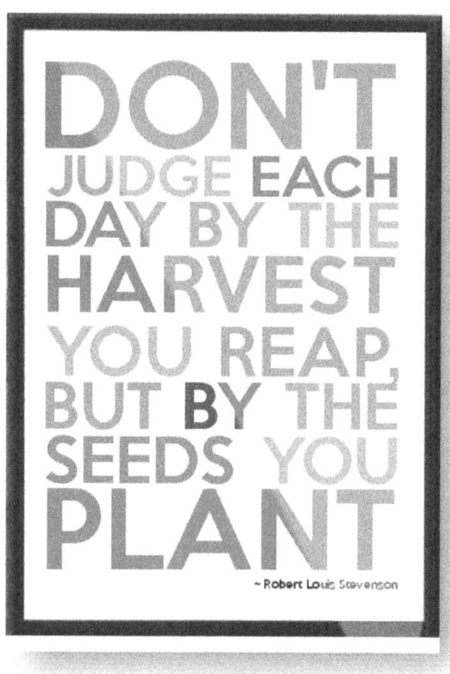

Table of Contents

Table of Contents Continued

Table of Contents Continued

> "The walk of faith
> is designed to be a walk of adventure,
> filled with periodic
> and delightful surprises –
> watch for them!"

Table of Contents Continued

Table of Contents Continued

Table of Contents Continued

"Either read or get out of the Ministry!"

John Wesley

INTRODUCTION

Another book on leadership! Why?

Well, let me explain. A few years ago, I was at a leadership conference with over 3,000 people in attendance in the country of Thailand.

The theme was pastoral or church leadership. The main idea presented was that a leader influences a church and a church influences society. Jesus taught this too. He said that as believers we are the light of the world and the salt of the earth. We bring truth and help to preserve society.   I think we all agree that society needs to be preserved today, especially since all signs point to the fact that the Lord is coming soon!

To deal with the present situation, we need leaders who are moral, honest, authentic, courageous, and seekers of God. We need men like the 200 leaders from the tribe of Issachar who understood the times and knew what Israel should do (I Chronicles 12:32). The Bible speaks of the difficulty of finding a good and faithful man (Proverbs 20:6). Who is the person that God can use to be a true world changer? Some say that leaders are born. Of course, we were all born. However, God has also chosen, called, and gifted certain individuals whom He wants to use. In a special way, we are all leaders whether we are mothers, fathers, presidents, company leaders, coaches, etc. But we must prepare ourselves if we sense God is calling us to lead.

> *"I will prepare myself*
> *and my time will come."*
> Abraham Lincoln

He read, studied, interacted with people and honed his speaking abilities. Billy Graham, the great evangelist, prepared for his future preaching ministry by selling Fuller brushes, and he practiced preaching in the woods. He would preach to the toads, the birds, and fish, (just for practice).

LEADERSHIP has been defined as influence, whether it is for good or for bad. It is the key to changing society. If you have good leadership in government, in business, in sports, or in religion, you can be assured of good success. Our goal, however, is not good success but great success.

> "The good is the enemy of the best."
> Jim Collins

Jim Colins, a leadership expert, wrote a book entitled *Good to Great: Why Some Companies Make the Leap and others Don't*. He examined businesses that were overwhelmingly successful because they sought greatness not just goodness.

Especially in the end times we need good leadership when expecting the soon return of Jesus. This should motivate us to occupy until He comes as He said in Luke 19.

The purpose of this book is to show the need for good leadership in the end times and to give 10 vital principles that can inform us and motivate us to be the leaders God wants us to be. It includes sections on great Biblical leaders and other leaders in the history of the church. We can also learn from secular leaders in every field who have led successful business, teams, and organizations. I will also share about some of the men who have mentored me either in person or through their books and messages.

The book ends with a vision and a plan that I believe can be used by God to bring change to this world.
However, in order to change the world we must first change ourselves.

Pastor Al Nucciarone
Jerusalem, Israel,
June 2021

Leadership Definition

1) 'The action of leading a group of people or an organization'; 'the state or position of being a leader' (NODE, 2001). The New Oxford Dictionary of English

2) 'The office or position of a leader, the capacity to lead, and the act or instance of leading' (Merriam-Webster, 2007).

3) "Leadership is the art of getting someone else to do something you want done because he wants to do it." Dwight D Eisenhower (1988)

4) 'An interaction between two or more members of a group that often involves a structuring or restructuring of the situation and the perceptions and expectations of members'.

5) 'The process of persuasion or example by which an individual (or leadership team) induces a group to pursue objectives held by the leader and his or her followers'.

6) 'A learnable set of practices'.

Many others have defined leadership in terms of behaviors, traits, competencies, activities and results of leaders.

The 5 Essential Qualities of a Great Leader:

1. Clarity
2. Decisiveness
3. Courage
4. Passion
5. Humility

The 7 Functions of Leadership:

1. Setting Goals
2. Organizing
3. Initiating Action
4. Co-Ordination
5. Direction and Motivation
6. Link between Management and Workers
7. Improving Motivation and Morale
8. Motivating Power to Group Efforts

PRINCIPLE 1

COMING AGAIN OF JESUS THE MESSIAH

One of the greatest themes in the Bible is the doctrine of the second coming of Jesus, the Messiah. The fact that we know Jesus is coming back should motivate us to serve the Lord and desire to have a high impact on society.   R.A. Torry the great pastor and evangelist, wrote about the lack of emphasis on this teaching in his book *The Return of Christ*. He emphasized these basics: Salvation, the Power of the Holy Spirit, World evangelization, and the Coming of the Lord.
Oswald J. Smith, famous pastor of the People's Church in Toronto wrote a book *The Man God Uses* in which he stated that he believed that the man or woman that God wants to use must be committed to three principles: The victorious Christian life, world evangelization, and the second coming of the Lord.

The importance of the second coming is seen in the fact that there are more verses in the Bible about the second coming of Christ than about His first coming. My book, *The Soon Return of Jesus the Messiah: Are you Ready?* talks about the prophecies about His first and second comings. Jesus taught us to look for His coming. The Bible gives us signs which we should look for which indicate His return is soon. Here are some significant signs of His second coming in recent news events.

THE SIGN OF ISRAEL

ISRAEL: THEIR DISPERSION

The modern state of Israel is a sign of Jesus' soon return. It is a miracle in itself. The Jews are God's beloved chosen people and they were promised a land and a people according to Genesis 12.

Under King David they became a monarchy and a nation. However, because of their disobedience they were scattered around the world. This was according to Scripture. Deuteronomy 28:64-68 speaks of the Lord scattering Israel among the nations. Because they worshipped other gods, they would find no repose or resting place for the soles of their feet. They would be anxious, and their eyes would be weary with longing, and they would have despairing hearts.

They would live in constant suspense and would be filled with dread, not sure of their life. They would see terror constantly. They would even offer themselves as slaves. This has already happened. In fact, it has happened twice. The first time they went into captivity in Babylon and again after Titus of Rome destroyed Jerusalem in 70 AD and the Jews were dispersed around the world.

THE RETURN OF THE JEWS TO ISRAEL

The return of the Jews to the land of Israel is also a sign that the return of Jesus is near. Here are three clear prophecies about their return.

1.	We read in Jeremiah 31:8-11 that God will bring Israel back to their land before the return of Jesus, *"See , I will bring them from the land of the north and gather them from the ends of the earth. Among them will be the blind and the lame, expectant mothers and women in labor; a great throng will return. They will come with weeping: they will pray as I bring them back. I will lead them beside streams of water on a level path where they will not stumble, because I am Israel's father, and Ephraim is my firstborn son. Hear the word of the Lord, O nations; proclaim it in distant coast lands: He who scattered Israel will gather them and will watch over his flock like a shepherd. For the Lord will ransom Jacob and redeem them from the hand of those stronger than they."*

This has already happened and is continuing to happen as Jews are still returning to Israel in large numbers.

2.   Jeremiah, the prophet, also gave us this prediction saying, *"You are saying about his city, 'By the sword, famine and plague it will be handed over to the king of Babylon,' but this is what the Lord, the God of Israel, says: I will surely gather them from all the lands where I banish them in my furious anger and great wrath ; I will bring them back to this place and let them live in safety. They will by my people, and I will be their God. I will give them singleness of heart and action, so that they will always fear me for their own good and the good of their children after them. I will make an everlasting covenant with them: I will never stop doing good to them, and I will inspire them to fear me, so that they will never turn away from me. I will rejoice in doing them good and will assuredly plant them in this land with all my heart and soul. This is what the Lord says: As I have brought all this great calamity on this people, so I will give them all the prosperity I have promised them."* (Jeremiah 32:36-42).

3.   The prophet Ezekiel affirmed this: *"and says to them, this is what the Sovereign Lord says: I will take the Israelites out of the nations where they have gone. I will gather them from all around and bring them back into their own land. I will make them one nation in the land, on the mountains of Israel. There will be one king over them and will never again be two nations*

or divided into two kingdoms." (Ezekiel 37:21,22).
These prophecies have already been fulfilled and are continuing to be fulfilled as Jews are still returning to Israel in large numbers.

ISRAEL, A NATION BORN IN A DAY

ZIONISTS PROCLAIM NEW STATE OF ISRAEL;
TRUMAN RECOGNIZES IT AND HOPES FOR PEACE;
TEL AVIV IS BOMBED, EGYPT ORDERS INVASION

Israel was established as a sovereign nation on May 14, 1948, recognized by the USA. other nations, and the UN.

This was the fulfillment of Isaiah 66:8 which says, *"Who has ever heard of such a thing? Who has ever seen such things? Can a country be born in a day or a nation be brought forth in a moment? Yet no sooner is Zion in labor than she gives birth to her children."*

ISRAEL TO SPEAK ONE LANGUAGE

Never before in history has a nation restored an ancient language. But Israel did. It happened when, Jews began arriving in Israel from all over the world and settled next to the Jews who were already in the land, most of whom were Arabic-speaking. All switched to use Hebrew as a *lingua franca*. Ben Yehuda is often viewed as the "reviver of the Hebrew language." [1]

An interesting fact about Ben Yehuda is that he insisted that his son, Ben Zion, be raised entirely in Hebrew, even berating his wife for singing a Russian lullaby to him. So, Ben Zion became the first native speaker of modern Hebrew with the language as his mother tongue. Hebrew is now the language of the nation of Israel.

---

[1] Wikipedia: Revival of the Hebrew language.

Zephaniah 3:9, predicted this. *"Then will I purify the lips of the peoples, that all of them may call on the name of the Lord and serve him shoulder to shoulder."*

ISRAEL BLOOMING LIKE A ROSE

Isaiah 35:1,2 gives us this description of Israel in the last days, *"The desert and the parched land will be glad; and the wilderness will rejoice and blossom. Like the crocus, it will burst into bloom; it will rejoice greatly and shout for joy. The glory of Lebanon will be given to it, and the splendor of Carmel and Sharon; they will see the glory of the Lord, and the splendor of our God."*

Lebanon, Carmel and Sharon are places well known for their lush beauty. [2] This is remarkable because in the 19th century Israel was a wasteland. After visiting Israel, Mark Twain described the country as, "a desolate country, given over wholly to weeds, a desolation. hardly a tree or shrub anywhere. We never saw a human being on the whole route."

Jesus said in his famous Olivet discourse, that when the twigs of the fig tree get tender and the leaves come off, you know that summer is near. In the same way, when these things happen the coming of the Lord is near (Matthew 32-36).

If you come to Israel today you will see the prosperity and fruitfulness of the country. The deserts bloom with trees and fruits (As Isaiah prophesied in Isaiah 35:1 and Isaiah 43:19-20).

Vineyards and forests cover much of the northern part of Israel and around Jerusalem. Of course, water is essential for fruitfulness.

The highest amount of rainfall occurred in 1948. This is remarkable.

Israeli desert agriculture

---

2 From Sermon Writer by Richard Donovan

There will be much rainfall in the last days as predicted by the prophet in Ezekiel 34:26-27, *"I will bless them and the places surrounding my hill. I will send down showers in season; there will be showers of blessing. The trees of the field will yield their fruit and the ground will yield its crops;..."*

ISRAEL AND THE JEWISH PEOPLE: Proof of God and the Bible [3]

In the 17th century, Louis XIV, King of France, asked Blaise Pascal, the great philosopher and thinker, to give him proof that there was a God. Pascal replied, "Why the Jews, your Majesty—the Jews."
Truly, the Jews are proof that there is a God. They have survived a 2000-year diaspora yet have remained distinct. No other people on earth have remained a distinct people. Do you ever hear of any Hittites, Jebusites, or Canaanites today? No. These people have not survived or remained distinct.

The Jews were driven from their homeland, scattered around the world, returned to their homeland, reestablished a state, and revived an ancient language. The Bible said that they would not cease to exist as a people (Jeremiah 31:35-37), and they have not. They were scattered around the world according to Deuteronomy 28:64, but they did not cease to exist as a people. It says in Genesis 12:3 that *"All the nations of the world will be blessed through you."* This has been fulfilled by the fact that Jewish people have been pioneers in medicine, technology, agriculture and science. As a people they have had more Nobel prizes proportionally than any other people.

They have also given us the Tanach or Old Testament, which has added moral value to our world and has fostered democracies, human dignity, peace, education, and honesty. Judeo-Christian values have been the bedrock of Western Civilization. God has also shown favor and blessing to nations which have blessed Israel and the Jews (Genesis 12:3). The United States is one such nation which has blessed the Jews throughout its history.

---

[4] Booklet, *Supernatural or Just Remarkable?* (Medabrim.org)

In spite of wars like the War of independence, the 6-day war, and the Yom Kippur war, Israel has miraculously survived (Micah 4:11-13). These facts all demonstrate that God exists, and that the Bible is true. We can trust God as our Lord and King.

THE INDESTRUCTIBLE JEWS

In a very revealing booklet, *The Indestructible Jews,* Max I. Dimont shares some amazing thoughts. He states,
- The King of Egypt could not Diminish Him (Exodus 1:9-12)
- The Waters of the Red Sea could not Drown Him ((Exodus 14:13-31)
- The Gallows of Haman could not Hang Him (Esther 5:14; 7:10;8)
- The Great Fish could not Digest Him (Jonah 1:17; 2:10)
- The Fiery Furnace could not Destroy Him (Daniel 3:16-28)
- The Lions of Babylon could not Devour Him (Daniel 6:3-28)
- Balaam could not Curse Him (Numbers 23:7,8)
- The Nations of the World could not Assimilate Him (Esther 3:8, Numbers 23:9; Deut. 33:27-29; Exodus 33:12-16
- The Dictators of the Nations cannot Annihilate Him (Isa. 14:1-5; Zech. 8:23,23).

Why is the Jew indestructible one may ask? Because God has promised that he will make them a great nation and will bless them and anyone who blesses them will be blessed and anyone who curses them will be cursed (Genesis 12:1-3, 22:18). God will not cast off the seed of Israel. His covenant will not be broken with David His servant who will have a son to reign upon the throne (Jeremiah 30:11, 31:35-37, 33:20-26).

The secret of this indestructibility is that God will bring into this destructible world an indestructible Savior, Jesus the Messiah. He will reign over the house of Jacob forever and His kingdom will never end (Rev. 19:16, Luke 1:31-33, Isaiah 9:6,7). He will bring peace on the earth (Isaiah 2:2-4).

The author concludes,

"Why is the Jew indestructible? Because the Jew is the vortex of all the plans and purposes of God, for the good of the whole human race, and if the Jew could be destroyed, then all of God's plans and purposes could be brought to an end by finite man which is unthinkable."

We must see why the nation of Israel is indestructible, and then turn to the Lord, in faith believing.

The city of Jerusalem is a significant element in God's prophetic plan.

THE SIGN OF JERUSALEM

Psalm 122 directs us to pray for the peace of Jerusalem. In Ezekiel 9, the prophet tells us that those who groan and weep for the sins of Jerusalem receive a mark. This mark protects them from judgement and destruction.

Christ's prayer for Jerusalem is found in Matthew 23:37-38. *"Oh Jerusalem, Jerusalem who kills the prophets who speak against it. How I wished to gather you to me as a hen gathers its chicks, but you were unwilling. I will not come until you say, 'Blessed is he who comes in the name of the Lord.'"*

I remember standing in the location where Jesus prayed over the city when I came in 1978 near the garden of Gethsemane. There were hardly any tourists. Now we have a record number of tourists who see the prosperity of the city and continue to pray for the peace of Jerusalem. It is amazing to see the arrival of many third world country folk. There has even been an invasion of Chinese tourists with direct flights from Shanghai. This is a sign that God is building His church in China and many are coming to the Lord and desire to see where Jesus lived, ministered, died and rose again.

Isaiah 62:6,7 states: *"I have posted watchmen on your wall, O Jerusalem; they will never be silent, day or night. You who will call on the Lord, give yourselves no rest, and give him no rest till he establishes Jerusalem and makes her the praise of the earth."*

In Zechariah 12:1-5 we read these words, *"This is the word of the Lord concerning Israel. The Lord, who stretches out the heavens, lays the foundation of the earth, and who forms the spirit of man within him, declares: 'I am going to make Jerusalem a cup that sends all of the surrounding peoples reeling. Judah will be besieged as well as Jerusalem. On that day when all the nations of the world are gathered against her, I will make Jerusalem an unmovable rock for all the nations. All who try to move it will injure themselves. On that day I will strike every horse with panic and its rider with madness, ' declares the Lord. I will keep a watchful eye over the house of Judah, but I will blind all the horses of the nations. The leaders of Judah will say in their hearts, 'The people of Jerusalem are strong because the Lord Almighty is their God.'"*

How true these words are today. Jerusalem is now prosperous and beautiful. It is being built up with many new apartment buildings. Beautiful shopping centers, plazas and cafes permeate the city. Yes, there is still tension because of the Arab, Israeli conflict. It is constantly in the news. However, it continues to grow and prosper and is now the fastest growing tourist destination in the world. God is wonderfully fulfilling His promise concerning the Holy City.

We anticipate the return of the Lord to reign in Jerusalem.

I like to read from Psalm 122 while standing with tour groups overlooking the Old City of Jerusalem and the Temple Mount about rejoicing that our feet are standing within the gates of Jerusalem. It is a city joined together where the tribes go to worship the Lord. It is in this context that the Psalmist exhorts us to pray for the peace of Jerusalem. He states as well, "May those who love you prosper and have peace."

Psalm 128 is often read at a child dedication, but we also read it while standing on top of the Mt. of Olives overlooking the great city. There are wonderful promises to the man who fears the Lord and walks in His ways. God will provide for him. All will go well. His wife will be fruitful, and his children will be like young olive trees. The Psalmist then concludes, *"May the Lord bless you from Zion, so that you will see the prosperity of Jerusalem all the days of your life and will see your children's children. Peace be with Israel."*

THE SIGNS OF THE NATIONS

In Ezekiel 38 it says that there will be an alliance among nations who will come down against Israel. The nations include Persia (Iran), Gomer (Turkey) and Put (Libya). It is interesting that Russia is now working with Iran to stabilize Syria. It is in the news because of their desire to influence the United States presidential election.

1) **Russia**
2) **China**
3) **Iran**
4) **Western Confederacy**
5) **Natural signs**
6) **Political signs**
7) **Sign of the Anti-Christ**
8) **Social signs**
9) **Religious signs**

China is in the news because of the Corona virus and their ambition to control the world with their economic might. They have a powerful communist government. The Bible speaks of an army of 200 million invading the Holy Land from the East. China has this kind of army.

Question:

Does China have a role in the end times?[1]

Answer: Many students of Bible prophecy consider Revelation 16:12–16 to possibly refer to China in the end times:

"The sixth angel poured out his bowl on the great river Euphrates, and its water was dried up to prepare the way for the kings from the East. Then . . . demonic spirits that perform signs . . . go out to the kings of the whole world, to gather them for the battle on the great day of God

---

[1] https://www.gotquestions.org/content_end-times_people.html

Almighty. . . . Then they gathered the kings together to the place that in Hebrew is called Armageddon." (Revelation 16:12–16)

This passage predicts a massive, climactic conflict known as the Battle of Armageddon. It occurs at the end of the tribulation, after the sixth bowl judgment. At that time, the Euphrates River will be dried up, allowing the "kings from the East" to invade the Near East and march toward Israel. It is the "kings from the East" identification that many associate with China. The Chinese army, or a Chinese-led coalition, will take advantage of the removal of a natural barrier and sweep westward to meet up with the forces of the Antichrist.

When the end-times' force from China joins with the armies of the Antichrist, the seventh and final bowl judgment will be poured out. The Lord Jesus will return, the most violent earthquake ever will shake the world, and the forces of the Antichrist and the armies of the East will be destroyed (Revelation 16:17–20; 19:11–21).

It is impossible to know for sure if the Eastern confederacy of the end times will include China; however, it seems likely that China will be involved. Recent years have seen a dramatic rise in China's power and influence. The development of enormous military strength; intimidation of Hong Kong, Tibet, Taiwan, and other regions; pursuit of global economic dominance; aggressive rhetoric on the world stage; and, of course, the persecution of Chinese Christians—all this has been characteristic of China. It is not hard to imagine that the "kings from the East" who one day march into Israel will include China.

Chinese Army

Some people identify another battle, mentioned earlier in Revelation, as a prophecy about China in the end times. The association hinges on the mention of an army of 200 million (Revelation 9:16) and occasional reports of China's capability of equipping such a vast army. There are a couple problems with this view.

One is that Revelation 9 says nothing of an army from the East; rather, it speaks of a demonic horde that destroys a third of mankind. The "horses" these beings ride are definitely not normal horses (verse 17). Also, the battle of Revelation 9 occurs after the sixth trumpet judgment; the battle of Revelation 16 involving the kings of the East occurs after the sixth bowl judgment, probably about three and a half years later.

In the end times, many nations, likely including China, will try their hand at conquest. Ultimately, their fight will be against God. The tribulation will be a tumultuous time of warfare, disasters, and divine judgment. But God has it all under control, as Psalm 2:2–6 assures: *"The kings of the earth rise up and the rulers band together against the Lord and against his anointed, saying, 'Let us break their chains and throw off their shackles.' The One enthroned in heaven laughs; the Lord scoffs at them. He rebukes them in his anger and terrifies them in his wrath, saying, 'I have installed my king on Zion, my holy mountain.'"*

IRAN

There is much in the news about Iran's desire to push Israel back into the sea. They are the number one state sponsor of terrorism working through proxies like Hamas and Hezbollah.
On a brief visit to Southern Lebanon I saw the home of a Hezbollah leader. At one time he had little money. Now he has a mansion and a nice boat in his driveway. Iran pays big money to carry on their terrorism.

Hezbollah logo

On the positive side, the fastest growing church in the world is the Iranian church, some within the country, some in other countries.
We had many Iranians visit our church in Vienna from 2000-2005.
They wanted to be followers of Christ. We baptized 80 former Muslims from Iran. The Bible does speak about Iran in Isaiah 45.
It is called the nation of Elam.

Question:
"What role does Iran play in the end times?"

Answer: There are several biblical prophecies of the end times that mention Iran, called Persia or Elam in the Bible. Given the fact that Iran is often in the news as a nation seeking armaments (possibly nuclear) and repeatedly issuing threats against Israel, students of Bible prophecy are taking note.

Iran does have a role to play in the end times, but, first, a little history of Iran and its neighborhood, as it relates to biblical history. Jeremiah prophesied that Elam, a nation east of Babylon, west of Persia, and south of Media, would be conquered and then rise to power again (Jeremiah 49:34–39). True to that prophecy, Babylon conquered Elam in 596 BC. But then Persia, under Cyrus the Great, took control of that area, and the Elamites and Medes became part of the Persian Empire. The Medo-Persian Empire ascended to power and conquered Babylon in 539 BC, fulfilling the prophecy of Isaiah 21:2. This happened during the time of Daniel (Daniel 5); in fact, Daniel later resided "in the province of Elam" in Persia (Daniel 8:2). Persia is the setting for the book of Esther and the first part of Nehemiah.

Alexander the Great's conquests put an end to Persia as a world power, fulfilling the prophecy of Daniel 8. In the following centuries, Persia was ruled by the Seleucids, the Parthians, the Sassanians, the Romans, the Byzantines, and finally, in AD 636, the Muslims. In 1501, the state of Iran was founded.

In the New Testament, men from Iran are mentioned indirectly as "Parthians, Medes and Elamites" were present in Jerusalem on the Day of Pentecost (Acts 2:9). All three of these people groups were Jews who lived in the area of ancient Persia, modern-day Iran, and they were present in Jerusalem to witness the birth of the church.

Iran's involvement in the end times will be as one of the nations involved in the battle of Gog and Magog, which probably occurs during the first half of the tribulation. Ezekiel 38:5 specifically mentions Persia as an ally of Magog/Russia. Other nations included in this coalition will be Sudan, Turkey, Libya, and others. This vast army will come against Israel, who at that time will be *"a peaceful and unsuspecting people."* (verse 11).

The outcome of this end-times invasion is predicted: God supernaturally intervenes, and Gog's coalition is utterly destroyed. *"On the mountains of Israel you will fall, you and all your troops and the nations with you. I will give you as food to all kinds of carrion birds and to the wild animals."* (Ezekiel 39:4–5).

Iran, allied with Russia, will think their invasion of Israel is a sure victory, but God has different plans. In protecting Jerusalem, God will send a strong message to the world:

"I will make known my holy name among my people Israel. I will no longer let my holy name be profaned, and the nations will know that I the Lord am the Holy One in Israel." (verse 7).

The Western Confederacy

The Western Confederacy under the Anti-Christ will also have a significant role in the last days. (Daniel 2, 7, II Thess. 3, Revelation 6,13).

Natural Signs

In Matthew 24 Jesus gives us the signs of His coming. His disciples asked, "Tell us when will this happen and what will be the sign of your coming and of the end of the age?" In this Olivet Discourse, he shares various signs. There are religious and political signs, and signs in nature. The signs in nature include famines and earthquakes in various places.

Revelation talks about plagues which will precede the coming of the Lord. Plagues are a sign of judgement.

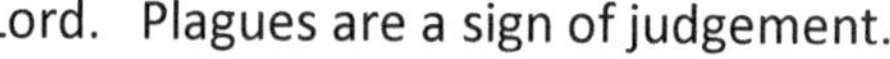

In Revelation 6 John mentions 4 horses. The first is a white horse. Its rider was given a crown. The second was a red horse whose rider had power to take peace from the earth and to make men kill each other. The third horse was a black horse. The fourth house was pale, and its rider was named Death. He had power to kill by sword, famine and plagues.

We are presently going through a crisis with the plague of coronavirus. It is a worldwide pandemic. Israel has closed its border to many nations, which has affected the tourist industry.

There have been other plagues in the past such as the Spanish Flu at the beginning of the 20th century which killed over 50 million people and the bubonic plague in the middle ages which killed a third of the population of Europe. There is a monument in Vienna, Austria, on one of the main pedestrian streets, which remembers those who died in that plague. It is interesting to observe that Jewish people were protected at the time of this plague. It was due to their sanitary kosher environment and because they basically separated themselves from other groups.

There is also the present plague of locusts in Africa. Years ago, we had the SARS epidemic. It could have been worse, but many believers prayed, and it ended. Should we not be praying for the coronavirus in the world and the locust invasion in Africa. Of course, there is also an increase in earthquakes and other natural disasters like hurricanes, tornadoes, and tsunamis. Certainly, the time of the coming of the Lord is soon.

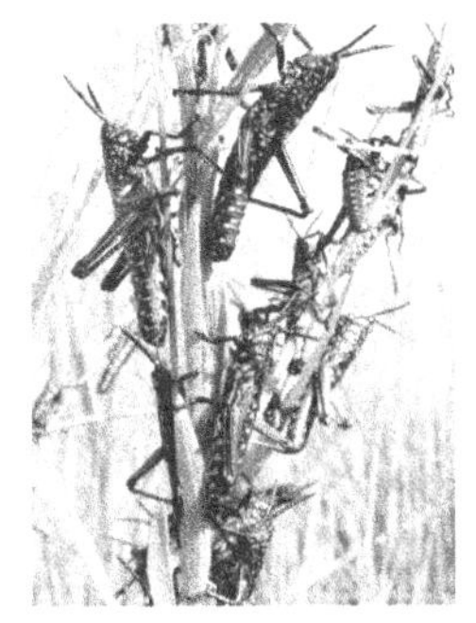

Political Signs

We live in a world which is deeply divided. In the USA it seems we are on the verge of a civil war between the right and the left. The issue of Brexit has affected Great Britain. Matthew 24 says that there will be wars and nation will go against nation. The word for nation is *"ethne,"* which refers to people groups. In America we still have a division between blacks and whites with people calling each other racists.

Sign of the Anti-Christ

Adolf Hitler was a type of anti-Christ. He was an evil leader who fooled the world. He built up the German economy, produced the Volkswagen and built up the German *autobahns* (highways). He was a bulwark against communism. He was praised by Joseph Kennedy, father of JFK, and hailed as a "man of peace" by Neville Chamberlain, prime minister of Great Britain. Then Hitler revealed his true nature as an evil dictator bent on ruling the world.

The Anti-Christ will be like a Hitler. He will be called a man of peace. He will head up a Western Confederation (probably the leader of the European Union). In II Thessalonians 3 the Apostle Paul gives a description of this coming world leader. He is called a man of lawlessness. He opposes and exalts himself over everything that is called God or is worshiped and sets himself up in God's temple, proclaiming himself to be God.

He will be empowered by Satan and do counterfeit miracles, signs, and wonders. He will be the great deceiver.

Revelation 13 speaks of the Beast coming out of the sea. He will survive a fatal wound. He will blaspheme God. He will be given authority to rule and to war against the saints. He will force all to receive a mark on their hands or foreheads, without which they will not be able to buy or sell. The number of the beast is 666. How can someone like this come to power? I believe the wars and conflicts in the world today will make the world look for a leader who can save them.

Social Signs

In II Timothy 3 and Matthew 24 (days of Noah), Jesus said that as it was in the days of Noah so it will be at the time of the coming of the Son of God. They were eating, drinking, and marrying. Yes, these were normal activities. However, they forgot about God and their accountability to Him. In II Timothy 3 the Apostle Paul, shares with Timothy the signs of the end times. It will be terrible times. People will be lovers of themselves and money. They will be proud and boastful. There will be abuse and disobedience to authorities. Brutality will characterize these times. People will be lovers of pleasure rather than lovers of God. They will also be religious hypocrites. They profess a faith but do not live accordingly. Certainly, these are characteristics of our society today. Mankind with all the technology available, is not able to change his basic nature. We are all sinners with corrupt and deceitful hearts. The fraud and deception we see in the recent USA elections prove that man's basic evil nature has remained the same. Only Jesus can change our hearts.

a. False Religions

Jesus began the Olivet Discourse with these words, *"Watch out that no one deceive you. For many will come in my name, claiming, "I am the Christ, and will deceive many. You will hear of wars and rumors of wars but see to it that you are not alarmed. Such things must happen, but the end is still to come."* (Matthew 24). He continues and says false Christs and teachers will appear and do great miracles and even deceive the elect if this was possible.

Peter anticipates these false prophets and teachers, *"But there were also false prophets among the people, just as there will be false teachers among you. They will secretly introduce destructive heresies, even denying the sovereign Lord who bought them--bringing swift destruction on themselves. Many will follow their shameful ways and will bring the way of truth into dispute. In their greed these teachers will exploit you with stories they have made up. Their condemnation has long been hanging over them, and their destruction has not been sleeping."* (II Peter 2:1-3).

Today there is the fake media which makes up stories and narratives to push their political agendas. There are also religious charlatans who deceive people with promises of

prosperity and success. They are greedy and seek only to fill their unholy pockets.

"A lie can travel around the world and back again while the truth is lacing up its boots."
Mark Twain

b. The preaching of the Gospel

In Matthew 24, Jesus shares a final sign. The Gospel of the kingdom will be preached in the whole world and then the end will come. We praise God for men like Billy Graham who have preached the Gospel in the whole world. Through TV and the internet, everyone today can be exposed to the Gospel.

WHAT THEN SHALL WE DO?

Considering the coming of the Lord, what are we commanded to do?

- ⇒ We must live holy lives according to II Peter 3.
- ⇒ We must be faithful until He comes (Matthew 25).
- ⇒ And, of course, we must occupy ourselves until He comes.
- ⇒ We preach Christ, the Hope of the world.

PRINCIPLE 2

CONDITION OF THE WORLD

II Timothy 3 says that there will be terrible times in the last days. We are living in terrible times. We have unending wars. Crime has infested the large cities of this world. Drugs are prevalent and there is increasing abuse. The Coronavirus has affected all of this. There is rampant homelessness in major population centers of the United States. There is violence in the streets and a movement to defund the police leading to further lawlessness. By tearing down our statues there is an attempt to savagely destroy our history and our culture in the USA. Is there no hope for peace?

In the Political world there is animosity and division. In the USA there is a war between the conservatives and liberals. In Israel, the political situation is very fragile with Netanyahu fighting for his political survival. Newspapers are exposing increasing anti-Semitism. Climate change has become a hot political topic.

What is the solution for these problems? Is it new leadership in the political world? Is it a total revolution? Do we need more social justice and monetary help? These are temporary solutions. However, what is the real root cause. The Bible says it is sin.

THE ROOT PROBLEM OF SIN

> *"The heart of the problem*
> *is the problem of the heart. "*

The Bible says that the heart is desperately wicked, who can understand it? (Jeremiah) To be an effective leader and influencer, we must understand the condition of the world and the real cause of our problems. James tells us the real cause of wars is the sin nature. It is our evil egotistic nature that always wants power and things. We crave these things. We steal and kill to get what we want.

What is the Biblical solution for the problem of sin? [1]

A. Understanding the Problem of sin

Sin is defined as transgression, evil, or a violation of an accepted moral code. It is lack of conformity to the character of God. It is a disease of the soul like leprosy is a disease of the body. It is part of our old nature.   It can be a thought, an act, or the fallen state or our nature.

B. Origin of Sin

Sin originated with Satan (Isaiah 14:12-14), who rebelled against God and wanted to be like God. Sin came into the world through the transgression of Adam and Eve who gave into Satan's temptation (Romans 5:12). We are tempted and enticed by our own sinful nature. We are drawn away by our lusts. Billy Graham identified 3 G's that can lead us astray - Gold, Girls, and Glory.

---

[1] Excerpt from *One Hundred Bible lessons* by Alban Douglas (OMF publishers (1966)

C. Manifestations of Sins

Sin has many names:

- **Transgression** or the overstepping of the law
- **Iniquity** is a breaking of a commandment
- **Trespass** is intruding our self-will into the sphere of God's authority.
- Lawlessness which means to be disobedient
- **Unbelief** is an insult to the divine veracity of God (Heb. 3:12).

D. List of Sins

The Bible lists many specific sins which are too numerous to mention here, but some significant sins include idolatry, murder, stealing, and lying. There are also the moral sins of adultery and fornication. We can also display wrath and anger. There are religious sins of heresy and witchcraft. Even spiritual leaders can be proud and hypocritical.

E. Sin Cannot be Hidden

Numbers 32:23 tells us, *"... be sure your sin will find you out."* Proverbs 28:23 tells us, *"He that covers his sins will not prosper, but whoever confesses his sins and forsakes them shall have mercy."*

F. The Results of Sin

There are many results of sin. First of all, there is death. Romans 6:23 says that the wages of sin is death. This is spiritual death or separation from God.   Luke 15:24 says that we are lost because of sin. We experience sickness, illness and eventual physical death because of sin. We are also condemned because of our sin. This is a judicial word. (John 3:18)

Obviously, we feel guilty when we sin and rightly so. There is also perdition or destruction and damnation. {I Tim 6:9) We also are punished because of our sin.

We read of those who are sent away into eternal punishment (Matthew 25:46). There is eternal fire as a sign of God's wrath (Jude 7). The Bible also speaks of hell which is the abode of the devil and those who follow him (Matthew 25:41). Those who do not follow the Lord and believe in Him will be sent there. A scary thought! Finally, there is the lake of fire or the second death (Revelation 20:14).

The Remedy for Sin

If sin is the root cause of all our personal and world problems, then what is the solution?

It is Christ and his atonement and resurrection. He is the Lamb of God who takes away the sin of the world (John 1:29) as declared by John the Baptist. No one can cleanse himself from sin. Job 9:30,31, says, *"Even if I wash myself with soap and my hands with cleansing powder, you would plunge me into a slime pit so that even my clothes would detest me."* Jeremiah 2:22 shares this: *"Although you wash yourself soap and use an abundance of cleansing powder, the stain of your guilt is still before me, declares the Sovereign Lord."* The only remedy for sin is forgiveness through the blood of Jesus Christ (Eph 1:7, I John 1:7).

We are all under sin (Romans 3:23, Galatians 3:22).
⇒   Have you put your faith in Christ who died for you?
⇒   Do you have the assurance of your salvation?

Here is a great verse that shows the effects of sin and the blessings of obedience.

"I am the Lord your God, who brought you up out of Egypt. Open wide your mouth and I will fill it. But My people would not listen to Me, and Israel would not submit to me. So, I gave them over to their stubborn hearts to follow their own devices. If my people would only listen to me, if Israel would only follow my ways, how quickly I would subdue their enemies and turn my hand against their foes! Those who hate the Lord would cringe before him, and their punishment would last forever. But you would be fed with the finest of wheat; with honey from the rock I would satisfy you." (Psalm 81:10-16)

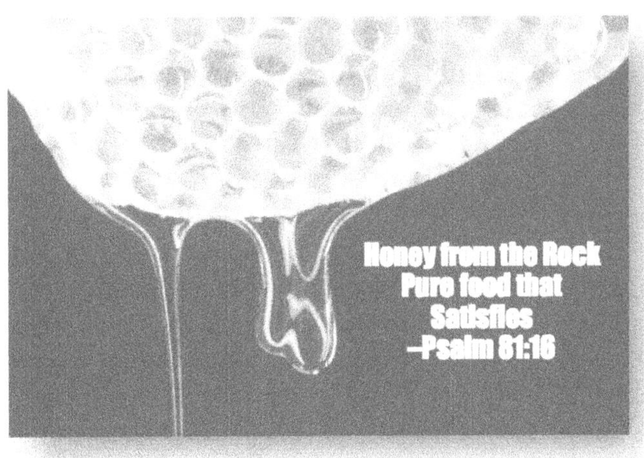

PRINCIPLE 3

CALLING FROM A HOLY, SOVEREIGN AND MERCIFUL GOD

A man or woman that God wants to use must believe in the sovereignty of God who chose him, saved him and called him. The God we serve is described in many ways in the Bible. He is a holy God who demands justice. He is also a loving and merciful God who provided His son to die for our sins. God is also a Sovereign God who created the world, sustains it and created us for a purpose. We know that God does not create robots who do things as the Master pulls the strings. We have freedom to believe or, or to obey or not.

The sovereignty of God and the responsibility of man are both clearly taught even though they may seem to be incongruous. It is hard to understand how both can be true. But these teachings are like a railroad tract. They run parallel to each other but somewhere in the distance they seem to meet and become one. Even though we may not understand it all, we must believe in both concepts.

ISRAEL AS A CHOSEN NATION

God chose the nation of Israel to be a particular people that would be a testimony to all nations (Isaiah 43:9). In the Old Testament God invited all nations to Jerusalem to pay homage to Him. The Jews were not commanded to go to the world (unlike the New Testament Commission given by Christ to His disciples), they were just commanded to be a holy nation and manifest the presence of God.

The news spread quickly that God was with them (Zechariah 8:23, Hab. 2:14). Many people see Israel as the Servant of the Lord mentioned in Isaiah 40-55. Some see this Servant as the Messiah who would take upon Himself all the sins of the world (Isaiah 53).

GOD CHOOSING AND USING THE CHURCH

God, in His sovereignty, saves people for a purpose. We are chosen to be part of the body of Christ, the church, and to be a bride for our Bridegroom. We are saved to serve and do good works as a testimony to our Great God. The book of Ephesians describes the church in all its glory. In the first two chapters we read of our inheritance in Christ, our position in Christ, and our past, present, and future. We see all the glory of God's salvation purposes, as He chose us, saved us, sanctifies us and uses us as a blessing to the world through our words and deeds.

OUR INHERITANCE IN CHRIST

In Ephesians 1:1-14 we see three reasons why we must praise God.

1)   The first is because of the work of God in eternity past in choosing us before the foundation of the world (vv. 4-6). The word "chosen" in verse 4 is in the aorist middle reflexive form in Greek indicating that He chose us at a precise time in eternity for Himself. Election is a truly Biblical concept. Israel was an elect nation (Exodus 6). Angels are chosen (I Timothy 5). Christ was elected (I Peter 2). We are chosen by God. Christ told His disciples in John 15:16, *"You did not choose me, but I have chosen you."* We are chosen before the foundation of the earth to have fellowship with God (1:14). He chose us because He loved us (4b, 5a). We became adopted children (v. 5) with all the rights of natural children. In Roman days an adopted child had every privilege that a natural child had.

2) The second reason we must praise God is because of the grace that we have received in Christ Jesus (vv. 7-12). We have been redeemed through His blood (v. 7). He has given us wisdom to understand His will (vv. 8-10). He has given us an inheritance (vv. 11-12). His purpose is to gather together all things in Christ.

3) The third reason why we must praise and thank God is because we have received the seal of the Holy Spirit (vv. 13-14). He is the guarantee of our future inheritance. This is our hope.

PRINCIPLES
TO
PONDER

1. We see here the principle of the sovereignty of God. He is the one who builds His church (Matthew 16:18). He chooses and adds to the church as He wills. This should encourage us to pray to the Lord of the harvest. How will a better understanding of the sovereignty of God help us in our prayer life?

2. An understanding of our position in Christ is essential for our growth as Christians. We are secure because He loves us. We are significant because we are children of the King. Once we accept ourselves, we are free to love others and share Christ's love. This principle can help us in our personal struggles.

3. An attitude of thanksgiving is essential to maintain a pure heart free of bitterness, jealousy, and envy. This attitude will attract people as they see Christ in us.

UNDERSTANDING OUR POSITION IN CHRIST

When I played guard on my high school American football team, I remember trying to do something spectacular with the end result that I tackled my own man. I did not play my position correctly. Whether it be a football team, an army unit, or a local church, every member must learn to play his position. As Christians, we have a very high position. God desires that we know our position and all the resources that are available to us to play that position. In other words, He wants us to know who we are and what He has provided for us to live as we should as Christians. This is the thought of the Apostle's prayer in Ephesians 1:15-23.

1. In this prayer Paul thanks God for the Ephesian believers and then shares with them the way he is interceding for them. He desires that they understand in their spirit the deep wisdom of God. He wants them to know God in a deep experiential way. He prays first that they may know the greatness of the plan of God (v. 18). God does indeed have a wonderful future for the believer. We have a hope that is based on the promises of God. Faithful is He who calls you and He will also bring it to pass (I Thessalonians 5:24).

We also have an inheritance and are co-heirs with Christ (Romans 8:17). Very often we get discouraged and frustrated because we feel we haven't done enough for God. The thing we need to hear is what God has done for us. We respond to His love for us.

2. The second thing Paul wanted them to know was the greatness of the power of God (vv. 19-20). In this passage He uses four Greek words to describe this power. The four words are: *dunamis* (power), *energeia* (working), *kratous* (might), and *iskus* (strength). It is the same power God used to raise Christ from the dead. Paul often speaks of the power God gave him to minister (Colossians 1:28,29). With this power he was able to do all things (Philippians 4:13).

3. The third thing Paul prays for is that they will realize the greatness of the Son of God (vv.21,22). Christ, not men, is the head of the Church, even though God uses men to mediate His rule. The body needs the head, but the head needs the body as well. Paul prays that these believers will understand the absolute supremacy of Jesus Christ.

**PRINCIPLES
TO
PONDER**

1. The content of our prayer for others is very important. The best way to pray for others is to use scriptural prayers.

2. Christ is the Head of the Church and will build it the way He pleases. He is to receive all the glory. What is our attitude towards our Head?

3. When we speak of the growth of the church we must speak of the dynamic relationship between Christ and His body. This a meaningful way to describe the church. It would seem that the body will grow as it correctly responds to the Head. Submission and obedience are absolutely essential.

4. We have the resurrection power available to us and to the church to live the Christian life.

OUR PAST, PRESENT, AND FUTURE (Ephesians 2:1-10)

A fortune teller purports to be able to see the past, the present, and the future. We know, of course, that there is no substance to their claims. God, however, who is omniscient, knows all about us. In eternity past He planned to elect a certain group of people to be His children (Ephesians 1:4). He knows our future. He has promised us an inheritance.

He understands our present situation and guides us everyday.

In Ephesians 2:1-10 we see another way God sees our past, present, and future. In this passage we see that our salvation is dynamic. Our past sinful condition has been changed. God has made us alive in Christ. He has made us to sit at His right hand. We await our final glorification when we will be given a new heavenly body. As far as our present condition is concerned, we are His workmanship created for good works. In this passage let us now look at 6 aspects of this salvation.

1. First, we see that salvation is from sin (2:1-3). We are born sinners.

A man is not a sinner because he sins. A man sins because he is a sinner. Paul uses two Greek words to describe sin.

The word translated "sin" is *harmatia* which means missing the mark or not hitting the bull's eye with an arrow.

The word translated "trespass" is *paratoma* and it means to go in a wrong direction. All men are in this condition. We are all under the control of Satan, the prince of this world. Satan dwells in the heavenly places above earth's atmosphere. Above him is a God who is in heaven. Unregenerate men who are on this earth are subject to the dominion of Satan.

As Satan's children, we were under the wrath of God (2:3). This is a very bleak picture which is seen in vivid contrast to the grace of God which delivered us from our past condition.

2. The second aspect of this salvation is that it was wrought in love (2:4). The Bible tells us that God is love. He saved us because He loves us.

3. The third aspect of this salvation is that it is unto life (2:5). God has made us alive. Paul speaks of this life in Galatians 2:20 when he says, "I have been crucified with Christ and it is no longer I who live but Christ lives in me."

4. The fourth aspect of this salvation is that it's purpose is to raise us up and seat us with Christ in order that God may manifest the riches of grace to all generations (2:6,7). God desires to put His attributes on display to glorify Himself.   The salvation that we have is a demonstration of His wisdom, compassion, love, and grace.

5. The fifth aspect of this salvation is that it is by faith (2:8,9). It is not by works (Titus 3:5).

6. The sixth aspect is that its end is that we might do good works (2:10). As one has said, "we are saved to serve." Since we have been made new creatures in Christ our inward desire is to do those things which are pleasing to Him. God had many purposes in mind when He saved us.

PRINCIPLES TO PONDER

1. Pray everyday for the salvation of a loved one.

2. Let us go out and tell people about Christ who died to liberate us from sin.

GOD'S CALLING DESCRIBED IN THE BOOK OF ROMANS

The book of Romans is a classic, doctrinal epistle penned by the Apostle Paul. The theme is the Gospel of Jesus Christ and salvation through Him. Paul says he is not ashamed of the Gospel of Jesus Christ because it is the power of God for salvation, for the Jew first and then to the Greek 1:16). He then deals with our sin and the deed of redemption (1:18-3:20). The Good News is that Christ died to pay the penalty for our sins and we are justified by faith in what He has done for us on the cross. This is called our justification.

In Romans 6:1-8:39 Paul explains our sanctification and the effects of redemption. We are unified with Christ (our identification with Him). But we still have a conflict between our two natures.

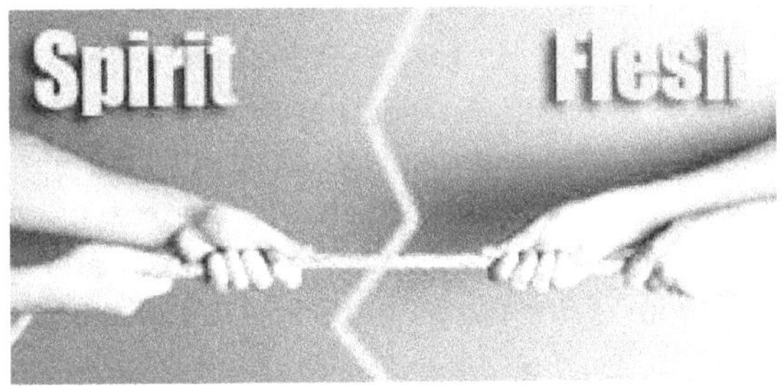

We have victory through the Holy Spirit. The Spirit witnesses to the believer that he is a son of God (8:16). We await our final redemption and adoption (8:23). God is in control and uses all things for our good (Romans 8:28).

God has also predestined us to be conformed to the image of Christ (Romans 8:29). In salvation, God predestines us, calls us, justifies us, and glorifies us (8:30).

In Romans 9:1-11:36, we see the plan of God for Jews and Gentiles. Israel is judged for their sin. However, they are given an offer of salvation (10:1-21). They are also promised a glorious future and restoration (11:1-36). This is for the believing remnant.

It is wonderful to know that God is sovereign and does what He desires. But, belief is still necessary for salvation. This salvation is all by grace.

In vv. 12:1-15:13, Paul describes the fruits of redemption. We are saved to serve God by using our gifts to build up one another. We must love each other. We must obey the governing authorities. In the church we must learn to accept one another knowing that only God is the righteous judge. The Holy Spirit fills our hearts with hope (15:13).

CALLING FROM A SOVEREIGN GOD

God calls a people unto Himself. It is His sovereign choice and it is by grace through faith. He also equips us with gifts and abilities to help build up the body of Christ. He raises up leaders to lead His people. Leaders can have a position or can be great people of influence.
We have looked at the theological concept of election and salvation. We have seen that God saves us for a purpose. It is to have a bride for the bridegroom (Christ). It is also to serve others. We are created to do good works for the glory of God (Ephesians 2:10).

Let us look now at some Biblical leaders who God chose to lead His people. They were chosen to serve through their leadership.

OLD TESTAMENT LEADERS

We begin with the father of the faith, and a man of great faith—Abraham! The three major religions of the world, Judaism, Islam, and Christianity, all look to Abraham as their spiritual father. Originally, he was from the city of Haran which was a center for moon worshippers. Then he moved to Ur with his father. There he received a call from God to leave and go to the promised land. It says in Hebrews 11 that by faith, when he was called, he obeyed and went out not knowing where he was going. That is true faith! When God called him as recorded in Genesis 12, He promised to bless whoever would bless Abraham, and to curse those who would curse him. This referred to his physical descendants, the Jewish people, as well as his spiritual descendants, the church of Jesus Christ (Romans 4). He believed in the Lord and it was counted to him as righteousness (Genesis 13). Abraham was also given the promise of a son even though he and Sara were old and beyond childbearing age. But the Bible says, "Yet with respect to the promise of God, he did not waver but grew strong in faith, giving glory to God, and being assured that what He had promised He was able to perform" (Romans 4:20, 21). God rewarded them with Isaac. Then he was tested. God told him to sacrifice his son Isaac. It was a difficult test of faith, but he believed God. Let us look to Abraham as a great man who believed God. But he was a sinner saved by grace. Do you remember when he told Sarah to lie and say she was his sister?

Moses was called by God to lead the people of God out of Egypt. Whom God calls He also prepares.

We all know how Moses was saved when all Jewish baby boys were supposed to be thrown into the river. By faith, his parents hid him and then he was found in the river and was brought up as the son of Pharaoh's daughter. His life was spared in an amazing way. God ordained all the particulars.

Moses had all the education of the Egyptians. However, before becoming a leader among the Jewish people, he had to be broken. After having killed an Egyptian soldier, he was found out, and escaped into the wilderness. There he became a sheep herder and was under the tutelage of Jethro, his father-in-law. This gave him the experience he needed to lead God's people who tended to go astray like sheep. When God called him from the burning bush, he responded in total honesty saying that he was not adequate for the job. He had a speech problem. God promised, however, that He would use Aaron to be his spokesman. By faith he accepted his assignment and boldly confronted Pharaoh. We all know how God used him to deliver the people out of Egypt.

> "Give your life to God;
> He can do more with it than you can!"
> D.L. Moody

God can use any one of us. He uses our backgrounds but needs our broken hearts. Moses had to be broken and humbled and we too need to be broken to be used of God. He did fail as he struck the rock for water. God told him to speak to the rock, but he disobeyed and in anger struck it. Because of this he was not allowed to enter the promised land. Are we broken and available for God to use?

The prophet Isaiah served a unique role in the history of Israel. He was God's spokesman. He warned and encouraged His people. He was used as a spiritual mentor to Hezekiah, the king of Judah, who brought real revival to the Jewish people.

Isaiah had a sovereign call from God. According to Isaiah 6, he had a vision of God who was holy. The angels proclaimed, holy, holy, holy. This was his look up. After seeing the holiness of God, he looked inward and stated, *"woe is me for I am a man of unclean lips and I dwell among a people of unclean lips."* He saw himself as a rotten sinner. We also need to understand the holiness of God and our own sinfulness. God then touched his mouth with burning coals and said, *"See this has touched your lips; your guilt is taken away and your sin atoned for."* (Isaiah 6:6,7).

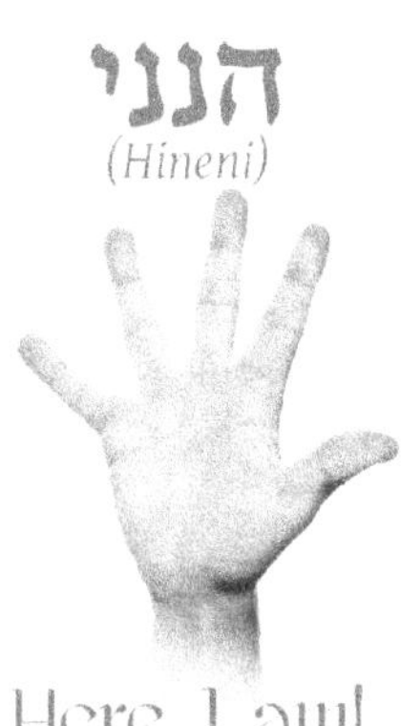

He was redeemed and saved. With the salvation came the fire within. He said, *"Here I am Lord, send me."* He knew what God wanted him to do. When we confront God, confessing our sin and turn to him in faith for salvation, we should immediately say, *"Here I am Lord. Use me as you wish."*

Jeremiah by Michelangelo

Jeremiah was "only a youth" when God called him. But God did wonderful things for Jeremiah even before he was born. He knew him. He formed him. He set him apart and appointed him as a prophet to the nations. This was long before Jeremiah drew his first breath or shed his first tear. Then He officially called him. Every Christian has a calling. There is a general call, of course, to believe in Jesus Christ. But everyone who believes in Christ also has a special calling to a particular sphere of obedience and ministry. We read of his calling in Jeremiah 1.

His response to God was, *"Oh no, Lord God! Look, I don't know how to speak since I am only a youth."* The rabbis called him "the weeping prophet." They said he began wailing the moment he was born. When Michelangelo painted him on the ceiling of the Sistine Chapel, he presented him in a posture of despair.

He looks like a man who has wept so long he has no tears left to shed. He is called the weeping prophet because of his lament over the sins of Jerusalem. He pleaded with the people, but they ignored him and even put him in a pit. Our calling begins with God even before we are born. This is a truly sovereign call.

When Jeremiah said that he didn't know how to speak, the Lord encouraged him and told him just to obey Him and speak. He had nothing to fear. God would put words in his mouth. God appointed him over the nations as an instrument to uproot and tear down, to destroy and overthrow, to build and to plant. At the end of Jeremiah 1 God told him to get ready and stand and tell the people whatever God commanded him. God made him a fortified city, an iron pillar and a bronze wall to stand against the whole land and the kings of Judah. They would fight against him, but they would not overcome him, for the Lord would be with him and would rescue him. He obeyed.

This passage has been an encouragement to me. While living In Vienna we used to go out preaching Jesus in the open air. Once we were confronted during a mass demonstration against America because of the bombing of Serbia. As I preached, I was called a CIA agent and screamed at. A man took my sketch board and threw it down. So, we stopped preaching.

The next week we were scheduled to go back. I felt afraid and thought I would just stay at home and watch a film with my family and eat a pizza. However, I read the passage at the end of Jeremiah 1:17-19 *"Get yourself ready! Stand up and say to them whatever I command you. Do not be terrified by them, or I will terrify you before them. Today I have made you a fortified city, an iron pillar and a bronze wall to stand against the whole land—against the kings of Judah, its officials, its priests and the people of the land. They will fight against you but will not overcome you, for I am with you and will rescue you," declares the Lord."*
God spoke to my heart. *Ok, Lord I will go.* I obeyed and the same thing happened.

However, after a few more Sundays my friend Phill Willer, a British evangelist, visited us. We went downtown together to preach. I told him what had happened other weeks, and he suggested approaching it in a different way. He said to help the protesters. So that's what we did. We helped them set up chairs. As we were doing that, the man who had thrown down my sketch board came to me and in a sense apologized and said he had just been doing his job. I believe God touched his heart.

I have always been encouraged by Jeremiah 20. Jeremiah complained to the Lord because of all the abuse he had encountered. He felt the Lord had deceived him. He was ridiculed all the time. Jeremiah proclaimed the truth and all it brought him was shame and reproach. He did not want to speak anymore. However, the word of the Lord was like fire in his soul. He could not hold it in. His friends rejected him, but he had to preach anyway. He knew the Lord was with him like a mighty warrior. His persecutors would stumble and not prevail. He asked God to show His vengeance to his enemies. He sang and began to rejoice in the Lord. [1]

During the period of the judges Israel was under constant attack. It was a period when every man did what was right in his own eyes. When Israel disobeyed, the Lord sent enemies against them. When they called on the Lord, he raised up deliverers. One was Gideon. When God called him, Gideon asked God how he could deliver Israel because his family was the weakest in Manasseh, and he was the youngest in his family. He didn't have a lot of confidence in himself. But God said, *"But I will be with you."* That was what made the difference. That's why he became a great leader.

THE MINISTRY OF JESUS CHRIST

Calling from a Sovereign God

In Mark 3:13-19 Jesus appointed the 12 Apostles. It says that after much prayer Jesus went up to the hills and called to Him those He wanted. He appointed the twelve. This was a sovereign choice. In the list of those he called, we see simple fishermen and a despised tax collector.

Paul said in I Corinthians 1:26-31: *"Brothers, think of what you were when you were called. Not many of you were wise by human standards; not many were influential; not many were of noble birth. But God chose the foolish things of the world to shame the wise; God chose the weak things of the world to shame the strong. He chose the lowly things of this world and the despised things--and the things that are not - to nullify the things that are, so that no-one may boast before Him. It is because of Him that you are in Christ Jesus, who has become for us wisdom from God - that is our righteousness, holiness, and redemption. Therefore, as it is written, "Let him who boasts boast in the Lord." (NIV).*

The 12 Apostles certainly fit this description. Yes, God can save Hollywood actors, sport stars, and presidents. However, most believers are just regular folk. Jesus appointed the disciples to be with Him and then sent them out to preach. They were called to fellowship with the Lord and learn from him. They were also appointed to serve the Lord by preaching, healing, casting out demons, and serving people. These men were saved to serve just like the prophets of the Old testament.

PAUL THE APOSTLE The apostle Paul received a sovereign call from God to preach the Gospel. We know that he was present at the stoning of Stephen. He kept all the garments. He was in hearty agreement.

Then as a Pharisee of Pharisee, he went out to persecute the church. However, our Sovereign God had other plans. We read of Paul's amazing conversion in Acts 9 and Acts 22. He was saved to serve.

In Acts 9 we read that Saul was breathing threats against the disciples. He sought approval by the high priest to go and capture believers to bring them to prison. However, on his way to Damascus, a light appeared in heaven. A voice said, *"Saul, Saul, why do you persecute Me?"* Was Paul actually persecuting Jesus? No, but when you touch the church, you are touching Jesus. Saul was told to get up and go to the city and then he would be told what to do. For three days he was blind. Then God called another man, Ananias, for a specific task, to go to Saul and place his hands on him so he would receive his sight. He didn't want to go because he had heard how Saul had harmed the saints in Jerusalem; but God told him that Saul was His chosen instrument to carry His name before the Gentiles, kings and the people of Israel. He would also be told how much he would suffer. Ananias obeyed God and went to Saul so he could receive his sight and be filled with the Spirit. Saul then regained his sight, and this began his earth-shaking ministry.

Again, in Acts 22, Saul recounted his testimony. He told about his religious past and his zeal for the Jewish nation. He said he persecuted the believers to their death. In other words, he was a murderer and a true terrorist. Then he shared about meeting the Lord on the road to Damascus and told how he came to faith and was told that He was to be a testimony to the Gentiles.

This story reminds me of Tass Saada. Tass is originally from Gaza and become a sniper for Yasser Arafat. He was a terrorist killing both Israeli's and Jordanians. However, God had a plan for him. He came to the States and worked in a restaurant where a client began to witness to him and pray for him. Tass met Jesus even though he was a hardened Muslim. He then began to witness for the Lord.

He went back to the Holy Land and established a ministry named Seeds of Hope to help both Jews and Arabs based in Jericho. He loves Israel and has established a kindergarten in Jerusalem. He also opened up a youth center in Jericho. and a palm tree business to help Palestinian people.

CALL TO THE LORD AND CALL TO MINISTRY

Those of us who have put our trust in the Lord are called to be His witnesses. We are His workmanship created in Christ Jesus for good works (Ephesians 2:10). However, there is a call to full time Christian service as a pastor or missionary. We call this a "call to ministry." These are leaders that God has called to lead the church. These men must have a calling, a true conversion, a commitment to a great cause, a character, and gifts for the ministry. These will be explored in the next few sections.

<blockquote>
"Do not enter the ministry
if you can help it."
Charles Spurgeon
</blockquote>

The sage advice of a divine to one who sought his judgment continued, *"If any student in this room could be content to be a newspaper editor, or a grocer, or a farmer, or a doctor, or a lawyer, or a senator, or a king, in the name of heaven and earth let him go his way."* [2]

Of course we all need wisdom to know if we are called to ministry or not. We seek counsel from the Word of God and from men.

MY PERSONAL TESTIMONY OF FAITH AND CALL TO MINISTRY

My story in a sense goes back to a lie. My father, a Protestant, married my mother, a Catholic. To get married he had to promise the priest that they would bring up the kids Catholic. My father crossed his fingers. When my sister and I were born we were baptized Presbyterians. So, I grew up a Protestant. My parents sent us to church. My mother went to her Catholic church. My father drove us to the Presbyterian Church then went home.

I must say I did learn something about Jesus at church and in Sunday School. I remember that our teacher gave us Bibles. I was involved in the youth group and enjoyed being with other young people, especially the girls.

Another event also had an impact. At eight years of age, my parents took us to Washington, D.C. We toured the FBI building and I thought it was so cool to see the agents at the shooting gallery. I decided that I wanted to be an FBI agent. Then we went over to the Capital. We sat in the balcony overlooking the Senate floor and seeing John F. Kennedy for the first time was also cool. Maybe I would be Senator? Well, either way I knew I had to study law. I went to college with that aim.

---

2 (Lectures to My Students, pg. 24).

During my high school years many things happened which God used to bring me to Himself. For a while, we had an Afro-American maid, named Janie, who was always cheerful and happy. I believe she prayed for me. Then, I had a French teacher named Miss Bonjour in 10th grade. She had been a missionary to France and had come back to Millburn High School to teach and help her mother. She was from Orange, New Jersey and went to high school with my father, aunt, and uncles. In the providence of God, after teaching me, she left Millburn High to teach at Columbia Bible College in South Carolina where my wife Billie was part of her class. Amazing how God works. I believe she also prayed for me.

During this time, I had a real self-image problem. I could not accept myself. When I wrote a very negative essay for my English class my teacher called me in and said, "Albert you have a negative view of yourself, you need a girlfriend." Well that was my assignment - to find a girlfriend. I found one and I felt so accepted and loved. Then, two years later, she dumped me. I was left depressed again. This was also

the time of the Vietnam War and I was afraid of being drafted. Two guys we knew from our hometown died there. It was during this time that I got a summer job in Richard Nixon's old law firm in New York City. It was a rather boring job. It was hard not to get depressed. I often looked out the window and thought, *what if I were to jump?* I knew my mother would be upset. Thank God for mothers.

Well at my lunch break one day I opened the New York Daily News. There was an advertisement for a Billy Graham Crusade that night in Shea Stadium (where the Mets played). I felt led to go. On the way there, I stopped by a bookstore and bought a cheap book (my hobby) for 10 cents. It was *Run, Baby, Run* by Nicky Cruz. I did not know who he was, but 10 cents is a good price.   When I got to the Crusade and sat down, the first testimony was by Nicky Cruz. He was a Porto Rican gang leader who got saved under the ministry of David Wilkerson of Teen Challenge.

When Billy Graham preached, the Lord touched me. I went forward at the invitation and a counselor met me. He shared John 3:16 with me, *"For God so loved the world that He gave his only begotten son that whoever believes in him should not perish but have eternal life."*

God spoke to me and I prayed to receive Jesus. Now I had somebody who would always love me and never leave me or forsake me.
My life was transformed.

I got involved with Campus Crusade for Christ at the University of Maryland. I was taught how to be filled with the Spirit, how to witness, and how to have a vision for world evangelization. Within one year of my conversion, I knew that God was calling me to full-time Christian service whether it be as a pastor, an evangelist or a missionary.

By the grace of God, He led me to Dallas Seminary where I learned how to study the Word and preach it. He also gave me a great vision to reach the world for Jesus. God used a group of seminary students who gathered for prayer every Friday night and for 40 mornings before my graduation. We prayed for wives and for the world. The Lord gave us wives and led us all around the world. I was led to serve in Milan, Italy. God gave me Billie as my life mate. We had met in Italy in 1975 as summer missionaries. God got us back together in 1978. We married in 1979 and then headed to Italy in 1980 where we spent 12 years in evangelism and church planting. I also pastored the Milan Bible Church. In 1992 we were led to serve in Vienna, Austria to pastor Grace Church and be involved in open air evangelism. Then in 2007 God led us to Jerusalem to pastor the Jerusalem Baptist Church and do sport ministry. See our complete story in our book, *Called to World Revolution* (the section on the Goodness of God). Also see the section in this book on Commitment to a Great cause.

AN EXPERT ON CHURCH GROWTH
SHARES ABOUT A CALL TO THE MINISTRY

Elmer Towns is one of the top experts on church growth. He was used of God to help Jerry Falwell begin Liberty University. He has written many books which examine the fastest growing churches and Sunday Schools in the world. In his book *Great Soul Churches*, he shared a chapter entitled, "The Call to the Ministry." I would like to share some of his insights.

The ministry is more than a job. It is a call from God. There is little money and sometimes constant criticism. So, what makes a preacher pray and preach Jesus constantly? It is the call of God.
Great churches are built by great men. What transforms average men into men of God? It is the call of God.

There are three calls of God in Scripture.

1. The call of God to repent of sin unto salvation.
The first call is to salvation. Jesus said, *"come to me, all who are weary and heavy laden, and I will give you rest"* (Matt. 11:28). Jesus is pictured as a Shepherd who leaves the 99 safely in the fold and pursues the one lost sheep.
Paul prayed in Ephesians that our eyes would be enlightened so that we may know what the hope of his calling is (Eph 1:18). This calling is for all. Paul states, *"For you see your calling, brethren, how that not many wise men after the flesh, not many mighty, not many noble, are called"* (I Cor. 1:26). The appeal of this call is to the heart, so it communicates to all.

2. The call of God to service
This call to serve Jesus Christ is a call to all. We all see the great need of men who are going to hell. We all realize the command of the Lord to make disciples of all nations. *"All have sinned and come short of the glory of God"* and *"the wages of sin is death."* (Rom. 3:23, 6:23).

The need of the world is the first step in the call of God to service. The command of Jesus Christ to "Go" is the second step in the call of God to service (Matthew 28:19). This is for all. However, there is another calling which is deeper and more compelling.

3. The high calling of God to full-time Christian service.
All who are called to be a pastor or evangelist believe that God called them specifically to their ministry. It seems to be an inner invitation from God. They also have a burden to preach the Gospel. Lastly, they have a desire to pastor a church. It cannot be put in a test tube and measured. It is internal. It is like being in love. You know it but have difficulty giving words to it.

Towns concludes,
> *"The call of God into full-time ministry is exactly that. It is God calling a young man to win souls, build churches, teach the Bible and serve Jesus Christ. A man knows he is called because of the burden God gives him to reach the lost. He knows God has given him a desire to preach. He has the inner assurance that he is to serve God. Just as he knows the fire is hot and up is up, so he knows God has called him to preach the Gospel and build a church. He responds as Isaiah did, 'Here am I, send me.'"*

PRINCIPLE 4

CONFESSION OF TRUE BIBLICAL FAITH

It certainly follows the concept that if God called us by His sovereign will, there will be signs of God's regenerative work in our lives. When we profess Christ and are truly born again, there will be evidence of this. In Romans 10, the Apostle shares these words, *"If you declare with your mouth, 'Jesus is Lord,' and believe in your heart that God raised him from the dead, you will be saved. For it is with your heart that you believe and are justified, and it is with your mouth that you profess your faith and are saved."* As Scripture says, "Anyone who believes in him will never be put to shame." He continues, *"Everyone who calls on the name of the Lord will be saved."* Those who believe have heard the Gospel by a preacher who is described as one whose feet are beautiful. They bring the good news. Faith comes by hearing the Word of God. This belief must come from a sincere heart. It is not just acknowledgement of who Jesus is. James tells us, *"Even the demons believe and tremble."*

FALSE BELIEVERS AND TEACHERS

It is not our words or our profession that indicate that we are truly believers. Jesus talks about this in Matthew 7. He says that there will be false prophets and teachers. They will bear bad fruit. A good tree will bear good fruit.
Not everyone who acknowledges the Lord will enter the kingdom of heaven, but only the one who does the will of the Father. People will say, *"Lord did we not prophesy in your name and in your name drive out demons and perform many miracles?"* Jesus will say to them:
"I never knew you. Get away from Me you evil doers."

In Matthew 24, Jesus spoke of false teachers and prophets who will be a sign of the last days.   II Peter 2 warns us of false teachers and prophets.   These people may say beautiful things, but they are like wolves in sheep's clothing.   Paul warned the Ephesian elders about this in Acts 20.   Satan is very deceptive.   He is like an angel of light as described in II Corinthians 11: 5-23.   False teachers can do miracles and duplicate things the Lord did during his ministry.

There are true believers all over.
What are the signs of true believers?   They are people who have put their whole trust in Christ. Their lives should change.
II Corinthians 5:17 tells us that, *"If anyone is in Christ, he is a new creature, the old things pass away, behold all things have become new."* After becoming a believer in Jesus, I noticed that I had more love for people. I stopped swearing and using God's name in vain.
I developed a desire to be with believers and not just hang out with my drinking friends. Of course, my attitude toward girls also changed.

A STANDARD TO EVALUATE

In my book, *Reformation and Revival, The Solution for the Middle East Crisis*, I share these thoughts about true and false believers (authentic or false). In Medieval times in European Cities, the cathedral became the center of the city. The rest of the city and the main thoroughfares circled around the cathedral. In Vienna, Austria, the center is dominated by St. Stephens Cathedral, a massive gothic structure. To the left of the entrance, right on the building, there are two curious looking symbols. One is a rod which is approximately one and a half yards long.

Official Viennese linen ell and drapery ell length standards embedded in the cathedral wall

The other is a figure of a bread roll imbedded into the building. These were standards for the city. If you bought a length of cloth, you could take it to the cathedral and find out if you had been given the correct length. If the merchant had cheated you, he would be dunked in the Danube River. In the same way, if you bought a bread roll, you could take it to the cathedral and compare it the roll etched there. If it did not conform to the size of the engraving near the door, you could tell the police and the merchant would be dunked. Standards are important.

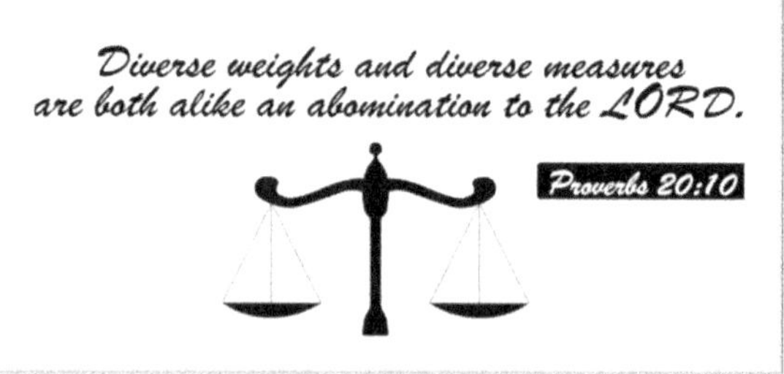

TESTS OF I JOHN IN THE NEW TESTAMENT

Jonathan Edwards was used of God to lead many people to Christ in the First Great Awakening. As people professed faith there were many tears and much repentance. As a good pastor, he wanted to make sure that those who professed Christ would demonstrate a genuine faith. He wrote a commentary on I John 4 in which he presented the Biblical tests for authentic faith in Jesus. In the book, John first encourages the believers to not believe every spirit but to test them whether they are from God.

How can we recognize a false prophet?

a.   The first test is whether this person acknowledges that Jesus Christ has come in the flesh? If not, then he is not from God. He then states that whoever listens to them (the apostles), knows God. This can mean today that it is those who listen to the Word of God who truly know God.

b.   The next test is love. Whoever does not love does not know God. If we say we love God, we must obey His commandments. If we have a desire to follow and obey the Lord, this is a good indication that we truly know the Lord. We also have the test of the spirit. Do we have the witness of the Spirit in our souls? (See Romans 8).

I John also suggests that these false prophets had been with the Apostles at one time, but did not remain and so proved their false profession. John says that Christ's true disciples will continue in their faith. Of course, believers may fall and stumble. However, they will not continue in their sin.

I close this section with an anecdote from the ministry of George Whitefield, the Great English Evangelist. He was once asked how many people had converted during one of his campaigns. He said, "I do not know. Ask me in a year!" We can say a person made a profession of faith. We will see if it was real as fruit is born.

VISION AND PASSION

Once a person comes to faith, he is given the Holy Spirit. In Romans 8 it states that the Holy Spirit testifies with our spirit that we are believers (Romans 8). The Spirit is a spirit of power and fire. He empowered Peter to preach an anointed message in Acts 2. Three thousand people came to the Lord. In John 14 Jesus shares these words with His disciples, *"Don't you believe that I am in the Father, and that the Father is in me? The words I say to you are not just my own. Rather, it is the Father, living in me, who is doing the work. Believe me when I say that I am in the Father and the Father is in me; or at least believe on the evidence of the miracles themselves. I tell you the truth, anyone who has faith in me will do what I have been doing. He will do even greater things than these, because I am going to the Father. And I will do whatever you ask in My name, so that the Son may bring glory to the Father. You may ask me for anything in my name, and I will do it. If you love me, you will obey what I command."* (vv. 10-15).

Luis Palau, the great evangelist, shared the following about these verses.

1.	We must dream great dreams and plan great plans (You will do greater things).
2.	We must pray great prayers (I will do whatever you ask).
3.	We must do great things (If you love me you will obey Me).

> "Never let the thought of failure stop you from reaching for your dreams."

Our vision is related to these dreams. We are to obey the Lord and go into all the world. Christ said that we would receive the Holy Spirit (fire of God) and that we would be witnesses in Jerusalem, Judea, and Samaria and to the utter most part of the earth. This is not just for special Christians, this is for all. We must be spirit filled vessels consecrated to God. He wants to use us in a cause that is greater than ourselves.

PRINCIPLE 5

COMMITMENT
TO THE GREATEST CAUSE ON EARTH

A great leadership expert said that his father had taught him three principles for living a successful life.

1. Have a dream.
2. Learn as much as you can.
3. Give yourself to a cause that is greater than yourself.

Great advice. Of course, we have to be careful what kind of cause we are giving ourselves to. An example of this is the communist movement. We know from history that it was supposed to make all people equal, which sounds like a noble cause. Many people gave themselves to this movement. It used every means possible, but 100 million people died as a result.

A TRUE PERSPECTIVE ON COMMUNISM

Many things have given rise to Communism. There is a definite climate of frustration in the world. There is the population explosion and the problem of food shortages in places like Ethiopia. Communism offers a solution and has done well in transforming backward agrarian nations into industrial powers. It offers mankind an international brotherhood. It appeals to the whole man. It appeals to young people who want to dedicate their lives to a planet-shaking movement.

Basic characteristics of communism

- State Ownership. The state owns all capital in a communist system including all land, machines, buildings and infrastructure.
- Central Planning
- Bureaucratic Elite
- "Common Good"
- Competition
- Austerity
- Single Party
- Repression

Today, however, in China, communism has produced oppression and political domination where the church is being persecuted. This is also true in North Korea, Cuba and Venezuela.

It is interesting to note that Vladimir Lenin studied to be an orthodox priest. He learned the discipleship methods of Jesus Christ. Jesus chose twelve men. Lenin chose a few followers who were willing to dedicate their whole lives to the communist cause.

A LETTER FROM A YOUNG COMMUNIST
TO HIS FIANCÉE ABOUT HIS TRUE COMMITMENT

"We communists have a high casualty rate. We are the ones who get shot and hung and ridiculed and fired from our jobs and in every other way made as uncomfortable as possible. A certain percentage of us get killed or imprisoned. We live in virtual poverty. We turn back to the party every penny we make above what is absolutely necessary to keep us alive. We communists do not have the time or the money for many movies, or concerts, or T-bone steaks, or decent homes, or new cars. We have been described as fanatics. We are fanatics. Our lives are dominated by one great overshadowing factor: The struggle for world communism. We communists have a philosophy of life that no amount of money can buy. We have a cause to fight for, a definite purpose in life. We subordinate our petty personal selves to the great movement of humanity; and if our personal lives seem hard or our egos appear to suffer through subordination to the party, then we are adequately compensated by the thought that each of us in his small way is contributing to something new and true and better for mankind.

There is one thing in which I am in dead earnest about, and that is the communist cause. It is my life, my business, my religion, my hobby, my sweetheart, my wife, and my mistress, my breath and meat. I work at it in the daytime and dream of it at night. Its hold on me grows, not lessens, as time goes on; therefore, I cannot carry on a friendship, a love affair, or even a conversation without relating it to this force that both drives and

CIVIL RIGHTS MOVEMENT

"One day men would not be judged
by the color of their skin,
but by the conduct of their character."
Dr. Martin Luther King Jr.

The 20th century also witnessed another revolution. It was the civil rights movement led by Dr. Martin Luther King Jr. His famous, "I have a dream" speech penetrated the minds and hearts of people around the world. It was a revolution for equality and it fought against discrimination and prejudice. His non-violent revolution was inspired by Mahatma Gandhi of India who also believed in peaceful change.

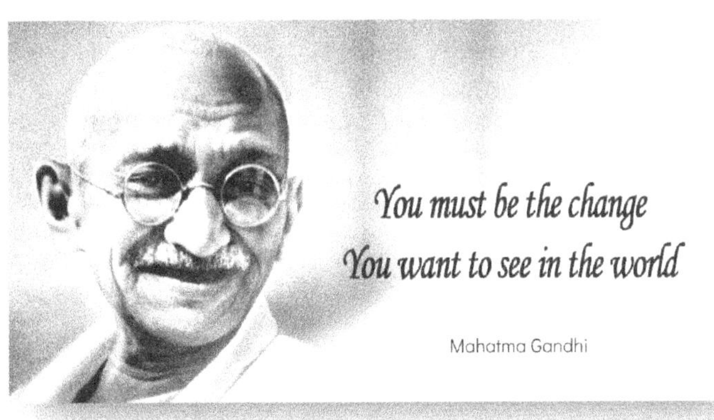

ISLAMIC REVOLUTIONARY

The Islamic Revolution challenges followers to give their lives to the cause of Allah. However, Islam brings Sharia law and total oppression and domination of society.

OUR CAUSE AS FOLLOWERS OF JESUS

As followers of Jesus, we have the greatest cause on earth, and there are no negative consequences.

This cause is to fulfill the Great Commission of Jesus Christ as stated in Matthew 28:18-20,
"All authority has been given to me on heaven and on earth. Therefore, go and make disciples of all nations, baptizing them in the name of the Father, the Son and the Holy Spirit, and teaching them to do all that I have commanded you."

Acts 1:8 further elaborates: *"But you shall receive power when the Holy Spirit comes upon you and you shall be my witnesses in Jerusalem, in Judea and Samaria, and to the uttermost part of the earth."*

To make followers of Jesus, we must first know and follow Jesus ourselves and then make Him known to others. This is the simple mantra of our cause. The Scripture gives us two basic goals. The first is our sanctification (to be more like Christ (I Thess. 3: 10).

The second is to preach the Gospel.

Jesus Christ challenged His disciples with these words when He saw the multitudes that were distressed and downcast like sheep without a shepherd. *"Pray the Lord of the Harvest to send forth laborers into the harvest field."* (Matthew 9).

Christ promised ultimate success for this cause. He said He would build His church and that the gates of hell would not prevail against it. (Matthew 16:18-20)

Our cause is the greatest cause on earth. We stand for truth. It is a truth revolution. We seek to know the truth, live the truth, and preach the truth. Jesus Christ is the way, the truth and the life, no one can come to the Father except by Him. (John 14)

SACRIFICIAL COMMITMENT TO THE CAUSE

Jesus taught that following him would not be easy. We must make sacrifices. But then he exemplified a life of sacrifice by giving His life for the church. I Peter 2:21 ff teaches, *"To this you were called, because Christ suffered for you, leaving you an example, that you should follow in His steps. He committed no sin, and no deceit was found in his mouth. When they hurled their insults at him, he did not retaliate; when he suffered, he made no threats. Instead, he entrusted himself to him who judges justly. He himself bore our sins in his body on the tree, so that we might die to sins and live for righteousness; by His wounds you have been healed."*

The Apostles showed great commitment to the cause of Christ as recounted in the book of Acts. Peter and John were courageous in their proclamation of the Gospel. They were put in jail for preaching Christ but refused to stop speaking about Jesus. They refused to obey their detractors and persecutors even when these were religious leaders.

The Apostle Paul was transformed by the power of the Gospel. Before knowing Christ, he was a zealous Jew who persecuted the church. Jesus transformed his life and he became a fully devoted follower of the Lord. He preached Christ in spite of persecution and suffering. In Acts 20, we read how he shared with the Ephesian elders about his suffering at the hands of the Jews. He did not hesitate to preach Jesus to them. He was heading to Jerusalem and knew what would occur. He knew prison and hardship awaited him there.

He shared, *"However, I consider my life worth nothing to me, if only I may finish the race and complete the task the Lord Jesus has given me- the task of testifying to the gospel of God's grace."*

In the end, he did give his life for the Gospel. This is what true commitment and sacrifice to the Cause is all about.

Paul said to Timothy that he must suffer hardship as a good soldier of Jesus Christ (II Timothy 2).

VISIONARY FAITH

Proverbs 29:18 states that without vision the people perish. Having visionary goals is the starting point for starting a church and seeing that church grow. Church growth experts speak of the necessity of having a conception in one's heart before attempting to start a church. Obviously, this vision must be born of prayer. Nehemiah had a vision for rebuilding the walls of Jerusalem. He did not share this with others until the proper time. First, he prayed. Then he surveyed the situation and established his plans. In other words, he saw the need, established the goals, and determined the means (materials, people, plans, etc.) whereby those goals would be achieved. The Bible is full of examples of men of vision. Paul, for example, had a vision to preach the gospel all over the known world. He and Barnabas had a specific goal to proclaim the Word of God (Acts 13:5). They sought to thoroughly saturate an untouched area like Paphos (Acts 13:13).

It is interesting to note that when persecution came their goals were changed (Acts 14:5,6). They learned to be flexible in their plans.

They also had a goal to disciple and teach as well as evangelize (Acts 13:22).

Men of God throughout history have followed their example.

William Carey (left) saw the whole world as his parish. He went to India to conquer that land for Jesus, while his fellow preachers at home in England were preoccupied with their own parishes.

Henry Martyn (center) saw India, Persia, and Arabia. He had a vision of the Muslim world while the church at home was engrossed in petty theological squabbles. It was said of **A.B. Simpson** (right) that his *"lifework seemed to be to push on alone, where his fellows had nothing to explore."* (J. Oswald Sanders, Spiritual Leadership).

It is obvious we need to be men of vision. We need to see opportunities and not difficulties.

> "Attempt something so impossible that unless God is in it, it is doomed to failure."
> John Haggai

We need to heed his advice.

> "Expect great things from God;
> Attempt great things for God."
> William Carey

I would like to share five essentials in capturing and maintaining a vision.

1.   The first essential is that we must have a clear-cut specific goal. We must see it clearly.

The Apostle Paul said, *"but one thing I do..."* (Phil. 3:13). He did not say 40 things I dabble in. Our goal should be in line with the Lord's command to make disciples of all nations (Matthew 28:18-20). We need to have personal, family, and ministry goals.

2.   The second essential is that we must want it desperately with a deep-seated desire.

I remember my great desire to play football in high school. I desired it so much that I disciplined my time well to enable me to prepare both mentally and physically. I made the team and played on the first squad.

3.   The third essential is that we must pursue it enthusiastically. Whatever we do we are to do it for the Lord and with all our hearts (Colossians 3:23).

I sold books one summer as my summer job. We had to memorize a phrase which really helped me to keep enthusiastic. It was: *"If you want to be enthusiastic you have to act enthusiastic."*

We have the greatest Book in the world, the Bible. We have a life changing message. The people we minister to are the greatest in the world, so we have every reason to be enthusiastic.

> "Rather than live with reluctance,
> let's live with exuberance.
> Instead of fearing what's ahead,
> let's face it head-on, with enthusiasm.
> And because life is so terribly short,
> let's do everything we can
> to make it sweet."
>
> Charles Swindoll

4.   The fourth essential is that we must follow it faithfully with a bulldog tenacity.

The Apostle Paul was a great example of this. He endured much for the cause of Jesus Christ (II Corinthians 4:7-12,) but never gave up.

Abraham Lincoln was a great example of one who pursued his goal with bulldog tenacity.

Look at his record:

In 1831 he failed in business;
1832 - defeated for the legislature;
1833 - failed in business again
1834 - elected to the legislature;
1835 - his sweetheart died;
1836 - he had a nervous breakdown; 1838 - defeated for legislative speaker;
1840 - defeated for elector;
1843 - defeated for Congress;
1846 - elected to Congress;
1848 - defeated for Congress;
1855 - defeated for Senate;
1856 - defeated for Vice-President;
1858 - defeated for Senate.
1860 - the record changed and Abraham Lincoln was elected as President of the United States. His example has influenced leaders around the world.

"We can complain
because rose bushes have thorns,
or rejoice because thorn bushes have roses."

Abraham Lincoln

5.   The fifth and last essential is to review, realign, and rededicate ourselves regularly. Situations change and therefore goals may change.

MEN OF GOD WITH A GREAT VISION AND A GREAT COMMITMENT

Throughout history, there have been many great church leaders and missionaries who have given their lives for the sake of the Gospel. John Knox, said, *"Give me Scotland or I die."* It was said that Mary Queen of Scots feared the prayers of John Knox more than the armies of the continent of Europe. He died preaching the gospel.

William Carey, the shoemaker from England, prayed over a map of India. He claimed it for Jesus. He also said, *"Give me India or I die."*
He went and shook a country for Christ.

Dwight L. Moody was a man totally dedicated to the cause of Christ.

"It was during his first visit to Britain that Moody heard the words which set him hungering and thirsting after a deeper Christian experience and which marked a new era in his life. These words were spoken to him by Mr. Henry Varley, the well-known evangelist, as they sat together on a seat in a public park in Dublin. The words were these: "The world has yet to see what God will do with and for and in and by the man who is fully consecrated to Him."
Moody thought, "he said, 'a man--, not a great man, or a learned man, or a smart man, but simply a man. I am a man, and it lies with the man himself whether he will or will not make that entire and full consecration. I will try my utmost to be that man.'
The words kept ringing in his mind and burning their way into his soul until finally he was led into the deeper, richer, fuller experience for which his soul yearned."
"The impression these words made was deepened soon afterward by words spoken by Mr. Brewley, of Dublin, Ireland, to whom he was introduced by a friend. "Is he out and out for Christ?" was the

question. From that time forward Moody's desire to be "O and O" for Christ was supreme." Out and Out means all in or totally committed to.

J. Oswald Sanders states:*" The real qualities of leadership are to be found in those who are willing to suffer for the sake of objectives great enough to demand their wholehearted obedience."*
Leadership has been defined as influence. Lord Montgomery stated: *"Leadership is the capacity and will to rally men and women to a common purpose and the character which inspires confidence."* (Unknown source)

CHARLES SIMEON: A PASTOR WITH A VISION OF GOD AND HIS GLORY - different insights

1. The Unripe Self

That is what I want to turn to now. First his trials, and then finally, the resources that enabled him to press on to the end and not give up. How was he able to be "patient in tribulation?"

The most fundamental trial that Simeon had — and that we all have — was himself. He had a somewhat harsh and self-assertive air about him.

One day, early in Simeon's ministry, he was visiting Henry Venn, who was a pastor 12 miles from Cambridge at Yelling. When he left to go home Venn's daughters complained to their 
father about his manner. Venn took the girls to the back yard and said, "Pick me one of those peaches." But it was early summer, and "the time of peaches was not yet." They asked why he would want the green, unripe fruit. Venn replied, "Well, my dears, it is green now, and we must wait; but a little more sun, and a few more showers, and the peach will be ripe and sweet. So, it is with Mr. Simeon."

Simeon came to know himself and his sin very deeply. He described his maturing in the ministry as a growing downward. We will come back to this as the key to his great perseverance and success.

2. The Unwanted Vicar

The vicar of Trinity Church died in October 1782, just as Charles Simeon was about to leave the university to live in his father's home. Simeon had often walked by the church, he tells us, and said to himself, "How should I rejoice if God were to give me that church, that I might preach the Gospel there and be a herald for Him in the University" (Moule, 37). His dream came true when Bishop Yorke appointed him "curate-in-charge" (being only ordained a deacon at the time). His wealthy father had nudged the Bishop and the pastor at St. Edwards, where Simeon preached that summer, gave him an endorsement. He preached his first sermon there November 10, 1782. But the parishioners did not want Simeon. They wanted the assistant curate Mr. Hammond. Simeon was willing to step out, but then the Bishop told him that even if he did decline the appointment, he would not appoint Hammond. So, Simeon stayed — for fifty-four years! And gradually — very gradually — overcame the opposition.

The first thing the congregation did in rebellion against Simeon was to refuse to let him be the Sunday afternoon lecturer. This was in their charge. It was like a second Sunday service. For five years they assigned the lecture to Mr. Hammond. Then when he left, instead of turning it over to their pastor of five years they gave it to another independent man for seven more years! Finally, in 1794, Simeon was chosen lecturer. Imagine serving for 12 years a church whose members were so resistant to your leadership they would not let you preach Sunday evenings, but hired an assistant to keep you out.
Simeon tried to start a later Sunday evening service and many townspeople came. But the churchwardens locked the doors while the people stood waiting in the street. Once Simeon had the doors opened by a locksmith, but when it happened again, he pulled back and dropped the service.

The second thing the church did was to lock the pew doors on Sunday mornings. The pewholders refused to come and refused to let others sit in their personal pews. Simeon set up seats in the aisles and nooks and corners at his own expense.

But the churchwardens took them out and threw them in the churchyard. When he tried to visit from house to house, hardly a door would open to him. This situation lasted at least ten years. The records show that in 1792 Simeon got a legal decision that the pewholders could not lock their pews and stay away indefinitely. But he didn't use it. He let his steady, relentless ministry of the word and prayer and community witness gradually overcome the resistance.

But I mustn't give the impression that all the troubles were over after the first 12 years. After years of peace, in 1812 (after he had been there 30 years!) there were again opponents in the congregation making the waters rough. He wrote to a friend, *"I used to sail in the Pacific; I am now learning to navigate the Red Sea that is full of shoals and rocks."* Who of us would not have immediately concluded at age 53, after thirty years in one church that an upsurge of opposition is a sure sign to move on? But again, he endured patiently and in 1816 he wrote that peace had come and the church was better attended than ever.

3. Despised in His Own University

As the students made their way to Trinity Church, they were prejudiced against the pastor by the hostile congregation, and for years he was slandered with all kinds of rumors. Basically, his enemies said that he was a bad man with a front of piety.
The students at Cambridge held Simeon in derision for his biblical preaching and his uncompromising stand as an evangelical. They repeatedly disrupted his services and caused a tumult in the streets.

One observer wrote from personal experience, *"For many years Trinity Church and the streets leading to it were the scenes of the most disgraceful tumults."* (Moule, 58).

On one occasion a band of undergraduates determined to assault Simeon personally as he left the church after service. They waited by the usual exit for him, but providentially he took another way home that day.

Students who were converted and wakened by Simeon's preaching were soon ostracized and ridiculed. They were called "Sims" — a term that lasted all the way to the 1860's and their way of thinking was derisively called "Simeonism."

But harder to bear than the insults of the students, was the ostracism and coldness of his peers in the university. One of the Fellows scheduled Greek classes on Sunday night to prevent students from going to Simeon's service. In another instance one of the students who looked up to Simeon was denied an academic prize because of his "Simeonism."

Sometimes Simeon felt utterly alone at the university where he lived. He looked back on those early years and wrote, *"I remember the time that I was quite surprised that a Fellow of my own College ventured to walk with me for a quarter of an hour on the grass-plot before Clare Hall; and for many years after I began my ministry I was 'as a man wondered at,' by reason of the paucity of those who showed any regard for true religion."* (Moule, 59).

Even after he had won the respect of many, there could be grave mistreatment. For example, even as late as 1816 (34 years into his ministry) he wrote to a missionary friend, *"Such conduct is observed towards me at this very hour by one of the Fellows of the College as, if practiced by me, would set not the College only but the whole town and University in a flame."* (Moule, 127).

4. Standing Strong in the Face of Opposition

When he was appointed as the pastor of a church in Cambridge, England, in 1783 Charles Simeon was delighted. The people of the church did not share his joy. Many of the prominent members of the church opposed his convictions on reaching the lost with the gospel. To show their displeasure they locked their pew boxes during the service and left them empty so that those who came to hear Simeon preach had to stand or sit in the aisles. Eventually God began to work, and Simeon's ministry had a powerful influence on the nation of England and the world through his efforts to encourage missionary work.

During the dark days of opposition Simeon wrote: *"In this state of things I saw no remedy but faith and patience.... It was painful indeed to see the church, with the exception of the aisles, almost forsaken; but I thought that if God would only give a double blessing to the congregation that did attend, there would on the whole be as much good done as if the congregation were doubled and the blessing limited to only half the amount. This comforted me many, many times, when without such a reflection, I should have sunk under my burden."*

Opposition does not mean that we are doing things wrong—often it is evidence that we are doing things right. If we allow ourselves to be deterred from doing anything unless we have complete approval, it is certain that we will never accomplish anything of value. Rather than being discouraged by opposition, we should take comfort in God's faithfulness and keep on doing what is right.

Bill Bright, founder of Campus Crusade for Christ (now CRU) had a vision to reach the world for Christ. I was transformed by this vision when I was involved with CRU.

George Verwer, the founder of Operation Mobilization wears a shirt with a world on it to remind himself to reach the world.

Oswald J. Smith started People's Church in Toronto to be a base for reaching the world for Christ. They support hundreds of missionaries and Dr. Smith travelled extensively to preach the gospel.

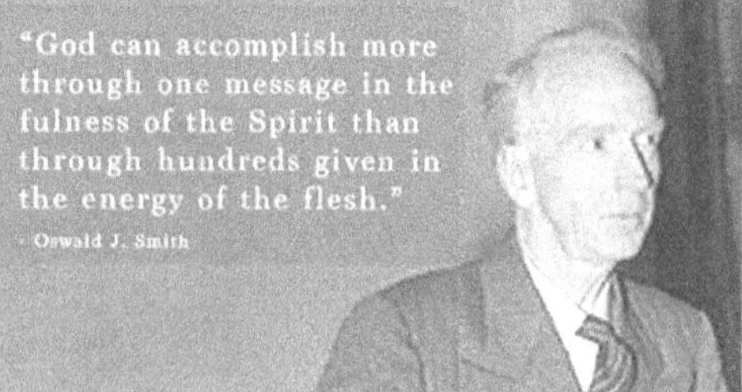

I want to add another leader whom I have known personally for 35 years. He is **Korky Davey.** We got to know Korky and Annie when they visited our home in the 1980's. He works with Open Air Campaigners and is the premier sketch board preacher in the world. He even taught open air sketch board  evangelism at the Billy Graham Evangelistic meetings in Amsterdam. He leads a team in Bristol, England and reaches 1000's of students a year in public schools. He also has ministry in Africa, Spain, Italy, Austria and Eastern Europe. He taught our missionaries in Italy and Austria and helped us begin Reach the City in Vienna which took place every year while we were there and helped to train 100's of believers.

Korkey is enthusiastic, funny, a great motivator and a conventional British gentleman. He loves his tea and brings his own bags and tea maker. Once while waiting at the airport in Entebbe, Uganda, at teatime, being a good Englishman, he took out his portable electric hot water maker, and plugged it into the nearest electrical socket to make tea. When he did this, the whole airport blacked out. He blew their fuse. He quickly put the machine away and quietly walked away.

Korky is also quite frugal or I should say he tries to be a good steward of God's finances. While with his team in Spain, they were all hungry and did not have much money. They went to a restaurant and were going to order a simple meal like French fries to split. When they arrived, they sat next to a couple who had a scrumptious meal in front of them. After eating half of their meal, the couple got up suddenly and left. The team with Korky looked at what was left and ate it. Much to their surprise, after a few minutes, the couple returned to their table. What a surprise! The team got a good laugh out of it and the story continues to be told around the world.

LOVE EUROPE (A Great Vision for a Great Continent)

Love Europe was organized by Operation Mobilization under George Verwer. We were able to attend two of them in 1988 and in 1990.

We gathered with 5000 young people for worship, prayer, training and outreach. In 1988 they prayed for the Berlin Wall to fall. It did and teams went to Poland, Czech Republic, Hungary, and Albania in 1990. When the wall came down, Eastern Europe opened up and the Gospel went forward in power.

The three emphases of Love Europe were,
1. to reach the big cities of the continent
2. to reach into Eastern Europe
3. to reach out to Muslims who live in Europe.

It was a great vision that captured our hearts. At that time, we were involved in a church planting ministry in Milan, Italy. This included open air ministry with Open Air Campaigners and an English-speaking ministry at the Milan Bible Church. As we prayed, God moved. He opened the door for us to move to Vienna, Austria (after receiving an invitation to lead an international congregation). We moved there and began to pastor and do open air work in the city square. God led Korky Davey to help us there, too. One of our young men, Stefan Hoefler, caught the vision and helped to establish Reach the City, a summer campaign with open air training and outreach.
It was unbelievable.

Stephan Hoefler

The Lord also led us to help with churches in Poland, Slovakia, and Hungary. We helped them in their evangelistic work. What a great joy.

In Vienna we ran into many Muslims bought there by God. We had had a few outreaches in Milan with Muslims from Morocco and there was also a group of Egyptian believers who were involved in one of our churches. In Vienna, however, God did great miracles. We had Iranians come to our church and seek salvation in Christ. They were Muslims who had seen the real side of Islam in Iran. The Mullahs had created hell on earth. It gave people a hunger for love, peace, and truth. These Muslims left Iran and traveled to Europe seeking a better life and truth. Many found Jesus. In fact, we baptized 80 Muslims.

As we look back, we see how God answered our prayers. We prayed for Love Europe and God enabled us to Reach the Cities, reach into Eastern Europe, and reach out to Muslims.

GO AND MAKE DISCIPLES

tekst/muziek: Val Howard
Matthéüs 28:19,20

QUESTION: What is the Prayer of Jabez?

Answer:

The prayer of Jabez is found in a historical note within a genealogy:

"Jabez was more honorable than his brothers. His mother had named him Jabez, saying, 'I gave birth to him in pain.' Jabez cried out to the God of Israel, 'Oh, that you would bless me and enlarge my territory! Let your hand be with me and keep me from harm so that I will be free from pain.' And God granted his request." (1 Chronicles 4:9–10)

The prayer has become well-known due to the publication of the best-selling book, *The Prayer of Jabez: Breaking Through to the Blessed Life* (2000), by Dr. Bruce Wilkinson with David Kopp.

Little is known of Jabez, other than that he was a descendant of Judah, he was an honorable man, and his mother named him "Jabez" (meaning "sorrowful" or "sorrow-maker") because his had been a painful birth. In his prayer, Jabez cries out to God for protection and blessing. Using a play on words, Jabez, the "man of sorrow," asks God to keep him from that sorrow that his name both recalled and foreboded.

The prayer of Jabez in 1 Chronicles 4:10 contains an urgent request for four things:

1) God's blessing. Jabez acknowledges that the God of Israel is the source of all blessing, and he asks God for His grace. No doubt, this request was based, at least in part, on God's promise of blessing to Abraham and his descendants (Genesis 22:17).

2) An expansion of territory. Jabez prays for victory and prosperity in all his endeavors and that his life would be marked by increase.

3) The presence of God's hand. This was Jabez's way of asking for the guidance of God and His strength to be evident in his daily existence.

4)   Protection from harm. Jesus taught His disciples to pray in this way: "Father in heaven . . . deliver us from the evil one" (Matthew 6:9, 13).

Jabez looks to God in confidence as his defender.
Jabez's goal in his prayer was to live free from sorrow, and the last thing we read about him is that God heard and answered his prayer. Like Solomon's humble prayer for wisdom (1 Kings 3:5–14), Jabez's devout prayer for blessing was answered. The success Jabez enjoyed outweighed the sorrow of his beginning. The prayer of Jabez overcame the name of Jabez.

The prayer of Jabez is a good example of how we should make prayer a priority in our lives. We should always look to God for our help in time of need, and we can take our requests straight to the throne of grace (Hebrews 4:16). Along with the prayers of Hannah, Jonah, Hezekiah, Paul—and of course our Lord's model prayer (Matthew 6:9–13)—the prayer of Jabez provides a wonderful instance of a child of God approaching the Majesty on High in humility, faith, and reliance upon God's goodness.

GOD'S BLESSING AS WE PRAY THE PRAYER OF JABEZ

Bruce Wilkerson's book *The Prayer of Jabez* was dynamite. Grace Church, where we were serving at that time, began to pray the prayer (see above). Another church, the Vienna Christian Center, put the verse in the front of the sanctuary behind the pulpit. Little did I realized how powerfully God was going to work.

We all remember Sept. 11, 2001, with the destruction of the World Trade Center and 3000 murdered. I heard the news while on a ministry trip in Prague, Czech Republic, and was shocked as everyone was. Prague was in panic mode. When I got back to my family in Vienna, we all mourned.

The next day I got a call from the Austrian newspaper, *the Standard*. The newspaper goes out to 7 million people. They wanted to interview me, an evangelical pastor, about my feelings toward the attack of 9/11. They also would interview a Rabbi and an Imam. The reporter came to our home with a photographer. I shared my feelings, and some of my testimony and that we wanted to minister to Muslims who need the Lord.

The day after the interview, I heard a reporter on CNN say that Americans overseas should keep a low profile. My wife and I panicked. Our names and picture would be in that newspaper.

We called *the Standard* to ask if they could not publish the article. They said it was too late. Well, the next day, the paper went out to seven million people with editions in German, Serbian, and Turkish. My testimony went out all over the country. Even my neighbors knew about it. I began to think maybe this was an answer to the Jabez prayer "to enlarge my territory". God works in a mysterious way.

God continued to enlarge our territory as the 80 Muslims mentioned above came to faith and were baptized. It is interesting that because of 9/11 the Iranians could not emigrate to the States. They had to stay in Vienna. God desires that no one should perish but that all should come to a knowledge of the truth. God's truth won out and He added to the church those who were saved. These folks also began to witness to their families and friends back in Iran.

I had to accompany the new Iranian believers, who wanted to stay in Austria, and testify before Magistrates. It was a great opportunity to witness to these immigration judges. One, magistrate asked to talk with me over coffee. He said he liked Bruce Springsteen and American culture. I also was called to speak to the head of indoctrination for the Roman Catholic Church in Vienna. The police called him to talk to me about these Iranians. I decided to bring my friend Amadeus, a Polish believer who had studied for the priesthood, because he spoke better German than I do. As we entered the office the head man recognized Amadeus. They had studied at seminary together. Wow!

In the office library I noticed that one of the sections was called "Sects." It included books about Mormons, Jehovah Witnesses, and Baptists. I knew I had a challenge. I then began to explain from the Bible why we baptized these former Muslims. He was enthralled and asked if he might visit our church. A great opportunity.

These new arrivals in our church brought some challenges. They were mostly men and these men began to approach the ladies in our church in a direct way, asking them to marry them (at first meeting). This was their culture. Whenever we had an *agape* or potluck at the church, they devoured it and not much was left for the rest of us. We understood that as refugees they did not have much money, but I had to instruct our folk, which included our new friends, to let women and children go first and to take small portions the first round.

LEADING TO ISRAEL

The story does not end there. God led us to work in Israel as pastor of Jerusalem Baptist Church and to be on staff with the Fellowship of Christian Athletes. The vision for the city and for Muslims continued. God sent us to Jerusalem. Jerusalem is one city with great two peoples, Jews and Arabs, and three major religions. Judaism, Islam, and Christianity. God has opened up ministry to Jews and Arabs as well as to internationals who visit the Holy Land. We have seen hundreds of Muslims make professions of faith through our sport ministry, and even some Jews have embraced Jesus as Messiah. It is amazing to see God open doors also to nominal Christians from all over who need to know about being born again. (See my second book on *Revolution* for more detail).

It all goes back to God. He answers prayer. It is an answer to the prayer for Love Europe. It is an answer to the prayer of Jabez that we prayed as well. It is an answer to our prayers for the peace of Jerusalem (commanded in Scripture). It is an answer to our times of prayer in college with Campus Crusade for Christ, and even an answer to the prayers of a few guys I met with at Dallas Seminary to pray for the world.

We met every Friday night praying for the city of Dallas and then praying over a map of the world. We decided to get together to pray at 5:00 in the morning for 40 days before I graduated. With our prayers for the world, we also prayed for wives (it is not good that man should be alone).

God sent us all around the world. Two went to India (one a native, one an American). I went to Italy. One went to Australia as an evangelist. One taught at Moody Bible School and one became a lawyer serving Christ in that field. God does more than we can ask or imagine (Ephesians 3:20).

THE SOUL WINNERS' FIRE

This is the name of a great book by John R. Rice, a famous evangelist and revivalist of the 20th century. The chapter on this fire ignited something in my soul. Jeremiah 20:8,9 states *"For since I spake, I cried out, I cried violence and spoil; because the word of the Lord was made a reproach unto me, and a derision, daily. "Then I said, I will not make mention of him, nor speak anymore in his name. but his word was in mine heart as a burning fire shut up in my bones, and I was weary with forbearing, and I could not stay."*

We need the fire from heaven to be an effective soul winner. Isaiah, the prophet, admitted he was a sinner. When he confessed this, a seraph took a coal of fire from off the alter in the temple, heavenly fire, and touched his lips, and said, *"Lo, this touched thy lips; and thine iniquity is taken away, and thy sin purged"* (Isaiah 6). Isaiah heard the call and said. *"Here I am Lord, send me."*

John the Baptist was a burning and shining light (John 5:35). Moses was called to his work by God who spoke to him from a burning bush, flaming but not consumed. Fire came in answer to the prayer of Elijah at Mt. Carmel. The people realized that, "The Lord--He is God!" The 120 disciples were filled with the Holy Ghost at Pentecost. There were tongues of fire.

The burden of ministry can be tough. When a preacher faces severe criticism, there are three choices.

1)   He can compromise, soft pedal and use smoother words. He would not speak so much about sin, repentance and judgment.

2)   A preacher may resign himself and suffer malice, reproach and the ridicule of wicked sinners and worldly church men and continue to preach.

3)   He can leave the ministry, which has been done by many. They have too much conscience and honesty to compromise Christ and dilute His Message. Jeremiah wanted to quit. He said, *"Then I said, I will not make mention of him, nor speak any more in his name."* (Jeremiah 20:9).

> "There is only one way to avoid criticism:
> Do nothing,
> Say nothing
> And be nothing."
>
> Aristotle

> "Do what you feel in your heart to be right for you'll be criticized anyway."
>
> Eleanor Roosevelt

JEREMIAH QUITS THE MINISTRY (for a moment)

Jeremiah prophesied that Judah would be carried away captive for their sins (Jer.18: 15-17; 19: 8,9; 20:4-6). The people agreed to not listen to him.

Pashur, a priest, got mad at Jeremiah and struck him. Even when he was imprisoned and then released, he continued to preach. He received more derision and did not want to speak any more. He figured that they would go their own way to destruction.

However, when he decided not to mention the Lord anymore, he found a seething volcano within himself. The Word of the Lord was in his heart like a burning fire shut up in his bones. He could not stand it anymore.

Outward circumstances and his relation to the people tempted him to quit, but inwardly, the fire of God was upon him and would not let him stop speaking. He was not only in the ministry, but the ministry was in him.

Too many preachers wait for a call and a job offer before beginning to preach. They forget that they can preach on the streets, in the jails and in shops and factories. There are enough dying men out there to reach. They do not need big auditoriums. The harvest is truly plentiful. I was at a revival conference one time and a man asked prayer because he was out of a preaching job. I wanted to tell him just to go outside and preach like the Lord did.

Mr. Rice continues,

> *"Our preachers are usually good men, often learned men, unselfish, self-sacrificing, sincere men, but that is not enough. Preachers lack the divine fire, the Christlike passion, the John the Baptist boldness, the Pauline urgency. We all need the Holy Spirit enduement of power that will fire the churches of God. We all need to have fire from Heaven, the fire in our bones that Jeremiah had. "*

Jeremiah had received a call from God in his youth even before he was born (Jeremiah 1:4-9). He said to the Lord that he could not speak because he was a child. God told him to speak. He said not to be afraid of people. The Lord touched his mouth and put words in it. This was his call. Moses, Isaiah and Elijah were called. Think about the call of Saul of Tarsus. Think about Jesus calling his fishermen to leave their nets. How has God called us? The early Christians received the Holy Spirit and began to preach with boldness. We need that call and we need to pray for boldness, and to be empowered by the Holy Spirit.

THE SOUL-WINNING PASSION

We must have a call and a passion for the work. Our message is from God. We must preach because we have fire in our bones.

Paul told Timothy to *"Preach the Word, be instant in season and out of season."* He was to preach when men heard and when they would not hear. Paul said, *"For though I preach the Gospel, I have nothing to glory of; for necessity is laid upon me; yea, woe is unto me if I do not preach the Gospel. For if I do this thing willingly, I have a reward; but if against my will, dispensation of the gospel is committed unto me."*

(I Cor. 9:16,17). Paul was a bond slave of Jesus Christ, enslaved by the gospel. He was miserable when he was not preaching. He was willing to die in order to see his fellow Jews saved (Romans 10). This is not something organizations give. It is divine and a consuming fire and comes from God Himself.

We must pray, confess our sins, and forsake them, until we get the anointing from heaven. Give us this holy passion, Lord.

GOD'S WORD IN THE PREACHER'S HEART-
THE SUPERNATURAL MESSAGE

Jeremiah received a Word from God. He wrote these words in a book. This proves the verbal inspiration of the Bible. But he did more. He spoke the words of the Lord. It was set aflame by the fire of the Holy Spirit. It takes the Spirit to preach the Word of God. It is the sword of the Spirit.

The Word must burn in the heart of the preacher. The Pharisees studied the Bible, taught the Bible but they were blind leaders of the blind. The letter of the law kills, but the Spirit makes alive. The Word of God which comes only through the brain and mouth of a preacher is blighting, fruitless, and powerless. The Word of God, in order to be blessed to the hearer must be preached from the heart.

Jeremiah said, *"His word was in mine heart as a burning fire shut up in my bones."* A preachers' heart is far more important than his head.

In Kansas City during the great Gipsy Smith revival years ago, an old preacher came into the room where Gipsy was sitting after the service. Thousands were being blessed and hundreds saved. The older minister placed his hands upon the evangelist's head and felt about it. "I am trying to find the secret of your success," he said.

"Too high! Too high! My friend, you are too high," Gipsy said. "The secret of whatever success God has given me is not up there but down here," and he placed his hand upon his heart!

The secret is the heart. The Word must be preached but we must pray much for God's anointing as we preach His Word. The Word must touch our hearts.

PRINCIPLE 6

CHARACTER DEVELOPMENT

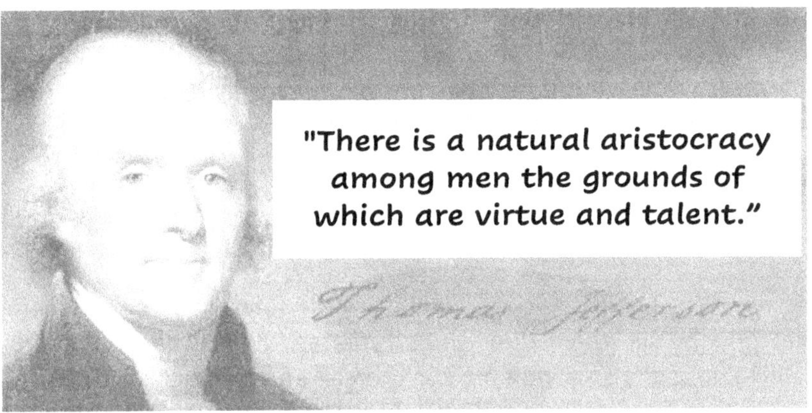

In other words, leaders standout for their character and their skills. Our basic goal as Christians is to be like Christ. This has to do with our character. God's purpose in saving us is given in Romans 8:29 where it says, *"For whom He foreknew, He also predestined to become conformed to the image of His Son."*   So, God predestined us to become like Christ.   But we also have a part or responsibility in becoming like Christ.   Philippians 2:12,13 puts these two ideas together. We read, *"work out your own salvation with fear and trembling because it is God who is at work in you both to will and to do of His good pleasure?"*

Let us look at God's work and then at what we must do in light of Scripture. God's goal for us is to be mature Christians reflecting His glory. He uses the Holy Spirit to lead, guide, and discipline us.
The Word is also used by God to help us to be like Christ (Psalm 19, Psalm 119). God uses trials to perfect us.

James 1 says, *"Consider it all joy my brethren, when you encounter various trials, knowing that the testing of your faith produces endurance. Let endurance have its perfect result that you may be perfect and complete, lacking in nothing."* Paul realized that God had given him a thorn in the flesh to keep him humble. When he was weak, he was strong (2 Corinthians 12). He was content with trials, persecutions, weaknesses, etc. These are examples of God's work to conform us to the image of Christ. In addition, Romans 5:3-5: tells us, *"Not only so, but we also rejoice in our suffering, because we know that suffering produces perseverance; perseverance, character; and character, hope. And hope does not disappoint us, because God has poured out his love into our hearts by the Holy Spirit, whom he has given us."*

God's Catfish

In one of his books Chuck Swindoll tells the following story. It seems that in the north-eastern United States, codfish are not only delectable, but also a very big commercial enterprise. A vast industry has grown up around catching, preparing and shipping codfish to every part of the country.

But the great demand for codfish posed a problem to the shippers. At first, they froze the codfish before shipping, but freezing them took away much of the flavor. Then they tried shipping the codfish alive in salt water, but that didn't work either.

Finally, someone hit on a creative solution. The codfish were placed in a shipping tank with their natural enemy—catfish. From the time the codfish left the east coast until they arrived at their destination, the catfish chased the codfish all over the tank!

When they arrived, the codfish were as fresh as when they were first caught with no loss of flavor or texture.

All of us live in a "tank" of particular circumstances. Into that tank God has placed a few divinely appointed "catfish" who chase us from morning till night. Who knows? You may be living with a catfish right now. You may see one at work tomorrow morning. You may live next door to one.

The catfish in your life are not sent to destroy you but to keep you healthy, alert, and always swimming. Without them, you would soon get fat and flabby. Your unique flavor and texture would soon disappear.

Losing Your "Unique Flavor and Texture"

Chuck Swindoll is right. We live in a world filled with catfish who chase us day and night. It's entirely possible that you've been swimming hard all week with a great big "catfish" nipping at your heels. To be honest about it, you may feel as if your "unique flavor and texture" disappeared sometime last Thursday morning.

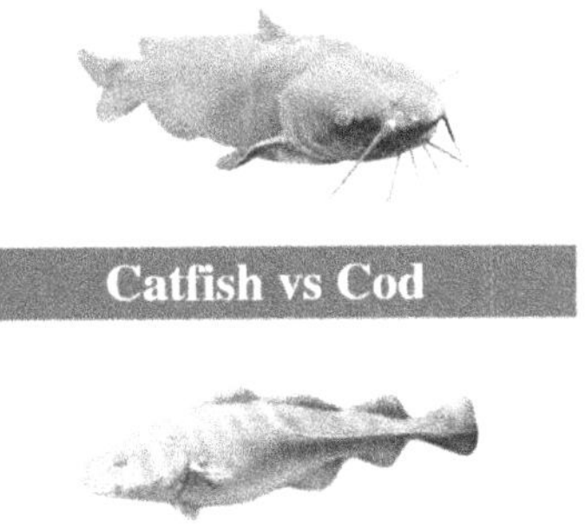

Here are three irrefutable facts about the catfish of life:

1. They make life difficult when it ought to be easy.
2. They always seem to catch us in our weaker moments.
3. They keep us swimming when we'd rather be resting.

That last point is very important. God has an important purpose for sending catfish into your life. He wants to keep you swimming.

"When you swim, you stay strong; when you stop swimming, you get fat and flabby." [1]

---

[1] (From Sermon by Pastor Ray Pritchard, Dallas Seminary grad and friend of mine.)

THE CHARACTER OF JESUS CHRIST OUR SERVANT LEADER

Today there is much written on the topic of leadership. Many corporate leaders whose goals are to get ahead by any means are held up as models of good leadership. Jesus taught, however, that to be a leader we must learn to be a servant. This is the key to unity in the church. Let us look at the example of Jesus.

1. Jesus Christ became a man and a servant. We read this in Philippians 2:1-11. We should look to the interests of others as Christ did. Christ was equal with God. He sat on the throne, but He did not regard equality with God a thing to be grasped. He did not reach for it or strive for it. He made Himself nothing and became a servant. What are the qualities of a good servant? The first is humility. Jesus humbled himself. We read in Proverbs 22, "By humility and the fear of the Lord are riches and honor and life." Isaiah 57:15 states: "For thus says the High and Lofty One who inhabits eternity, whose name is Holy: I dwell in the high and holy place with him who has a contrite and humble spirit, to revive the spirit of the humble, and to revive the heart of the contrite ones." Our attitude should be that of a child (Matthew 18:4). King Solomon recognized this at the beginning of his reign. Solomon said in I Kings 3:7: "Now oh Lord my God, You have made your servant king instead of my father David, but I am a little child; I do not know how to go out or come in." He asked for wisdom.

2. The second quality of a servant is obedience and submission. Christ submitted Himself to the will of the Father. He became a servant to all and went to the cross. He submitted himself to help his disciples. He washed their feet (John 13:5).

3. The third quality is sacrifice. During his earthly sojourn, Christ gave up the conveniences that many of us assume. He said, "The foxes have holes, and the birds of the air have nests, but the Son of Man has nowhere to lay His head."

A.   **Jesus was the perfect model of a servant leader.**

He was humble, He was obedient to His Father, and he sacrificed Himself for us. If we want to be good leaders, we also must be humble, be obedient to the Lord, and be willing to sacrifice ourselves for Him. In I Peter 5, the Apostle exhorts leaders to humble themselves and to be examples.

George Verwer, the founder of Operation Mobilization, was distributing tracts in Mumbai, India late one night, when he became tired and wanted to quit and sleep. Then he thought of Jesus who went the extra mile and so he continued to bring aid and tracts to the poor who were sleeping on the streets.

Hebrews 11 tells about Moses who had the privilege of being a prince in Egypt, but he was willing to give it up to identify with the children of Israel. He gave up all the riches of Egypt to follow Christ in his suffering.

God puts a premium on humility. In James 2 we are warned not to be like those who show their preference for the rich and noble and give them preferred seats of honor. He exhorts the believer to remember the poor and needy. I remember hearing about a church that had a special section in the front for important people. When Elizabeth Taylor and her husband John Warner visited the church, they were quickly escorted to that special section.

One of my assignments while I was in seminary was to spend a weekend in downtown Dallas with just $5.00 and a  toothbrush. I went with a friend. We stayed in the Salvation Army the first night and the Union Gospel Rescue mission the second night. We decided to visit a church on Sunday morning and went to one of the historic churches.

We went to a Sunday school class and, believe it or not, the lesson was from James 2. Unfortunately, the word did not affect them. No one greeted us.

Thank God that there are also some good examples of humility. In a

church in California two hippie types entered, walked right to the front, sat down on the floor in front of the pulpit, and began to worship God. This upset many of the members who were glad when they saw a church elder head down the aisle after them. Imagine their surprise, however, when the elder sat down next to them and began to raise his hands and worship the Lord with them.

Billy Graham was another good example. He heard of two long haired hippie guys who were coming into his crusade. The ushers wanted to keep them out, but He said, "Who are we to stop two men who look like Jesus?"

Jesus He was obedient. He went to the cross as a great act of sacrifice.

B. Jesus serves as a High Priest.

We read in Hebrews 5 that Christ become our great high priest and can thus understand our weaknesses. He has gone through the heavens. But he can sympathize because he was tempted in all things like we are.   He offered up prayers and petitions during his earthly sojourn and was heard because of his reverent submission. He learned obedience from what he suffered.

C. Christ suffered and submitted.

We read in I Peter 2:13-25 of Christ's example. We are to submit to those over us, and even bear up under unjust suffering. Christ became our example of suffering. He committed no sin and no deceit was found in his mouth. When they insulted him, he did not retaliate.   When he suffered, he uttered no threats. He entrusted Himself to the one who judges rightly. He bore our sins in his body so that we may die to sin and live for righteousness.

OUR HEARTS: BROKEN AND PURE

Our part in being conformed to the image of His Son is to obey. We are to watch over our hearts.

The Apostle Paul shared many ideas about the need to not only preach Christ, but to display Christ. He called us living epistles read by men (II Corinthians 2). Of course, the character we display comes out of our hearts. Proverbs 4:23. tells us to watch over our hearts because out of it flow the issues of life.

"A broken heart, wet eyes, and bended knees."

Stephen Olford on characteristics of a great leader.

TAKE HEED TO YOURSELF AND TO YOUR TEACHING

I Timothy 4:16 says, "Pay close attention to yourself and to your teaching, persevere in these things, for as you do this you will insure salvation for yourself and for those who hear you." In this chapter Paul is sharing with Timothy about the dangers he faces in Ephesus with many evil doctrines being taught. He exhorts Timothy to nourish himself in the Word and to be an example. If he does this, he will be used as an instrument of God to save others. Dr. Albert Martin, a great Reformed Baptist preacher, said in his booklet, *What is Wrong with Preaching Today,* that the problem with preaching is either in the character of the preacher or in the message that he preaches.

We should have sound lives and sound doctrine.

In Acts 20, Paul gave instructions to the elders in Ephesus. Giving his own testimony, he said he had served the Lord with humility and with tears. This was first. He said he had been courageous in preaching the truth. The truth is the Gospel which says that men must turn to God in repentance. He was willing to sacrifice his own life for the sake of the Gospel (verse 24).

In Acts 20:28, Paul continues telling the elders to keep watch over

themselves and the flock. They were to shepherd them and warn them to be careful of savage wolves who come to attack the believers. These wolves distort the truth in order to get other disciples to follow them. He said he had been warning them for three years.

Then he said he was free from greed. He said, *"It is more blessed to give than to receive,"* and proceeded to be an example of this by his hard work. Before we can preach Christ, we must be the right kind of people.

In Galatians 5, Paul exhorts believers to walk in the spirit. He says that the fruit of the Spirit is *"love, joy, peace, patience, kindness, goodness, faithfulness, gentleness and self-control."* The first three qualities are inner qualities. I Corinthians 13 speaks about the importance of love. It says that we can have knowledge, preach well, and sacrifice ourselves, BUT, if we do not have love, we are nothing.

He puts our teaching together with the importance of love or the right attitude. II Timothy 2:24-26 says, *"And the Lord's servant, must not quarrel; instead, he must be kind to everyone, able to teach, not resentful. Those who oppose him he must gently instruct in the hope that God will grant them repentance leading them to a knowledge of the truth and that they will come to their senses and escape from the trap of the devil, who has taken them captive to do his will."*

LESSONS FROM THE PASTORAL EPISTLES[2]

The Pastoral Epistles are full of great teaching for leaders. They include the characteristics of good leaders in the church. Let me share the qualifications of an elder as described in I Timothy 3:1-7, Titus 1:5-9, and other passages from the pastorals.

I Timothy 3:1-7

1. First, he must seek the responsibility (v. 1).
2. General Qualification: He must be above reproach (v. 2a).
It doesn't mean he has to be perfect. If he has done any wrong in the past against God or someone else, he must be a person who has made things right. Living in Israel is like being in a fishbowl. People watch us.

One time I accidently bumped into a car in my garage. I tried to wipe off the stain but there was more damage. As the day passed on, I realized I had to put a note on the car admitting my guilt. A short time later I got a call from the owner. He said that here in Israel nobody admits this. I was able to pay for the repair and also give a testimony of integrity to one of my neighbors. I see him often and am glad the Lord helped me to do the right thing.

3. Moral qualifications: (2b).
He must be the husband of one wife. This does not exclude a bachelor or a widower. It says an elder should not be divorced, even though I know that some churches accept divorcés as elders because of their view on divorce and re-marriage.
4. Mental Qualifications: (v2).
   a. He must be temperate. This means to be clear thinking and stable. We would say he must have his head on his shoulders. He must be mentally well balanced.
   b. He must be prudent or sober-minded. This means he is in control of himself or self-disciplined.

---

2 Help from lectures by Bill Standridge of Rome, Italy.

c. He must be respectable. He must show dignity. He must show courtesy, especially to non-Christians.

d. He must be able to teach. He should have an excellent knowledge of the Scriptures plus be able to communicate it clearly.

5. Personal Qualifications (vv. 2,3)

a. He must be hospitable. This means he must love strangers.

b. He must not be given to much wine. He must not be a drunkard.

c. He must not be violent but in control of his anger.

d. He must be gentle. This means he must be patient and able to bear up under provocations and the slights of men.

e. He must not be quarrelsome. He must not insist on his rights. He must not insist on always having his own way.

f. He must not be a lover of money. He should not seek to be rich or to use his position for gain.

6. Family qualification: He must govern his own family well. He must have his children under control (v. 4).

7. Spiritual maturity: He must not be a new convert. The church at Ephesus was founded 12 years before. He must have some maturity (v. 6).

8. He must also be esteemed by non-Christians (v. 7). He must be known for his honesty, integrity, and meekness.

TITUS 1:5-9

1. General Qualification: He must be blameless (v. 6).

2. Family Qualification: He must be the husband of one wife and have children who believe and who are obedient (v. 6).

3. Personal Qualifications:

a. He must not be arrogant (v. 7). An arrogant man refuses to listen to the advice of others.

b. He must not be quick tempered (v. 7).

c. He must not be given to much wine (v. 7).

d. He does not pursue dishonest gain (v.7). This is also a requirement for a deacon (I Tim. 3:8).

e. He must be hospitable (v. 8).

f. He must love what is good (v. 8). He is ready to help anyone who does good.

4. Mental Qualifications
   a. He must be prudent (v.8).
5. Moral and Spiritual Qualifications:
   a. He must be upright (v. 8). He lives rightly before God.
   b. He must be holy (v. 8). His life must conform to His high calling.
   c. He must be temperate or disciplined (v. 8). He is in control of his desires and appetite.
   d. He must hold firm to the Word (v.9). He defends the Word and obeys it.
   e. He is capable of exhorting with sound doctrine (v. 9). He has a good knowledge of the Word and has a gift of communicating it.
   f. He is capable of refuting with sound doctrine (v. 9). He must be able to recognize and refute   false doctrine.

OTHER VERSES THAT CAN BE APPLIED TO ELDERS

1. II Timothy 2:25 (Gentle, capable of teaching, patient)
2. I Timothy 1:5 (a pure heart, a good conscience, and a sincere faith).
3. I Timothy 4:6 (nourished on the Word of God and sound doctrine)
4. I Timothy 6:11 (He must pursue righteousness, godliness, faith, love, endurance and gentleness).
5. II Timothy 1:7 (He must be a man full of power, love, and a sound mind).

A SYNTHESIS OF THOSE QUALITIES WHICH ARE ESSENTIAL FOR A PASTOR/TEACHER ELDER

I Timothy 4:16

1. An exemplary spiritual life.
2. A deep, articulate, and systematic knowledge of the Word of God.

CHARACTER AND THE FOUR SEASONS

I heard a lecture on the importance of character by a great business guru, Jim Rohn. It can apply to us as believers. The main thesis is the importance of working on our character. With God's help, we can change ourselves. He shared that we can change, but certain circumstances cannot. As an example of such circumstances, he said that the seasons cannot be changed, and he compares these seasons  to diverse circumstances in our lives.

We must adapt and work with the different seasons of our lives. He uses the illustration of farming. In winter, for example, we cannot do much as far as going out and working the fields.

However, we can sharpen our tools.

We can work on our lives and skills and work to improve ourselves.

Then, in spring, we sow the seed.

We must take advantage of opportunities to plow the fields and plant the seed. We can preach the Word and do good as a testimony. In summer, we must continue to water and fight insects, vermin, and other factors that would try to attack the crop. In the same way, we need to take out the weeds in our lives, getting rid of sin in our lives which attacks our souls. Then comes fall. This is the time of harvest. We need to reap with care and work hard to take advantage of the opportunity to bear fruit. We must maximize this time.

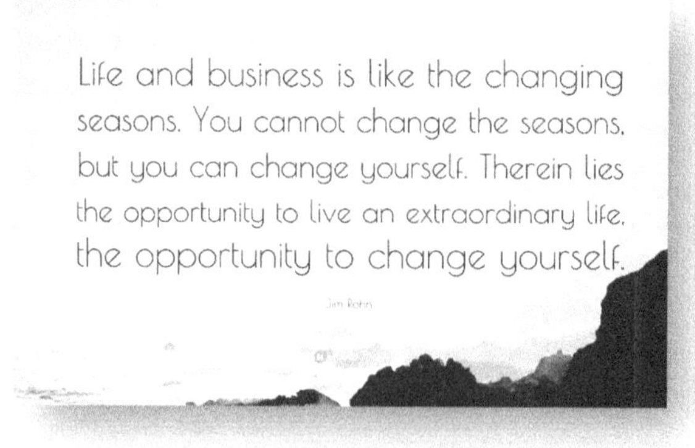

MEASURE OF A MAN

Faith, Hope, and Love. These are three qualities that the Apostle Paul emphasized in his letters as he wrote to churches (I Thessalonians 1). He did not commend churches for their attendance, budget, or building. He spoke of faith, hope, and love. God looks at the heart of man and the "heart" of a church. These are spiritual qualities which cannot be measured by a calculator or a scale. We leave it to God to evaluate. However, we can pray and aim for perfection (II Corinthians 13) and ask God to make these real in our lives and ministries.

TERRIBLE TIMES IN THE END DAYS:
WHAT SHOULD THE RIGHTEOUS DO?

The Apostle Paul spent time in Mamertine Prison in Rome. He was in a real hole and in chains. Food and drink were lowered to him. He knew he was facing death. While in this horrific situation he wrote a letter of encouragement and warning to Timothy, his son in the faith. He was aware that the Lord is coming and of what Timothy and further generations must do in light of His coming.

In II Timothy 3 and 4 he gave the condition of the world and what the man of God must be and do in these days. In the first part of chapter 3 we read of the terrible times that will come (3:1-9).

Men will be unholy, disobedient, ruthless, undisciplined, and selfish. In general, they will be true to their nature. Some will even have a veneer of righteousness and religiosity. However, their hearts will be far from God.

We see these conditions today in the violence in the cities of America. Mobs are looting stores and killing people. Paid protestors are supplying bricks to young people to wreak havoc. These are anarchists who want to bring down America. What must we do?

"When the foundations are shaken, what will the righteous do?" (Psalms 11:3)

Paul then shared with Timothy the need to follow his example of faith, love, perseverance, godliness, etc. Our first duty is our character. It is a matter of the heart (3:10-17). God is looking for men who will stand in the gap (Ezekiel 22:30). The Lord seeks a man after his own heart (I Sam 13:14). Jeremiah 4:25 states, *"I beheld and lo, there was no man."* Jeremiah 5:1 tells us, *"Run ye to and fro through the streets of Jerusalem and see… if you find a man… that executes judgement, that seeks the truth, and I will pardon it."*

Along with seeking after godliness, comes persecution. All those who live godly in Christ Jesus will suffer persecution (II Timothy 3:12). It is part of the cost of following Christ.

"The real qualities of leadership are to be found in those who are willing to suffer for the sake of objectives great enough to demand their wholehearted obedience."

J. Oswald Sanders

Not only are we to live for Christ and grow in character, but we must also preach Christ. Paul states in II Timothy 4:1-5 that in light of the coming of the Lord, Timothy is to preach the Word. This is the Word, meaning the Scriptures ((Timothy 3:16), or the Word meaning Christ Himself (the Living Word). He is to preach it in season and out of season, whether it is convenient or not. Inside the church and outside the church. He is to proclaim it clearly and boldly. We must tell it like it is. In the end times, men will prefer to have their ears tickled with soft theology and a watered-down Gospel.

Besides persecution from without there are also attacks from within. Paul experienced the desertion of workers and betrayal by friends as well as a vicious attack by Alexander, the Coppersmith (4:9-16).
He stated that in the end, all deserted him. However, he had encouragement. He knew of his promised reward in the crown of righteousness (4:8) but also of the power of the Gospel and God's enablement to preach it. He said that in spite of it all, Christ was with him and gave him the strength to proclaim the message of Christ. Here we see the conquest of the Gospel. Finally, Paul acknowledged the comforting hand of God. He knew that the Lord would lead him to the promised Kingdom by His hand and His grace. The Lord would protect him until his time to depart was at hand (4:17-18).

"Preach the Gospel at all times
And when necessary, use words."

Francis of Assisi

A PAINFUL BUT NECESSARY LESSON TO LEARN ABOUT CHARACTER

The Apostle charges Timothy to follow certain qualities. First, he tells Timothy to pursue righteousness. This means to do the right thing. Whatever, the consequences we should always seek to do the right thing in every situation. When I was a young believer, I was taking a class in philosophy at the University of Maryland. When I took an exam one day, I felt that I would fail, so I put a fake name like Superman on the exam thinking I could take it again later. The next day the professor shared that there were some interesting people in our class like Superman, Mickey Mouse, Batman. Others had done the same thing I did.

I was able to take the test again and passed the course. I went on to graduate from the University of Maryland and then went to Dallas Seminary to prepare for the ministry.

God called me to serve in Italy as a missionary. We left the USA and moved to Florence, Italy to learn Italian. While we were there, I was having my quiet time one day, when the Lord convicted me of my wrongdoing at the university 10 years before. I knew I had to make it right. So… I wrote the Philosophy department and confessed my wrongdoing. I feared that they would take away my degree.

One month later I got a response from the department. They said, *"Mr. Nucciarone, thank you for your letter. You realize that what you have done was wrong and could have caused you to be suspended. However, since you have suffered for 10 years, we forgive you."*

What a relief. However, they said, *"As an act of penance, you can contribute money to the philosophy department."*

I sent in $20. The letter continued saying, *"We have made an example of your letter. We have published your letter in the university newspaper (which went out to 30,000 students and faculty, of course without my name). We wanted to tell them it is always good to do the right thing."*

As believers, we must seek to do the right thing at all times.

After leading Israel out of Egypt, Moses assumed the posture of God at the waters of Meribah-Kadesh and so was denied the privilege of entering the Promised Land. David, the "man after God's own heart," bungled his way into the Bathsheba-Uriah disaster with his eyes wide open.   Solomon, with his unparalleled wisdom and legendary accomplishments, wound up collecting women like toys—and following other gods.

The list of failures of great men of God goes on ad nauseum. Howard McGlamery (Grace Chapel of Ladson) gives us a priceless contrast between three Christian leaders in our day:

"It was in 1945 that Billy Graham seemingly came out of nowhere and began filling auditoriums across America, preaching to as many as thirty thousand per night. But in 1945 there were two other preachers who were packing auditoriums. Their names were Chuck Templeton and Bron Clifford. Both were accomplishing the same thing as Billy Graham and even more.

"One seminary president, after hearing Templeton preach to an audience of thousands, called him 'the most gifted and talented young man in America today for preaching.'

In 1946, the National Association of Evangelicals published an article on men who were 'best used of God in that organization's five-year existence. The article highlighted the ministry of Chuck Templeton. Billy Graham was not even mentioned.

| Chuck Templeton | Bron Clifford | Billy Graham |

"Bron Clifford was a twenty-five-year-old fireball. In 1945, many believed Clifford was the most gifted preacher the church had seen in centuries. That same year, Clifford preached to a packed auditorium in Miami, Florida. People lined up ten deep outside the auditorium trying to get in. One wrote, 'At the age of twenty-five, young Clifford touched more lives, influenced more leaders, and set more attendance records than any other clergyman his age in American history. National leaders vied for his attention.' "Now we all know the name Billy Graham, but I doubt that many know the names Chuck Templeton and Bron Clifford. All three began their ministries in 1945 and all came out of the starting block like rockets. Why is it then that we are not familiar with the names Templeton and Clifford?

"Just five years later, Templeton left the ministry to pursue a career as a radio and television commentator and newspaper columnist. Templeton had decided he was no longer a believer in Christ in the orthodox sense of the term. By 1950, he no longer believed in the validity of the claims of Jesus Christ. Clifford, also, by 1954, had lost his family, his ministry, his health, and then—his life by 1954. Alcohol and financial irresponsibility had done him in. He wound up leaving his wife and their two children. At just thirty-five years of age, this once great preacher died from cirrhosis of the liver in a run-down motel on the edge of Amarillo, Texas. Some pastors in Amarillo took up a collection among themselves in order to purchase a casket so his body could be shipped back East for burial in a cemetery for the poor." (Excerpt from sermon by James Rutz.)

DON'T COMPARE YOURSELF TO OTHERS
OR BE JEALOUS OR ENVIOUS

This a real trap for a man of God.

We should always be comparing our life to Christ. We must seek to be like Him.

However, at times, we look to others and envy their successes in the ministry. We look at those with big churches and big budgets. When ministers get together, they often ask each other how big their churches are, how their offerings are, and how big their building is.

The Bible says we are not to compare ourselves to others.

Oh yes, I can be jealous in many ways. While walking to my economy seat on airplanes, through the first-class section, I have often thought how nice it would be to be famous and rich like the people sitting in first class. I must admit I did pray that just once in my life I could travel first class. Of course, I did not want to pay extra for it. Well it happened. While living in Austria, I was invited to speak at a mission's conference in the States. One of the members of the church said they could give me their air miles. Now I knew I had airmiles that were expiring, so I asked him if I could take his air miles and add mine to them and get a first-class seat. He was so nice and offered me enough air miles for business class on British Air (like first class). I took the offer. Of course, I dressed up professionally and enjoyed the perks which included the entrance into the British Air club at the airport.

I took my seat in the business section and enjoyed steak and fish.

Wonder how it felt? Oh well, just once is OK.

●　●●　●

LESSONS ON FAITH FROM MEN AND WOMEN OF GOD

I have benefitted from working with men and women of faith. In my book *Called to World Revolution* I mentioned two leaders who are men of vision and faith. They are Marian Pawlas from Palowice, Poland, and Manoj Magar from Mumbai, India. Read about their lives and ministries.

I have also learned a lot from my African brothers and sisters. They are great people of faith. They really believe in prayer and the reality of spiritual warfare. If you have an international church, you need to have Africans and Filipinos.

When we were serving in Milan, Italy, we had two African musicians in our church - Ezy and Isaac, both from Nigeria. Ezy played the guitar and Isaac the saxophone. They both sang. They were so positive and great men of faith. Ezy got married to Gillian, an Australian girl and had a little girl, Rhoda. The Lord led them to leave Italy and go to Africa. They were to fly from Amsterdam and would take a train from Milan to Amsterdam. They spent the night before with us. At around 6 pm I took them to the train station and sent them on their way. At around 11:00 pm I got a knock on our door. It was Ezy. I thought it was an angel. He came in and explained that he was stopped at the border with Switzerland because he did not have a transit visa. Gillian and Rhoda continued the journey. It was amazing to see his peace and tranquility. He was not at all worried and knew God had a plan. What faith! We prayed, then informed our field leader Ray Whitlock, who came up with a solution. Since he needed no visa to fly to Amsterdam, he offered to buy a one-way ticket for Ezy. God had planned it all. Ezy flew the next day, reunited with his family, and want on his way to Nigeria. What a lesson on trusting God.

> "Keep trusting God.
> He is always in control even when your
> circumstances may seem out of control."

TRUST AND OBEY FOR THERE'S NO OTHER WAY

When I am with a group on the Sea of Galilee, I like to share this insight.

Jesus taught many lessons to His disciples while he was ministering around the sea of Galilee. His base was Capernaum from which He preached and performed miracles and worked with His

disciples. There are two basic lessons. First, he called Peter and John, who were fishermen, saying, *"I will make you fishers of men"* (Matthew 4).

It says that they immediately left their nets and followed him. This is the lesson of obedience. He then taught them about faith.

He was with His disciples on a boat when a storm developed. He was sleeping. The disciples were worried.   When they woke Him, he calmed the storm and they all marveled at the one who could perform this miracle over nature. He said to them, *"Oh men of little faith."*

He also walked on the water and called Peter to do the same. Peter got out of the boat and walked on the water as he focused on Jesus. When his eyes looked elsewhere, he sank. Jesus also multiplied the fish and bread at Tabgha showing His disciples that they must trust Him.

Here are the two lessons: **Trust and Obey**. Just like the song we often sing. These are the two greatest lessons of the Christian life as told to us by Elizabeth Elliot Leach.

"When we walk with the Lord,
in the light of His Word,
what a glory He sheds on our
way! While we do His good will,
He abides with us still,
and with all who will
trust and obey."

CHARACTER IN SPORTS: PRIORITY OF COACH AND PLAYER

Building the Perfect Player
By Dan Bauer

In the 1985 film "Weird Science", two nerdy teenage boys build the

perfect woman. The main characters, Gary and Wyatt, sit in their dimly lit room with bras on their heads and feed vital information into their computer that happens to be wired to a Barbie doll. They succeed and Kelly LeBrock emerges from a haze-filled closet. It didn't win any Academy Awards but did score a 6.6 rating on IMBd.com.

As coaches, we partake in a similar exercise as we strive to create the perfect player. We are constantly striving to find new training methods, drills and motivation to improve our athletes. Which leads me to the question that I ask when speaking at coaching clinics:

"If we could build the perfect player, what would they look like? What are the five or six most important traits they should possess?"

Coaches willingly jump into the trap I have set with great answers like work ethic, coachability, competitive drive, positive attitude, heart, unselfishness, leadership and other high character traits.

"I have a job to do that is not very complicated, but it is often difficult: to get a group of men to do what they don't want to do so they can achieve the one thing they have wanted all their lives."

Dallas Cowboys Coach Tom Landry on discipline

For every ten answers like these I will get one answer addressing the fictional player's physical skills. It seems that if the consensus is that 90% of the most important characteristics of a great player fall into what we would define as character traits.

So why do we spend 90% of our time coaching their physical skills? That is the million-dollar question.

The answer can be found in the science behind the 3D framework of coaching where building the perfect player starts with building the perfect coach. This is where worthwhile science has studied and unlocked the keys to the heart and soul of our athletes. Those coaches looking to gain that edge in building player relationships and improving team unity are taking the journey through the 3D blueprint. They are moving past the 1st Dimension of physical skills and exploring the cerebral 2nd and 3rd Dimensions of the 3D framework. It involves tearing down the traditional walls of intimidation and building a relationship of mutual respect with our players.

Obviously, I am not advocating that we stop practicing the physical skills to play the game, but I am asking that you evaluate how you are building character in your athletes. The reasons are fairly clear as we have all had that ultra-skilled athlete that is either selfish or lazy or undisciplined. Or perhaps their sport IQ is so low that they struggle with even the simplest decisions in a contest. Finding a place for these athletes to play can be a nightmare. They can suck the life out of a team and drain a coach's patience.

Agreeing that skills are important, let's consider the opposite scenario. You have a moderately skilled player that has great work ethic, is unselfish, disciplined and is very coachable. How hard is it to find a place for this kid to play? Not very hard. In fact, we often consider these blue-collar grinders as the heart and soul of our teams. They lead by example, they are great teammates, they accept and excel at their role no matter what it is, and they always put the team first. If they play two minutes or the entire game, you get the same attitude and effort. Those are the type of, behind the scenes players, that are the core of every successful team.

They understand that being on a team is about something bigger than their own personal agendas.

The proof is consistently revealed in the post-season comments of championship teams. They instinctively spread credit throughout their team and always talk about the "family" atmosphere that enabled them to come together and focus on their goals. They bang the drum of their role players as strongly as they do their star players. They seldom talk about their talent level being superior, but always acclaim their unbreakable team unity. And when we look back at the projected pre-season favorites, they are rarely the ones holding the trophy.

The Six Pillars of Character

When character building is the foundation of our coaching philosophy, we build not only successful players, but resilient, hardworking and optimistic people that will use those traits for the rest of their life.

"Athletics must be the training ground for life;
it is the charcoal
that leads to the diamonds of the future."
Dan Bauer

When we focus on the process, which at times can be difficult and sometimes painful, we learn the valuable life lessons. That process must go deeper than the traditional emphasis on physical skills and challenges. We must tap into the hearts and souls of our players.

Despite all our technological advances since 1985, we still don't have a computer program to magically build the perfect player. What we do have is a framework, built by 3D Institute, that gives you the resources and road map to be a transformational coach who can, in turn, build character driven athletes.

That is a formula for success in athletics and in life.

When our athletes believe in our message and buy into our purpose, they take ownership. It becomes something bigger than just them and they will commit their heart and soul to the cause.

No weird science in that equation.

If you have never taken the 3D journey, you can sample the 3D Coaching training for free at www.becomea3dcoach.com.

"Success is built on the ABILITY to do better than GOOD ENOUGH."

"A true leader has the confidence to stand along, the courage to make tough decisions, and the compassion to listen to the needs of others." Douglas McArthur

"You can do what I cannot do. I can do what you cannot do. Together we can do great things." Mother Teresa

The most important thing about GOALS is having one ⟶

PRINCIPLE 7

Competence in and Cultivation of Basic Biblical Gifts and Skills

Introduction

For our basic needs in life we rely on skilled people. Of course, we want the best. We want those who are skilled in their professions. We certainly go to medical doctors who have the right training and experience. For our automobiles we go to a mechanic who is capable and honest. Everywhere I have lived, whether in Italy, Austria, or Israel, I have found great mechanics who know how to work on cars and are very trustworthy. My mechanic in Austria was even an artist (very detailed).

If we fly on planes, we put our trust in experienced pilots who have a good track record. When I was in Seminary, Dr. Ryrie recommended taking a tour of the Delta Training Center. He felt it would inspire us to train well in our ministerial endeavors.

Of course, in all jobs, in our country, and in our schools, we need honest, competent leaders and administrators.

""There is a natural aristocracy among men the grounds of which are virtue and talent."

Thomas Jefferson

In other words, those who rise to the top will have good character and be skilled in their profession. This is especially relevant to those of us in Christian ministry. If the church is the light of the world and the salt of the earth, we need men and women who are people of strong character and who are highly skilled. Character development, however, should be our prime pursuit. Our ministry is eternity related.

At birth, we are all born with different traits and abilities. These are natural. Some people are gifted to work with people. Some have good technical skills. As believers in Jesus Christ, we are bestowed with spiritual gifts. We probably all have a few but some do stand out. Let us look at some of these gifts.

BIBLICAL SPIRITUAL GIFTS

The Bible describes the church as a body with different members. (I Corinthians 12).
Each member has at least one gift he can use to help the body. We must all know our gifts and exercise our gifts. I Corinthians 12 gives us an extensive list. There are different gifts but the same Spirit. The Spirit gives them and empowers us to use our gifts for the good of the Body. There is wisdom and knowledge. There is the gift of faith and healing. There is prophecy, which is preaching today. There is discernment and tongues (maybe for today or not). Paul also mentions the gift of apostleship (which could be church planters today). There is also teaching and administration (important for leaders). These gifts are given sovereignly by God. (See also Romans 12).

In Ephesians 4, Paul also mentions pastoral gifts. Some think of this as the five-fold ministry to prepare God's people for service so that the church will be built up and there will be unity in the Body and we will be more mature in Christ. These gifts include apostleship, prophecy, evangelism, pastoring, and teaching.

Peter gives us a perspective on gifts in his first epistle. He said we are in the last days and need to be clear minded, self-controlled, and love deeply. He encouraged us to be hospitable.   He then says, *"Each one should use whatever gift he has received to serve others, faithfully administering God's grace in its various forms. If anyone speaks, he should do it as one speaking the very words of God. If anyone serves, He should do it with the strength God provides, so that in all things God may be praised through Jesus Christ. To him be the glory and the power for ever and ever, Amen."* (I Peter 4:10,11)

DEVELOPMENT OF OUR GIFTS

We must seek to develop our gifts. Practice makes perfect as they say. However, the practice must be evaluated (good to have mentors). It takes time to be a world class artist or performer. One day a lady met Picasso. She asked the artist to make her a drawing on a piece of paper, and he did so. She thanked him and started to walk away.

Picasso then said, "Excuse me. That will cost you 1 million dollars." She responded, "Mr. Picasso, that took you 30 seconds to draw."

He said, "Miss, it took me 30 years to be able to draw that in 30 seconds." How profound!

Demosthenes, the great Greek orator, had a speech problem in his youth. He was determined to become a great orator, so he began practicing speaking every day with pebbles in his mouth. Billy Graham practiced his preaching in the woods by a stream. The frogs and birds became his audience. Robert Kennedy would listen to Shakespeare as he did his pushups. It helped him to elevate his vocabulary.

As preachers of the Word, we need to cultivate our research abilities and communication gifts.   We can learn from lawyers and investigative reporters. We can also observe great communicators like Rush Limbaugh and Oprah Winfrey (empathy).

Of course, Billy Graham and John McArthur are great examples. I find it helpful as a pastor and preacher to sing hymns as well as preach in the open air. Praying out loud is beneficial as well. Also, it is good to discuss your topic with your wife or friends to get their input.

BIBLICAL CONCEPT OF STEWARDSHIP

When Peter says, *"Each one should use whatever gift he has received to serve others, faithfully administering God's grace in its various forms"* (I Peter 4:10), he is giving us a good definition of stewardship.
It is like being the manager of a household, a company, a church or a country. We manage the people and the resources we have, to help build up the body and evangelize the world.
Besides using the gifts God has given us, we must also administer the other things God has given us. First of all, we must manage ourselves. We must be good stewards of our time, treasure, and talents.

TIME MANAGEMENT

As far as time is concerned, Ephesians says we must redeem the time because the days are evil (Ephesians 5:15,16). We should seek the will of God (John 17:4).   We must then prioritize our time and buy up every opportunity to serve Christ.
We need to delegate responsibility (Matthew 25:14-30).

We need to analyze our use of time.
There are three possibilities why we might not have enough time to do what we should.

1) We are doing too much. We need wisdom from God on this (James 1:6).
2) We are doing the wrong things. The good is always the enemy of the best.
3) We are doing things the wrong way. We need to work smarter not harder.

We need to establish our priorities and make use of a schedule.

How are we to redeem time? Here are some basic concepts.

1. We must plan ahead, make lists, and bring things to do or read along with us for when we are waiting in line, etc.
2. We must pour eternity into time (Psalm 90:12).
3. We must plug the leaks.
4. We must relax when possible. It is not wasted time. We need to restore our bodies, minds and souls.

MONEY MANAGEMENT

In this day of financial pressure and the deterioration of our economies, we must be wise in our use of money. Regarding money, we must live responsibly, simply, and generously. Matthew 6:33 states that we are to seek first the kingdom of God and his righteousness and all these things shall be added to us. These "things" are our basic needs like food and clothing. We must do the will of God. According to 2 Thessalonians 3, if a person will not work then he should not eat. We must work.

For one summer job during university I worked at the Prudential Insurance Company. Sometimes after lunch I would find an isolated room and take a snooze under some cardboard boxes. This was thievery. I stole from the company. When I became a believer, my work habits changed. As I began to see work as a stewardship for the Lord, I worked hard.

We must also live simply. In Luke 10, the Lord sent out his followers two by two. They were to carry with them only those things that were necessary. In essence, they were to carry things that would provide for them for one day. They were not to worry about the next day.

We are told to be content with food and clothing. (Philippians 4, Proverbs 30:8,9, Hebrews 13). One day when they told John Wesley that his house had been burned down, he said, *"O well, that is one less thing to worry about."* In these days of the coronavirus and the economic crises, we need to live simply and not worry about tomorrow.

We must also give generously. Honor the Lord from your wealth and your barns will be filled (Proverbs 3). In Malachi 3, we are told that if we tithe, the Lord will, *"open the floodgates of heaven and pour out so much blessing that you may not have room enough for it."*

"We make a living by what we get, but we make a life by what we give."

Our daughter, Libby, experienced this personally. When she was a senior in high school, our family got lice. It was horrible. Because we were traveling during this time, it took us a long time to get rid of them. Libby was especially distraught over the situation.
One day she came to us and shared why she thought she had lice. While having her devotions she read a verse that said, *"You are infested because you have withheld your tithes and offering from Me."* (Malachi 3:8-10).
She learned a great lesson from this experience and has seen God bless her financially as she obeys Him in this area.

We are told in 2 Corinthians 8:8,9 and in Luke 6 that we are to give generously from the heart. When we obey, He will give back.
CT. Studd was the best athlete in England and earned a lot of money. When he got married, he decided to give all their money away except for $25,000. When he told his wife about his actions, she said., "Didn't the Lord say to give it all? Let us start marriage with nothing."

During my seminary days, I was in an accident and received about $6000 in workman's compensation. I decided to give 20% of the money to the Lord. When I moved back home to New Jersey from Dallas, my car died immediately. My father saw the situation and decided to give me his new Chevy Impala which was worth $7000. Wow! God provides! We cannot out give God. From the original $6000 I also had money for a trip to Israel which is something I had been praying about, and money to buy an engagement ring for Billie.

THE STEWARDSHIP OF OUR BODY

God has also given us our bodies to be used for His glory. Our bodies are a temple of the Holy Spirit (I Corinthians 6). Jesus grew in stature (Luke 2:52). He ate well and was constantly on the move. He was walking not taking public transportation. He had enough strength to overturn the tables of the money changers.

Lewis Sperry Chafer, the founder of Dallas Seminary, said that it is important to keep our bodies healthy and sound. If we are healthy, then we can pray better and read the Bible more attentively. Obviously, we will have more strength to serve the Lord.

God has given us the Gospel to be believed on and preached. We are to guard it, protect it, and proclaim it faithfully and accurately. On many occasions Paul spoke of himself as a servant of the Gospel. It is a great treasure to be cherished and shared. (I Corinthians 9:17, Galatians 2:7, Colossians 1:25, I Thess. 2:4, I Timothy 1:11, Titus 1:3). The gospel is powerful. Let us see what it has done in the Middle East.

A HARVEST IN LEBANON

I met a great brother, Pastor J., from Beirut, Lebanon. I got his name from a brother in the States who visited in Israel. Pastor J has an amazing ministry working with Syrian refugees, Lebanese, and international workers and students. We met and he invited me to sponsor a lunch at Kentucky Fried Chicken for nine Syrian Muslim refugee women.

Of course, before the lunch, we met with them in a hotel meeting room, where I shared my testimony with them and then concluded with the Gospel. While I was speaking and Pastor J. was translating, a lady outside the room came in and asked if she could listen. She was a Lebanese lady who worked at the hotel. I shared my story and then gave the Gospel. Praise the Lord all 10 of them made professions of faith. What a revival. Do pray for them.

The next week, Pastor J brought me to Biblos, which is where the name Bible comes from and where our alphabet was developed.

We even travelled up to Tripoli. When there, I asked how far it was to the Syrian border. So, he invited me to come with him the next day to drive to the Baaka Valley on the eastern border with Syria.

We arrived there and it was very interesting. There were gypsies around who were waiting to return to their families in Syria. They have a problem because they are without passports. We bought

them some cakes. We then drove to some refugee camps of Syrians who were living in tents. He told me that many there were the wives and children of ISIS men. We stopped by an improvised school made up of Syrian kids and run by a Korean missionary with whom Pastor J works. What a joy to see these kids reciting Bible verses. They also hold church services at the school. Many of the Syrian Muslim refugees have come to believe in the Lord Jesus.

We also bought some milk to bring to a family. As we entered their

tent, we had to be careful because it had just rained and there was almost a little pond in from of the entrance to the tent. We walked in and sat on the floor where we were served some tea.

The mother was there with her three children and her nephew. Her nephew escaped from Syria and was now in Lebanon illegally. I shared my testimony and the Gospel, and they all made professions of faith. This was amazing because the nephew had prayed to God the day before, asking for someone to help him in his quest for God's help. He was so happy.

Wow, God is really working!

We left rejoicing because of these open doors and the opportunity to see God work in the lives of people. Pastor J. wants to start a small school with a TV monitor in this home. Pray for this and for growth for these people.

> "God's work done in God's way
> will never lack God's supply."
> Hudson Taylor

ELIMINATE AND CONCENTRATE

Billie and I attended a conference where Ray and Anne Ortlund spoke. He was a pastor from California who wrote a book entitled, *Lord make my Life a Miracle.* The conference was life changing. They taught on the three priorities for the believer.

Ray and Anne Ortlund

1)	We are to put God first and worship Him.
2)	We are to love the brethren.
3)	We are love the world and share Christ with unbelievers.

Anne also wrote a book on the priority of worship. At the conference, she spoke of the "Eliminate and Concentrate" concept. She said that when she got home every day she would empty her purse and eliminate the things that were not important.

A great concept. We can apply it to so many areas.

a.	We can clean-up our finances and eliminate unnecessary expenses.
b.	We can eliminate calories by eating better.
c.	We can eliminate activities that are a waste of time. We should concentrate on our priorities like worship, study of the Bible, and outreach.
d.	We can clean up our cellar and house and throw out things we do not need (or sell them if we can get some needed cash).

AWARENESS, ATTITUDES, ACTIONS

In my book, *Called to World Revolution, God's Path to Total Victory,* I share three concepts that we must keep in mind as we think of gifts and all that God has given us to use for His glory.

1.	**AWARENESS**. We are to know the gifts and seek to discern what are our gifts and abilities. We may have one or multiple gifts. We see these in Ephesians, 4, I Corinthians 12, Romans 12, and I Peter 4. We can call these our strengths or the things we are passionate about. For me it is preaching and leadership.

2.   **ATTITUDES.** We must have the right attitudes in exercising our
     gifts. We are not to be proud and look down on others. We must
     seek the good of the team, the body of Christ. We must display
     the fruit of the Spirit.   After Paul mentions the gifts in I
     Corinthians 12, he concludes saying, " I will show you a better
     way." That way is love, as described in I Corinthians 13. After
     Paul mentions gifts in Romans 12, he exhorts the believers to
     love deeply and care for one another.
3.   **ACTIONS.** We must obey the Lord and use our gifts to edify one
     another. I Peter 4:10 encourages us to use the gifts God has
     given us.

We read in I Corinthians 4:1,2: *"So then, men ought to regard us as
servants of Christ and as those entrusted with the secret things of God.
Now it is required that those who have been given a trust must prove
faithful."* So then, we must know our gifts, have the right attitudes,
and spring into action. Finally, we must depend on the Holy Spirit who
energizes us as we exercise our gifts.

ANATOMY OF A CHURCH

In my book, *Called to World Revolution,* I share about a series on the
church by Dr. John MacArthur called, "The Anatomy of a Church."
The concepts put together some of the truths shared in this chapter.

Dr. MacArthur compares the church to a body.
1.   The skeleton of the body. This is the basic structure. These are
     the foundational principles which include a High View of God, a
     High View of Scripture, Doctrinal Clarity, Holiness, and Spiritual
     Authority.
2.   The living systems like the heart, the kidney, and the other
     organs. These refer to our attitudes. They include love, joy,
     unity, obedience, etc.
3.   The muscles. These are the things we do. These are the
     spiritual gifts we have that we exercise. They include
     preaching, teaching, praying evangelizing. These are the gifts
     and talents we cultivate.

4.   The head. Christ is the Sovereign head of the church.

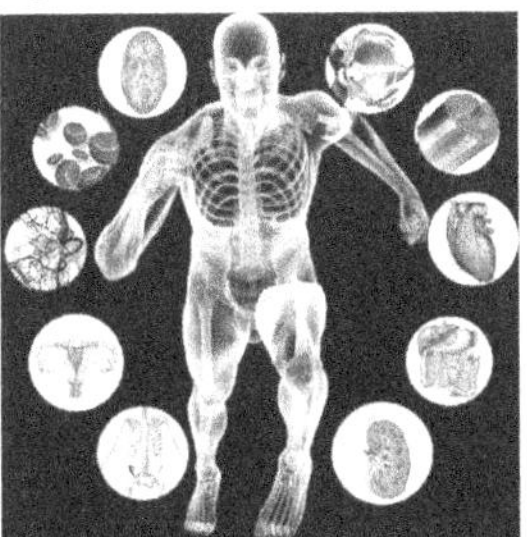

THE LEADER IN THE ROLE OF PROPHET, PRIEST AND KING

Jesus Christ fulfilled His role as prophet, priest, and king. He was the Word made flesh. He spoke the Word and lived the Word perfectly. He also is our Great High Priest. He sacrificed Himself for us on the cross to pay the penalty for our sin. He also intercedes for us now, seated at the right hand of the Father (Romans 8:34, John 17). Finally, He is our Lord and the King of the Universe.

As Pastors and leaders, we follow the Lord. We serve as prophets as we preach the Word of God. We serve as priests as we pray for others. We serve as God's managers, leaders, and administrators (like a Kingly role). Of course, in a church a pastor may have all three roles or just one. The other roles can be fulfilled by others.

SHEPHERDING: THE GREAT WORK OF A CHRISTIAN LEADER

Probably there is no greater image that describes the work of a Christian leader than that of a Shepherd.

What is shepherding? It is the task of the pastor or elder in caring for the total body of the church.

It involves caring for their spiritual, psychological, and physical needs. We see the aspects of the life and work of a shepherd in Psalm 23. In this Psalm the shepherd cares for the needs of the sheep, guides them, and protects them from harm. This is the ministry of the pastor or elder in the local church.

SELECTED BIBLICAL REFERENCES TO SHEPHERD/SHEPHERDING

1. Jeremiah 23:1,2 *"Woe to the shepherds who are destroying and scattering the sheep of my pasture!" declares the Lord. Therefore this is what the Lord, the God of Israel, says to the shepherds who tend my people: "Because you have scattered my flock and driven them away and have not bestowed care on them, I will bestow punishment on you for the evil you have done." declares the Lord."* What a convicting passage. We have a great responsibility.

2. Zechariah 11:15-17: "Then the Lord said to me, *'Take again the equipment of a foolish shepherd. for I am going to raise up a shepherd over the land who will not care for the lost, or seek the young, or heal the injured, or feed the healthy, but will eat the meat of choice sheep, tearing off their hooves. Woe to the worthless shepherd, who deserts the flock! May the sword strike his arm and his right eye! May his arm be completely withered, his right eye totally blinded!'"* This reminds me of some prosperity gospel preachers who like to fleece the sheep.

3. John 21:15-19: *"When they had finished eating, Jesus said to Simon Peter, 'Simon son of John, do you love me more than these? Yes, Lord,' he said, 'you know that I love you,' Jesus said, 'Feed my lambs.' Again, Jesus said, 'Simon son of John, do you love me?' He answered, 'Yes Lord, you know that I love you.' Jesus said, 'Take care of my sheep.' The third time he said to him, 'Simon son of John, do you love me?' He said, 'Lord, you know all things; you know that I love you.' Jesus said, 'Feed my sheep. Truly, truly I tell you, when you were younger you*

dressed yourself and went where you wanted; but when you are old you will stretch out your hands, and someone else will dress you and lead you where you do not want to go.' Jesus said this to indicate the kind of death by which Peter would glorify God. Then he said to him, 'Follow Me.'"

4. Acts 20:28: *"Keep watch over yourselves and all the flock of which the Holy Spirit has made you overseers. Be shepherds of the church of God, which He bought with his own blood."* This is a great verse for a pastor. It makes it simple. Watch your life and your doctrine (what you teach to the flock). See I Timothy 4:16.

5. Colossians 1:28: *"He is the one we proclaim, admonishing and teaching everyone with all wisdom, so that we may present everyone fully mature in Christ."* This verse says it all. We must teach, proclaim, and admonish with wisdom. Goal: Help to mature all.

6. I Peter 5. Here it says the shepherds are to care for the flock and watch over them. They are to do it with an open, honest heart and with enthusiasm. They should not lord over others. They are to be examples. The Lord will reward them.

THE SCOPE OF THE SHEPHERDING TASK

1. The Shepherd is an inspector. This has the idea of taking measures to inspect and attend to whatever condition one discovers out of concern.

2. It is a comprehensive care and discipline of a flock, not just the teaching of them.

THE HEART OF A SHEPHERD

1. Care/Empathy (I Thess. 2.) Paul cared for the believers as a mother would care for her children (verse 7).

2. Love: He loved them and wanted to share his life with them (8).

3. Self-Sacrifice (8)

4. Objectives: He wanted them to become imitators of him.

THE SKILLS OF A SHEPHERD

1. Feeding: This involves feeding them from the Word of God. The pastor needs to spend time studying the Word.
2. Counseling: This is a ministry on a one-to-one basis which seeks to solve personal problems.
3. Caring: This is seeking to meet the total needs of a person which include physical needs, spiritual needs, and emotional needs (for love and acceptance).

WE MUST USE AND DEVELOP WHAT GOD HAS GIVEN US

The great violinist, Niccolo Paganini willed his marvelous violin to the city of Genoa, Italy, on the condition that it must never be played. The wood of such an instrument, while used and handled, wears only slightly, but set aside, it begins to decay. Paganini's lovely violin has today become worm-eaten and useless, except as a relic.

> "A Christian's unwillingness to serve may soon destroy his capacity for usefulness."
> Carl Laney

GOD, OUR MASTER, CAN USE US AS WE RELY ON HIM

A little girl wanted to become a great pianist, but all she could play on the piano was the simple little tune, "Chopsticks." No matter how hard she tried, that was the best she could do. Her parents decided after some time to arrange for a great maestro to teach her to play properly. Of course, the little girl was delighted.

When the little girl and her parents arrived at the maestro's mansion for the first lesson, they were escorted by the butler into the parlor, where they saw a beautiful concert grand piano.

Immediately, the little girl dashed over to the piano and began playing "Chopsticks." Her embarrassed parents started across the room to tell her to stop, but as she played, the maestro entered the room and encouraged the little girl to continue. The maestro then took a seat on the piano bench next to the little girl, listening to her play. After a moment he began to play along with her, adding chords, runs, and arpeggios. The little girl continued to play "Chopsticks."
The parents couldn't believe their ears. They were hearing a beautiful piano duet, played by their daughter and the maestro, and amazingly enough, the central theme of it was still "Chopsticks."

At times you may feel like you're a nobody, that you will never accomplish great things. But think of that little girl. All she could play was "Chopsticks." Nobody wanted to hear "Chopsticks." It was an embarrassment to her parents and annoying to everyone else. Yet the maestro encouraged her to keep on playing.

God knows what you can do. He created you with gifts and talents. Sure, compared to some people's abilities, your gifts and talents may seem like "Chopsticks,"-not very original and not very spectacular. But God says, "Keep on playing-and make some room on the piano bench for Me." God is able to take the little that we are able to do and turn it into something beautiful.

LITTLE IS MUCH WHEN GOD IS IN IT

A story is told of how Paganini once came into the concert room, took the violin, and touched the strings. First one string broke, and a smile went around the room; then another string broke, and there was more audible expression of mockery; when a third string broke, many people laughed outright at his discomfort.
But Paganini stood forth with his violin as though nothing had happened and played on the one string, and the people ceased to smile, but listened spellbound.

Some of those who had derided him began to weep, and some even prayed. (Encyclopedia of Illustrations - #2618).

SEEKING MASTERY IN ALL WE DO

With all that God has given us to use for His glory, we are responsible to cultivate the gifts and abilities with all our heart, soul, mind and strength. Steve Martin was asked by a young comedian how he could attract as much attention as the famous comedian.
Mr. Martin replied, "Be so good at what you do that people will not take their eyes off you."

Even to his dying day at the age of 100, my grandfather, Albert Sr., pursued excellence in his profession and interests. He was the oldest practicing architect in the world at age 95. Nobody has disputed this. He lived with my family for more than 30 years. He was at the drawing board by four o'clock in the morning. His architectural designs were works of art. He designed things to last. He was an artist and a skilled carpenter. He was also a musician and played the piano by ear. He loved opera and knew all the verses of their songs (His voice was not the greatest). He was a competitive bocce player and built his own bocce court in our back yard. He played with his friends every Thursday night. His team was called "The Short Hills Bombers." What a living example to me of a perfect Renaissance Man like Leonardo DaVinci. Unfortunately, I did not receive his gift of art. He designed church buildings.

Note: of course the real buildings were 'straight', unlike these pictures.

I try to build churches according to God's design in the Bible in a spiritual sense.

In all we do to develop our gifts and abilities, we must be aware that it must be done in the power of the Spirit of God. We do all in His power and for His glory.

A story, often told by Howard Hendricks, says it all.

The great Italian conductor, Arturo Toscanini was leading a famous Beethoven piece and ended with a great crescendo. The audience responded with wild enthusiasm. He then responded. "It is not me, it is Beethoven."

For us, in all we do, it should not be us, but Christ in us.

THE DISCOVERY OF PARETO'S LAW
The 80/20 Rule - Different Perspectives

Vilfredo Pareto (1848-1923), an Italian economist, first observed the 80/20 principle when researching wealth and income distribution in nineteenth-century Italy.

Pareto noted that broadly 20 percent of the people owned 80 percent of the wealth and subsequently discovered the principle can be applied to virtually all other distribution scenarios as well.

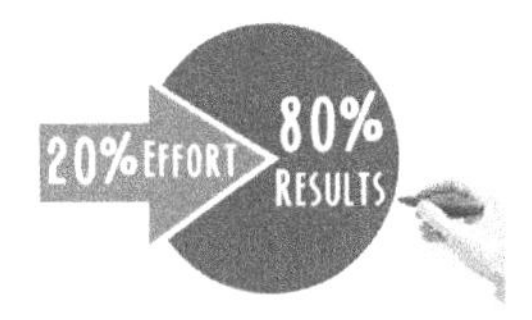

Here are some examples of Pareto's Law as it applies to various situations in any given organization or business. Remember it's a guide rather than a scientific certainty.

- 80 percent of results come from 20 percent of efforts
- 80 percent of activity will require 20 percent of resources
- 80 percent of usage is by 20 percent of users
- 80 percent of revenue comes from 20 percent of customers
- 80 percent of problems come from 20 percent of causes
- 80 percent of profit comes from 20 percent of the products
- 80 percent of complaints come from 20 percent of customers
- 80 percent of sales will come from 20 percent of sales people. The precise ratios for specific situations can be different than 80/20, but the principle applies nevertheless that a minority is typically creating a majority.

1. THE 80/20 PRINCIPLE IN ACTION

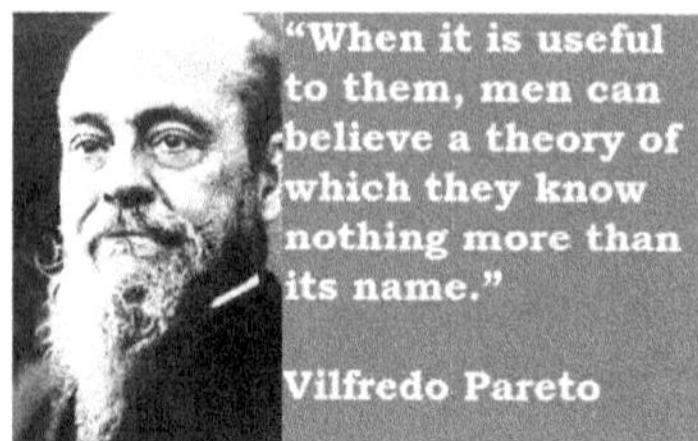

Leadership experts have often taught the 80/20 principle developed by the Italian economist Vilfredo Pareto.

He demonstrated that 80% of the land in Italy was owned by 20% of the population.

This principle can be applied in many situations. In a company we can say that 20% of the people do 80% of the work. We should then concentrate on the 20%. One leadership expert says we should spend one on one time with this 20% and group time with the 80%.

It is interesting to note that Jesus used this method. Maybe he invented it. In His last three years of ministry he spent more time with his 12 disciples than with the multitudes. He gave them his personal time, taught them and demonstrated to them how to be fishers of men and, how to disciple others.

Even Lenin used this principle (he studied theology at a Seminary). He developed and trained a small group of disciples who would train others in the ways of communism. Here are different articles which explain this concept. Excuse the repetition. We need the reinforcement for an in-depth understanding.

2. What's the 80/20 rule in business? Are you doing it right?

The Pareto Principle, better known as the 80/20 rule, has been making the rounds in business psychology for decades. It basically states that 80% of outcomes result from 20% of all causes for a given event. In layperson's terms, this means 80% of your results should come from 20% of effort, not more. The staying power of 80/20 rule in business comes from the fact that it can help business owners, managers and employees identify and prioritize the most productive and crucial business tasks that yield the best results.

"Give me a fruitful error anytime, full of seeds, bursting with its own corrections." Vilfredo Pareto

So how do you use the 80/20 rule in business?
If you're already adopting the Pareto Principle in your daily life, are you doing it right?

3. Understanding the 80/20 rule in business

The 80-20 rule is basically simple cause and effect. 80% of outcomes are from 20% of causes. It all came about when Italian sociologist and economist Vilfredo de Pareto realized that in general, 80% of a nation's income was in the hands of only 20% of the population.
Extrapolating this concept, Pareto defined a rule that became known as the Pareto Principle, or 80/20 rule, that 80% of results are produced by 20% of causes.
This rule is most often used in business to illustrate that 80% of a company's revenue is generated by 20% of its customers. This means that businesses would benefit the most from focusing on retaining the 20% of clients that bring in 80% of sales, while attracting new clients like the golden 20%. The principle makes it easier to hone-in on what matters to the business and adapt new strategies with a clearer focus.

The Secret to Success
by Achieving More with Less

4, Pareto Principle: What it essentially means

At its core, the 80/20 rule is about identifying your company's best assets and using them efficiently to create maximum value. Using the clients and revenue example, identifying the 20% of clients that generate the most revenue for your business can help you plan your sales, marketing and customer experience strategies to keep those clients happy. That doesn't mean that you drop the 80% of clients or ignore their needs when planning ahead.
This is why the 80/20 rule is often misinterpreted. It's not a hard-and-fast mathematical law, but a general principle that can help those in decision-making roles streamline their processes.

5. Examples of the 80/20 rule in business

The 80/20 rule helps managers focus on what is most important and/ or urgent to the business. Here are some key examples of how the 80/20 rule can help you streamline your business.
- 20% of customers equal 80% of sales
- 20% of the marketing efforts represent 80% of the results
- 20% of software development efforts account for 80% of the program's functionality
- 80% of the quality failures originate from 20% of the tasks

6. The 80/20 rule and time management

Small business owners are notoriously time-poor. Tasks like running to the post office, or stocking up the pantry with tea and biscuits for the week, frequently cuts into the work day and mental space of the small business owner just starting out. In fact, a 2017 study revealed that UK small businesses waste up to 120 days a year (!) on admin tasks. While these business owners are so caught up on these '£10 an hour' admin tasks, they end up forgoing the activities that are truly crucial to their business, that could earn them £1,000 an hour (like sending the right email to the right person, for example, or finally fixing a time to meet a potential client).

This is where the same 80/20 principle can come into play. It applies to every dimension of business, including arguably the most important entrepreneurial skill of them all: time management.

7. The 80/20 Rule And How It Can Transform Your Church

Known by various names, including Pareto's Law, Pareto's Principle, the 80/20 Rule, and The Law of Disproportionate Distribution, the 80/20 Rule is a powerful and simple tool for analyzing and optimizing choices involving distribution of any kind.

By the numbers it means that 80 percent of your outcomes come from 20 percent of your inputs. The concept is especially useful in business and personal matters by causing us to focus on the 20% that really matters. This concept can be applied to:

- Prioritization
- Planning
- Evaluation
- Decision Making
- Problem Solving
- Selling
- Marketing
- Budgeting
- Resource Allocation
- Change Leadership
- Project Management

8. Applying Pareto's 80/20 Rule in the Church

The 80/20 Rule is counter-intuitive to how most ministers think. They assume the critical 20% is doing OK, so they should spend their time on the 80% that is not doing, giving or attending as much in comparison.

The life of Jesus provides a clear example of wisely applying the 80/20 Rule in his time and teaching. Jesus spent time daily with the crowds but spent focused time with the 12 disciples, and took Peter, James and John apart for even more intentional instruction and delegated responsibility. And clearly, Jesus loves and longs for each sheep.

The fact is that ministers can't afford to ignore either the 20% or the 80%. Both should be closely monitored and provided time and attention. But, Pareto's Law is dramatically effective when applied to distribution decisions in the local church, because it encourages a focus of activity, resources, time and effort that usually produces quick and noticeable improvements.

Below are examples of how to apply this principle in ways that could potentially change your church.

9. Program Priorities

80% of your ministry results that measurably impact the mission and vision of the church comes from 20% of your programs, emphases and initiatives. Therefore, program impact could be improved by carrying out a quick and simple 'Pareto analysis' to clearly see at-a-glance where to direct your program efforts, and probably also see many programs that could be discontinued.

A. **Outreach:** 80% of your prospects are generated from 20% of your outreach efforts. Therefore, outreach results will improve if you identify which strategies produces most of the new prospects, and use the identified most-effective strategies more often (and use the less-effective strategies less often, or not at all).

And typically, only 20% of a congregation has the gift of "Evangelism," therefore focusing more training and resources on these 20% will garner more results than a commensurate amount of training and resources spent on the other 80%.

B. Budget Allocation: 80% of the biggest Kingdom impact of your church's budget comes from 20% of the dollars allocated. In most churches 80% of the budget is spent internally and only 20% externally.

Therefore, Kingdom impact will increase the more you reallocate dollars to line items that produce greater results, which are usually those that are focused outside the walls of the church.

C. Giving: 80% of your church's revenue comes from 20% of your giving units.

Therefore, giving will increase significantly if you identify your top 20% giving units and focus developmental strategies on those who have the "gift of giving" and are committed to biblical stewardship.

D. Leadership: 80% of your church's leadership effectiveness comes from 20% of your volunteer and staff leaders.

Therefore, providing increased opportunities and intensified training and resources for the top 20% of your leaders will increase effectiveness more rapidly than spending a commensurate amount of training and resources on the remaining 80% of leaders.

E. Website: 80 percent of time spent on your church's website will be spent on 20 percent of the website pages. Therefore, identifying the pages of your website that generate the most traffic and investing new resources to make them more prominent and engaging will have the greatest impact on website traffic.

F. Publicity: Members receive 80% of their information about the church from 20% of your promotion efforts. Therefore, surveying your congregation to determine the top two ways they prefer receiving information from the church and reallocating your messages accordingly will focus and enhance congregational communication.

G. Core Competencies and Passions: 80% of your member's service should be spent in areas of competency and passion. Spend more than 20% of your time serving in areas outside your skills and passions and motivation and output declines significantly.

Therefore, providing a process for church members to identify and connect with ministries that play to their gifts and passions will increase ministry effectiveness and volunteer retention.

H. Time Management: 80% of your results that help you accomplish your job description comes from 20% of your time. Therefore, prioritize and focus on the handful of activities that you do every day that produce the most results.

What others would you add?

10. Pareto Principle for Christian Churches [1]

Vilfredo Pareto noticed about 20% of the peapods in his garden contained 80% of the peas.

To put it more generally, it says that 80% of the effects come from 20% of the causes. to put it more concretely:

- 80% of property is owned by 20% of the population
- 80% of sales come from 20% of the clients
- 80% of complaints come from 20% of a company's customers
- 80% of problems come from 20% of causes.

Unless companies are aware of the 80/20 law, they can unwittingly expend 80% of their time and efforts on the 20% of customers who are producing 80% of the complaints and problems. This leaves only 20% of their time and effort to expend on the customers who are producing 80% of their sales and profits. But churches and pastors can also succumb to this tendency of devoting the majority of their attention to problems and complaints at the expense of the vast majority who are living steady godly lives and serving the Lord fruitfully.

While we must not run away from problems and we must address legitimate complaints, church leaders must be resolute in their determination to prevent problems and complaints setting the agenda and dominating their time and attention.

Perhaps we could re-write the Pareto principle for churches. Give a maximum 20% of your time to the problems and a minimum 80% of your time to the fruitful and the faithful.

---

[1] by ChurchInfluence.Com

11. The Pareto Principle and the Church

The 80/20 Rule (Pareto Principle) states that 20% of the people in an organization will produce 80% of the work and production. If you've experienced the frustration of this reality, you undoubtedly dislike this rule. Unfortunately, most of us have found it to be painfully true in almost all the organizations we're associated with, whether professional, social, or religious. It is particularly frustrating when you see it played out in churches — true to the rule's percentages.

Jesus obviously anticipated that throughout the growth of His Church, this sort of problem would exist. As evidenced by His words recorded at Luke 10:2... Jesus said to them, *"The harvest is plentiful, but the laborers are few. Therefore, pray earnestly to the Lord of the harvest to send out laborers into his harvest."* ESV (Also Matthew 9:37-38; John 4:35) Notice He doesn't say "believers" are "few", just that those who really get engaged in the work and mission of the church, the

harvesting of souls, would be few in number. Notice too... the urgency implied in his message. By using the metaphor of "a harvest" Jesus implies an urgent work that requires immediate attention. When a harvest is ready, you can't wait, you have to move quickly and decisively to bring in the crops.

Maybe therein lies the problem in our churches. Perhaps we have failed to communicate the sense of urgency in what we are attempting to accomplish. "Urgency" tends to require visualization of a pending disaster to motivate some people. For example, if a building is on fire we know that rescue efforts have to move quickly or people could possibly die. Firefighters are motivated and aggressive in rescuing people and using their equipment and skills to put out fires before loss of life and property.

Perhaps in our churches, people are not fully realizing the consequences of inaction, and even if they have some sense of the consequence, they are convinced that someone else will deal with it.

Christians... we have a raging fire that demands our total unencumbered attention. It's the work of harvesting souls, bringing people to Christ... it's God's command to urgent action... the Great Commission. People are dying minute by minute without friends, without hope, without help, without belief, without care.

Just as surely as that fireman sees a child in a second story window of a burning structure, we are witnessing people who are in imminent danger of an eternal destiny apart from hope and apart from God.

Can you imagine a firefighter who would stand outside that burning house and say, "I am safe and comfortable right here. I'll just watch. One of the other firemen will get in there and help those people."

Most of our churched members are thinking to themselves, "That's the preacher's job, the elder's job, a missionary's job, not mine."

PRINCIPLES TO PONDER

What if the 80/20 rule were reversed? What if 80% of the people produced, not 20% of the work that needs to be done, but 100%? Okay, maybe given the lesson of history, that's a naive assumption. So, let's reduce those expectations just a bit. If the 20% are producing 80%, then what if we could get 40% to accomplish 100%? What if 50% got involved? If the 20% can do so many good things, then what if we could just get half of the people in our churches passionately motivated to participate in the work and mission of God? No doubt the results would astound us!

Maybe your church is a small one. If you're one of the leaders, you may be frustrated that only five, six or seven folks show any desire or ability to help move things forward. No matter what you try, what you do, how you encourage and motivate, you just can't get more people to

participate. You don't have to be a small church to experience the 80/20 Rule... larger and even mega churches experience the same problem.

I know this next statement is going to sound very odd, and it should not be viewed as an excuse for the majority to shirk their responsibility for the Great Commission. If you're a frustrated small church leader... you should consider yourself fortunate that you have that many willing servants, five, six or seven souls ready, willing and able to work for the interests of God's mission.

Fortunately for us, God rarely needs more than a few to get the ball rolling and keep it moving. Remember... Jesus changed the whole world with twelve disciples, plus Paul.

Christianity in terms of active participation, has always been a minority movement. Jesus occasionally attracted multitudes, but his transformative work was achieved through a small group of disciples who influenced many.

So, if you're one of those leaders who is frustrated by a lack of participation... maybe this "idea" is a new way of seeing your situation. Don't be frustrated, build around those who have stepped up to do the work of the church. Remember, through your preaching truth, shepherding and counselling efforts you're planting seeds that may very well grow over time to inspire wider and deeper levels of participation and engagement.

We should be exceedingly thankful to God that we don't have to wait until 60%, or 80% or 90% of regular members decide to get involved. God can work through something as seemingly small and insignificant as a mustard seed to grow His Kingdom.

Jesus saw the "crowds" who assembled to hear His messages and recognized the extreme urgency of the situation.

He didn't wait until a large "army of believers" could be assembled, over months and years, to carry out the work of spreading the gospel. He "launched the mission" with something akin to a "mustard seed," a small group of men filled with the Spirit. They, in-turn, inspired and passionate for Christ and His Kingdom, responded to a continuously evolving vision of not only what needed to be done, but what it would take to get it done. They went out and did it... one, two or three to the entire known world of their day!

There's a "mustard seed" in every congregation of God's Church. It's small but it can do great things. Of course, more "workers in the harvest" are always welcome.

PRINCIPLE 8

CALL TO ARMS

The Film "War Room" had a great impact on the Christian world.

In the military, the war room is the place where the President and the heads of all the military services gather to plan their strategy for battle. In the political world the war room is where the parties get together to plan their election campaign which includes how to defeat the enemy (their opponent).

In the world of sports, the coaches plan their strategy for winning the game watching films of their opponents. In the business world, presidents, CEO's, and board members gather in the war room to set their goals and marketing strategy including ways to beat the competition.

For Christians, the war room is where we come to the Lord, fellowship with Him, and begin to intercede for people and other needs. The wonderful thing about this is that we don't really need a room, we can do this anywhere, although it is good to have a place dedicated to this. We do this alone with the Lord or with others and the Lord. We are at war. It is not an analogy but a reality. We must recognize that we have an enemy. Paul says that we should not be ignorant of his (the devil's) strategies (II Corinthians 2:11). We have an enemy who prowls around like a roaring lion seeking whom he may devour (I Peter 5). We wage war not on a fleshly basis. We fight against the foe who tries to affect our minds and thoughts (II Corinthians 10). We fight against spiritual forces in the heavenly places (Ephesians 6).

We are called to be good soldiers of Jesus Christ (II Timothy 2) and to fight the good fight of faith (I Timothy 6). In this study we shall look at this war. We shall examine the enemy. We shall understand fully our call to arms. We shall also learn of all that God has given us to fight the good fight. We will examine principles of real warfare that we will relate to our spiritual battles. We will then conclude with a study of techniques of the marines, the navy seals, and the Israeli Defense Forces that can help us in our war against the spiritual forces of evil.

THE SPIRITUAL BATTLE

There is a spiritual battle raging. We see it not only in obvious ways, but also in more subtle ways as Satan seeks to destroy the testimony of believers in our Lord Jesus Christ. Satan introduces false doctrine in the church and uses problems between Christians to divide churches. He causes Christians to fall into temptation. He also blinds the minds (II Cor. 4:4) of the unbelievers and influences them to steal, kill, and destroy (John 10). He is a liar and plants his lies in the minds of people (John 8). It is an all-out attack. We must know our enemy, his strategy, and respond to the Lord's call to arms. We must rely upon our Commander in Chief and take up the armour of God. We turn to the Bible to see who our enemy is and what he tries to do to destroy. (see my book, *Called to World Revolution*, the section of Knowing Your Enemy for a more detailed analysis).

WHO IS SATAN AND WHAT DOES HE DO?

1. He is a created being who rebelled against God's rule (Isaiah 14). He was Lucifer, the choir director of heaven, however, he wanted to be like God. He said, "I will be like the Most High." Pride was his downfall. Ezekiel 28 describes him as a beautiful cherub. He can deceive with his appearance and sweet words. This reminds me of some of the cults that are propagating their pernicious doctrines. Some are very nice in personality and appearance.

2. He is called by various names in Scripture like, "evil one," (I John 5:19). He is the source of all evil. He is the tempter (I Thess. 3:5). He tempts us like he tempted Adam and Eve. He is the prince of this world (John 12:31). He controls leaders of this world who do not know Christ. Thankfully, our Lord is the King of the Universe. Satan is the god of this age (II Corinthians 4:4). He blinds the mind of people to the truth of the Gospel. This is why we need to ask God to open the eyes of people. He is the prince of the power of the air (Ephesians 2:2). His domain is a spiritual domain. We were under his control until Jesus delivered us (when we believed in Him). He is also the accuser of the brethren. He mocks us and makes us feel guilty for things we have not done (Rev. 12:10). We overcome him by the Word of the Lord and the blood of Jesus.

3. He tried to hinder Christ from going to the Cross. The Cross meant his defeat. Christ came to destroy the works of the devil.

4. He deceives the nations (Rev. 20:3), as the Anti-Christ will do.

5. He blinds the mind of unbelievers (II Corinthians 4:4). In Jesus time, the religious Pharisees thought they were doing the work of God in persecuting Jesus. They were blind.

6. He uses men to oppose God' work (Rev. 2:13). They will persecute the church. Fox's Book of Martyrs describes the history of this.

7. He tempts the Christian (Acts 5:3). Ananias and Saphira were deceived by Satan. He filled their hearts with evil intentions (I Cor. 7:5). Satan can lead us to commit acts of immorality.

WHAT IS OUR DEFENSE AGAINST SATAN?

We need an understanding of what we must do as soldiers of Christ to defeat Satan.

1. Thank God we have Christ who is interceding for us (24/7) at the right hand of the Father (John 17). He is praying that we will be sanctified in the truth (his Word is truth). He prays that we will be protected from the evil one. He prays for our unity in Him. We can let Christ pray this through us.
2. We must thank the Lord for the Holy Spirit who dwells within us. He fills us, strengthens us, guides us, teaches us, and comforts us. We must always seek to be filled with the Holy Spirit (Ephesians 5:18). When we are filled with God's Spirit we are really being clothed with Christ. I like to refer to the Holy Spirit as the fire of God. We ignite His explosive work in us through prayer.
3. We must call on the Lord to send His angels to help us and fight for us (Psalm 91). He will give his angels charge over us to guard us in all our ways.
4. We must submit to God's perfect will. God may use Satan for beneficial purposes in our lives (II Corinthians 12:7). God allows Satan to work as a thorn in the flesh to keep us humble and to help us rely on His power and strength.
5. We should never speak of Satan contemptuously (Jude 8,9).
6. We should always be on guard against him (I Peter 5:8).
7. We must use the armor of God (Ephesians 6).
8. We must fight the good fight together with other members of the body (I Cor. 12.) We are all part of God's team or army (Acts 2:42, Acts 5:23-31).

... some are called to battle.

THE SIGN OF DEMON ACTIVITY

The Apostle Paul gave this warning to Timothy, *"But the Holy Spirit explicitly and unmistakably declares that in later times some will turn away from the faith, paying attention instead to deceitful and seductive spirits and doctrines of demons, by the hypocrisy of liars whose consciences are seared as with a branding iron, who forbid marriage and advocate abstaining from certain kinds of foods which God has created to be gratefully shared by those who believe and have a clear knowledge of the truth."* (1 Timothy 4:1-3).

What are demons?

Many scholars believe demons are part of the army of Lucifer who rebelled against God (Luke 14, Ezekiel 28). They are part of Satan's forces who attack and can possess people. They can also influence people to teach strange doctrines. These are the false teachers mentioned in II Peter 2. They are also involved in sorcery and sexual immorality. John makes this vivid description in Revelation 9:20:

"The rest of mankind that were not killed by these plagues still did not repent of the work of their hands; they did not stop worshiping demons, and idols of gold, silver, bronze, stone and wood-idols that cannot see or hear or walk. Nor did they repent of their murders, their magic arts, their sexual immorality or their thefts."

This sorcery can also be drug use.

The Illuminati is a group of men dedicated to Satan who wish to create a new world order. In this Luciferian world order, they say there would be peace and security for all. However, we know that Satan and his army of demons masquerade themselves as angels of light. Their purpose is to deceive (II Corinthians 11). 

In II Timothy 3 we have a description of the terrible times which will come in the last days. There will be immorality, violence, debauchery and a false religious covering. Let us walk in truth and not be deceived and understand the schemes of the devil (II Corinthians 2).

SPIRITUAL WARFARE: THE ARMOR OF GOD

Introduction

In our path to total victory and, in the midst of spiritual warfare, we must be aware of the armor of God available to us. We need to fight with spiritual weapons (II Corinthians 10). A spiritual battle is raging. How can we be prepared against these attacks? God has given us the necessary armor to fight the battle. We see this in Ephesians 6:10-20.

Discussion

The first thing we need to know regarding spiritual warfare is that we fight in the strength of God and not in our own strength (vs. 10). It is through His mighty power that the battle is won. We are called to action. No military-like leaves are permitted. We must report for duty. Each one must put on the full armor of God.

Our struggle takes place on the spiritual level. We fight not against flesh and blood, not against people, but against the spiritual forces of wickedness in the heavenly places (vs. 12). When we hear about the Middle East Conflict, the Russian conflict, and the possibility of a cold war with China, we must realize that behind it all there is a battle between the forces of Satan and the God of Abraham, Isaac, and Jacob.

God has provided a complete set of armor for us to use in the battle with Satan. When he wrote this, Paul was thinking of the armor of a Roman soldier. The first piece in our armor is the belt of truth. This belt was used to hold in place the soldier's tunic so that he would be able to fight unhampered. Truth here is either the Word of God or a truthful attitude (sincerity). It can also mean total sincere commitment. It is being authentic. We should be people who have nothing to hide.

I had a Jewish friend here in Jerusalem who was very close to me. We trusted each other. I let him use my car and he picked up my mail when I was away. I even let him read my mail, in case I had to pay something. Really, I have nothing to hide. (He is now deceased and hopefully with Jesus).

Then there is the breastplate of righteousness. This is not self-righteousness or imputed righteousness but practical righteousness. A pure life is a holy weapon in the hands of God.

A righteous man will do the right thing.

"It is Never Wrong to Do the Right Thing ."

You've probably heard of Al Capone, the notorious Chicago mobster of the 1920s and 30s. But have you heard about the man nicknamed "Easy Eddie," who was Capone's business partner in crime?

Easy Eddie was a rich, successful lawyer and businessman before he moved to Chicago, who increased his wealth helping run Capone's crime syndicate.

One day Eddie had a change of heart. He volunteered to become a secret informant for the government, and his testimony helped put Al Capone in prison. Nobody knows for sure what caused Eddie to go straight. Some think we has just tired of

Eddie & Butch O'Hare

working with thugs. Others say he wanted to avoid being arrested and sent to prison. And some believe Eddie decided to straighten up and try to be a better example for his only son who was his pride and joy. Whatever his reasons were, Eddie stepped up and did the right thing. Several years later he paid a great price for his good deed. He was gunned down in a gangland-style execution. He did the right thing and it cost him his life.

Here's another true example of doing the right thing. Lt. Commander E.H. "Butch" O'Hare was a decorated naval hero in World War II. One day Butch O'Hare and five other fighter pilots took off from the U.S.S. Lexington to protect the carrier from approaching Japanese bombers.

When Butch and his wingman spotted enemy planes, the other members of their squad were out of range. Even though they were outnumbered nine to two, Butch and his partner had to start the attack alone. Right away the wingman's guns jammed, shrinking the odds to nine against one. Nobody would have blamed Butch for calling off the attack until the other fighters arrived. But if they didn't attack right away, some of the bombers might get through to the Lexington. Butch decided to take on all nine enemy planes alone, knowing he would be a sitting duck for the bombers' gunners. By the time the other fighter planes arrived, Butch O'Hare had shot down five enemy bombers and damaged a sixth. His heroic effort has been called one of the most daring achievements in the history of combat

The O'Hares: A Story Of Redemption Between Father And Son Easy Eddie And Butch O'Hare

aviation. Butch was awarded the Medal of Honor for doing the right thing in the face of deadly odds.

Less than two years later, Lt. Commander O'Hare was shot down and perished during combat over the South Pacific. O'Hare International Airport was named in tribute to Edward H. "Butch" O'Hare in the same city-- Chicago, Illinois - where Butch's dad, Edward J. "Easy Eddie" O'Hare paid the ultimate price to bring down Al Capone. We'll never know for sure, but I suspect that Butch O'Hare's heroics may have been inspired by his father's decision to do the "right thing."

Here's what I want to emphasize: It doesn't matter what your dreams or calling from God are - it won't come easy. You will have to battle for God's best in your life. And a big part of that battle will be "doing the right thing" consistently against all odds.

Do the right thing. It will gratify some people and astonish the rest.

Mark Twain

WELL FITTED COMBAT BOOTS

Roman soldiers also had well fitted, durable combat boots with cleats because of the hard terrain. These represent the need to be ready to share the gospel. It can also mean the peace of God which is in our hearts. The Gospel brings peace with God and with each other.

A CITY TRANSFORMED BY THE GOSPEL

A few years ago, a film came out entitled *Woodlawn*. It was about a high school during the process of integration in the city of Birmingham, Alabama. It became a very tense issue during the days of racial conflict. Once the team was integrated, tensions rose. A faithful man connected with the Fellowship of Christian Athletes came onto the scene. He had just been to

Explo 72, a young peoples' Christian conference in Dallas. I was there as well. One night there was a very moving service where Billy Graham spoke, and we began to light candles and spread the light.

This young man, Hank Erwin, got a burden to reach out to Woodlawn High School. He asked permission to meet with the team at Woodlawn. When he preached the Gospel, revival broke out. Almost the whole team came to Christ. The team began to win and win. They even had joint prayer gatherings with members of the opposing team and had a joint camp with their main adversary. It changed the face of the city. Soon other schools were integrated including the University of Alabama. This is the power of the Gospel.

THE BLESSINGS OF THE SOUL WINNER
by Dr. C. L. Cagan, Deacon

A sermon preached at the Baptist Tabernacle of Los Angeles
Lord's Day Morning, January 23, 2011

"Go ye therefore, and teach [make disciples of] all nations, baptizing them in the name of the Father, and of the Son, and of the Holy Ghost: Teaching them to observe all things whatsoever I have commanded you: and, lo, I am with you always, even unto the end of the world." (Matthew 28:19-20).

Christ gave this command after His resurrection. Some have incorrectly said that this command was given only to the Apostles and has nothing to do with us today. One bad man even split a church using this false doctrine. But that doctrine is not true! It is for *"always, even unto the end of the world."* It has been in the Bible for two thousand years, as a command to all Christians, "always," down to the end of this age. All Christians are commanded to do soul winning, to attempt to win other people to Jesus Christ. The command is for all Christians, not just the Apostles in the first century.

How could all Christians in the first century take part in soul winning when not all of them were Apostles? How can all Christians today take part in soul winning when not all of them are pastors, evangelists, or missionaries? The answer is simple. The work of soul winning has many parts. Speaking of that work, the Apostle Paul said, *"I have planted, Apollos watered; but God gave the increase."* (I Corinthians 3:6).

And so it is today. A Christian invites a lost person – a friend, a relative, or a stranger – to church. Perhaps another Christian telephones that lost person and brings him to church in his car. There the pastor preaches the Gospel, the Bible truth that "Christ died for our sins according to the scriptures; And that he was buried, and that he rose again the third day according to the scriptures" (I Corinthians 15:3-4). The pastor and the deacons and Christian workers explain the Gospel to the lost person individually, making sure that he understands salvation and that he comes to Jesus Christ.

At the same time, other Christians are being friendly to that lost person, showing him Christian love in the church, and praying for him. Here we see that there are many people that go into soul winning. In soul winning, one person plants, another waters, and it is God who produces the fruit! And indeed, a lost person converted to Jesus Christ is a beautiful and sweet fruit, which makes all our time and trouble worthwhile. Soul winning is the highest service a Christian can do!

This sermon is adapted from Chapters 14 and 15 of *The Golden Path to Successful Personal Soul Winning* by Dr. John R. Rice (Sword of the Lord Publishers, 1961). I want to bring out two points from Dr. Rice's book: first, the earthly blessings of the soul winner; and second, the heavenly rewards of the soul winner.

"The Christian who wins souls has special blessings which [others], who do not win souls, never have."

(Rice, ibid., p. 275).

I. The earthly blessings of the soul winner.

God has many special blessings for the Christian who works hard to win souls. Yes, the soul winner has many blessings in this life.

Christ promised the soul winner He would be present with him always in a special way. Our text says,

"Go ye therefore, and teach all nations, baptizing them in the name of the Father, and of the Son, and of the Holy Ghost, and, lo, I am with you always, even unto the end of the world." (Matthew 28:19-20).

This promise of Christ's presence was given together with His command to win souls. The promise and the command go together. His presence is promised in a special way to those who do this work.

Christ said that He will show His love to the Christian who obeys Him and wins souls. He said,

"He that hath my commandments, and keepeth them, he it is that loveth me: and he that loveth me shall be loved of my Father, and I will love him, and will manifest myself to him." (John 14:21).

Remember that soul winning is a command of Christ. Taking up the work of soul winning is obeying a command of Christ. The Christian who obeys his Lord and works hard to win souls will experience the presence and love of Christ in a special way.

Then, also, special joy is promised to the soul winner. When a Christian works to win souls, praying even with tears for souls, he will rejoice when lost sinners are converted to Jesus Christ. The Bible says, *"They that sow in tears shall reap in joy. He that goeth forth and weepeth, bearing precious seed, shall doubtless come again with rejoicing, bringing his sheaves with him."* (Psalm 126:5-6).

Who will rejoice? When a soul is converted, everyone who had a part in that work will rejoice. Yes, one person plants and another waters, but everyone rejoices! Jesus said, *"that both he that soweth and he that reapeth may rejoice together."* (John 4:36). When a lost soul is converted, the Christian who invited him to church rejoices. The Christian who telephoned him and brought him to church rejoices.

The Christians who showed him Christian love and friendship rejoice. The pastor who preached the Gospel to him rejoices.

"He that soweth and he that reapeth...rejoice together!"

There is no greater happiness and rejoicing than to see someone you have spoken to, prayed for, and cared for converted to Christ. The Apostle Paul called the Christians in the church at Philippi, *"My brethren dearly beloved and longed for, my joy and crown."* (Philippians 4:1).

Again, the Apostle Paul wrote to the Christians in the church at Thessalonica, *"For what is our hope, or joy, or crown of rejoicing? Are not even ye in the presence of our Lord Jesus Christ at his coming? For ye are our glory and joy."* (I Thessalonians 2:19-20).

What tender words! What happiness! What rejoicing! Yes, there are blessings and joys for the soul winner – blessings and joys in this life, here and now!

II. Second, the heavenly rewards of the soul winner.

Beyond this life on earth, the Bible promises heavenly rewards to those who win souls. When Christ comes to set up His Kingdom, the faithful soul winner will receive honor and rewards from the Saviour Himself. When He comes, Jesus will say to the faithful soul winner, *"Well done, thou good and faithful servant: thou hast been faithful over a few things, I will make thee ruler over many things: enter thou into the joy of thy lord."* (Matthew 25:21).

The Christian who is faithful in soul winning will have abundant rewards and a high position in the Kingdom of Jesus Christ, living and reigning with Him for a thousand years (see Revelation 20:4, 6).

But the rewards of the soul winner go on for much more than a thousand years! The soul winner will shine like the stars for ever and ever. God said through the prophet Daniel that this heavenly glory would specifically be given to soul winners:

"They that be wise shall shine as the brightness of the firmament; and they that turn many to righteousness as the stars for ever and ever." (Daniel 12:3).

What does it mean to *"turn many to righteousness"*? What does it mean to turn people to righteousness? It means to win souls! Lost people are certainly not living righteous lives – and they are not righteous in the sight of God, since their sins are written in God's books (Revelation 20:12), not covered and cleansed by the Blood of Christ. When lost people are converted to Christ, they turn *"to God from idols to serve the living and true God."* (I Thessalonians 1:9). From a life of unrighteousness, they are born into a new life of righteousness.

Even more important, when lost people are converted to Christ, they are declared eternally righteous. Christ's death pays for their sins and His blood covers and cleanses those sins in the sight of God. God declares that they are righteous and treats them that way. The Bible says that *"the righteousness of God...is by faith of Jesus Christ unto all and upon all them that believe."* (Romans 3:22). Yes, if you come to Jesus, you will be *"justified freely by his grace through the redemption that is in Christ Jesus: Whom God hath set forth to be a propitiation through faith in his blood."* (Romans 3:24-25).

If you come to Jesus, you will be "justified" (Romans 3:28), forgiven, declared eternally righteous in the courtroom of God, because the penalty of your sin is paid by Jesus Christ.

What does it mean, then, to be turned to righteousness – to a new life, and most of all to be counted as righteous before God? Why, it means to be converted – to be won to Christ! And who are the human instruments that God uses to turn people to righteousness? Soul winners! Who are those who will shine as the stars for ever and ever? Soul winners!

And now, my Christian friend, what rewards will you have? Will you look to Christ's command, and to the eternal rewards? Will you be a zealous, active and faithful soul winner, or will you just sit in church and not throw yourself into the work of Christ? Will you obey the command of Christ to win souls or will you hang back from His words? The Apostle Paul spoke of the coming judgment of Christians. Yes, Christians will stand and be judged – not for salvation but for rewards in Christ's Kingdom. In the passage of Scripture which Dr. Chan read, the Apostle said, *"For other foundation can no man lay than that is laid, which is Jesus Christ. Now if any man build upon this foundation gold, silver, precious stones, wood, hay, stubble; Every man's work shall be made manifest: for the day shall declare it, because it shall be revealed by fire; and the fire shall try every man's work of what sort it is. If any man's work abide which he hath built thereupon, he shall receive a reward. If any man's work shall be burned, he shall suffer loss: but he himself shall be saved; yet so as by fire."* (I Corinthians 3:11-15).

These verses speak to Christians, for verse 11 says *"other foundation can no man lay than that is laid, which is Jesus Christ."*

So, the rest of the verses speak to those who have their foundation laid in Jesus Christ – to people who are converted.

But how will you build upon that foundation? What will you do with your Christian life? Will you live a faithful, zealous, holy, soul-winning life – will you build with "gold, silver, precious stones"? If you do, you "shall receive a reward."

But if you live your Christian life sitting in church without throwing yourself wholeheartedly into the work of soul winning, just enjoying the fellowship of your friends, you are building only "wood, hay, stubble" and your work "shall be burned." If you are converted you yourself "shall be saved" by Christ, but you will have no rewards in the coming Kingdom, no crowns from the Saviour.

Earthly pleasures and treasures will count for nothing in that Kingdom. But souls who are won to Christ, and the rewards that He gives to soul winners, will remain forever. As Dr. Rice said in the song that Mr. Griffith sang a moment ago,

> *"The treasures of earth, oh, how vain and how fleeting; They vanish like mist and they wither like leaves; But souls who are won by our tears and our pleading, Will remain for our reaping up there. The price of revival, the cost of soul winning Is repaid at the reaping up there!"*
> (*The Price of Revival* by Dr. John R. Rice, 1895-1980).

Now let me say a word to those of you who are not yet converted. Jesus died on the Cross to pay for your sins. He gave His Blood to wash away your sins. Jesus Christ rose from the dead to give you eternal life. The Gospel of Jesus Christ was given by the Apostle Paul, *"Christ died for our sins according to the scriptures; And that he was buried, and that he rose again the third day according to the scriptures."* (I Corinthians 15:3-4).

If you are hoping to get to Heaven by your own goodness, you will fail and go to Hell. If you are hoping to get to Heaven by coming to church, you will fail and go to Hell.

If you are hoping to get to Heaven by studying the Bible and learning Christian doctrine, you will fail and go to Hell.

The only way to be saved is by coming to Jesus Christ Himself.

And, my Christian friend, will you be a faithful soul winner in the weeks ahead? Do you want to please your Saviour Jesus? Do you want Him to reward you when He comes again? Do you want to shine as the stars for ever and ever? Then throw yourself into the work of soul winning! Bring your friends and relatives to church. Go to evangelism 

with us. Go out on your own to the colleges and malls and do personal evangelism. Bring the names in! Help us bring the people in! That is the work of soul winning!

Let's go out evangelize this afternoon! Let's go out and evangelize during the week! Let's do evangelism! If you will dedicate yourself to do evangelism this winter and spring, come forward and kneel down and Mr. Prudhomme will pray for you (he prays).

Let us stand and sing "Evangelize! Evangelize!" It's the last song on your song sheet. Don't just sing the words of the song – obey them!

"Evangelize! Evangelize!" Words by Dr. Oswald J. Smith, (1889-1986); sung to the tune of "And Can It Be?" by Charles Wesley, (1707-1788).

Give us a watchword for the hour, A thrilling word, a word of power, A battle cry, a flaming breath That calls to conquest or to death. A word to rouse the church from rest, To heed the Master's strong request. The call is given, Ye hosts, arise, Our watchword is, evangelize!

The glad evangel now proclaim, Through all the earth, in Jesus' name; This word is ringing through the skies: Evangelize! Evangelize! To dying men, a fallen race, Make known the gift of Gospel grace; The world that now in darkness lies, Evangelize! Evangelize!

Go out and evangelize – this afternoon, and at every opportunity. May God bless you as you do it!

THE OUTLINE OF THE BLESSINGS OF THE SOUL WINNER
by Dr. C. L. Cagan

"Go ye therefore, and teach [make disciples of] all nations, baptizing them in the name of the Father, and of the Son, and of the Holy Ghost: Teaching them to observe all things whatsoever I have commanded you: and, lo, I am with you alway, even unto the end of the world." (Matthew 28:19-20) ; I Corinthians 3:6; 15:3-4

1. The earthly blessings of the soul winner, Matthew 28:19-20; John 14:21; Psalm 126:5-6; John 4:36; Philippians 4:1; I Thessalonians 2:19-20.
2. The heavenly rewards of the soul winner, Matthew 25:21; Revelation 20:4, 6; Daniel 12:3; Revelation 20:12; I Thessalonians 1:9; Romans 3:22, 24-25, 28; I Corinthians 3:11-15; 15:3-4.

THE SHIELD OF FAITH AND HELMET OF SALVATION - DEFENSIVE WEAPONS

The **shield of faith** is to be wielded against the fiery darts of the wicked one. These darts are temptations which include the lust of the flesh, the lust of the eyes, and the boastful pride of life. It is most probably the dart of doubt which must be thwarted by the shield of faith. The **helmet of salvation** must be put on to protect against the doubts cast upon us by the devil. The sword of the spirit is the Word of God, a powerful offensive weapon in the hand of God.

OFFENSIVE WEAPONS

Finally, a soldier must keep in contact with his commander. We need to pray and keep in contact with Christ our Lord. Both the Word and prayer are our offensive weapons.

When attacked we have to go on the offensive, not just put up a defense. One time while living in Milan I was attacked by 10 gypsy kids in front of the main train station. They wanted to rob me. I instinctively went into a Karate stand (just like *Karate Kid*), and they fled in haste. On the way back, after picking up my friends, we walked by the same place of the attack and the kids were still there. They were now imitating me with their Karate Kid stances. It was good that when attacked, I did not flee. I stood my ground and went on the attack (at least in my threatening position).

THE POWER OF PRAYER

Prayer is the first weapon.
We begin here. When the early church was attacked by the religious establishment, they came together to pray. They prayed for continued boldness to preach the Gospel. Then they went out in courageous witness.

Charles Feinberg, a great Jewish believer and scholar, attributes his salvation to an Afro-American lady who prayed for him. Then, after being prayed for, he met another Jewish believer who shared the Gospel with Him. Lon Solomon, a Jewish believer and former pastor of McLean Bible Church, in McLean, Virginia, shared how his family maid sang gospel hymns when he was growing up. He believes she was the one who prayed for his salvation. Years later at the University of North Carolina, he met an evangelist who shared the gospel with him, and he came to faith.

Our family also had an Afro-American maid (once a week) who was so happy. She was a believer and I believe she really prayed for me. Then, when I was in 10th grade, my French teacher, Miss Bonjour, was a former missionary with Greater Europe Mission. I believe she also prayed for me. An interesting side note is that Miss Bonjour later went to teach at Columbia Bible College and was the French teacher for my wife, Billie. God is amazing.

I commend us all to read Ezekiel 9 and Isaiah 62. You will begin to pray for Jerusalem in a fresh new way.

Blessed are those who are called to the marriage supper of the Lamb!

Revelation 19:9

DESTINED FOR THE THRONE

Revelation 20:4, II Timothy 2:12, Ephesians 1:20-23.

Introduction

1.   Preparation of a companion for Christ (A Royal Romance)
     Jesus died to purchase us to become His bride (Importance of
     Calvary).
     Our present position in Christ (Colossians 3:1, Ephesians 2:4-6).
     Spiritual preparation of the Bride of Christ through the Word
     and through trials. (Ephesians 5:22-27, John 17, James 1:2-4,
     Romans 5:3-5).
2.   The Wedding Feast and Supper (Revelation 19:9, 21:9)
3.   We will reign with Him and judge the world (I Corinthians 6:2,3;
     II Timothy 2:12).
4.   The Reward of the Overcomers (Revelation 2-3).
     Churches: Historical, Prophetic, Local churches today.
     Summary of each letter: Commendation, Condemnation,
     Reward.

a. We will eat from the tree of life (2:7).

b. We will not be harmed by the second death (2:11).

c. We will have hidden manna. We will have a white stone with a new name inscribed on it that no one knows except us.

d. We will have authority over the nations. We will have the morning star (2:26-28).

e. We will be dressed in white clothes. Our names will never be erased from the book of life. Jesus will acknowledge our names before the Father and His angels (Revelation 3:5).

f. We will be given a pillar in the sanctuary of our God. God's name will be written on us. The name of Jerusalem will be written on us. This will be the new Jerusalem which comes down out of heaven from God (Revelation 3:12).

g. We will be given the right to sit with Christ on His throne just as He also won the victory and sat down with the Father on His throne (Revelation 3:21).

5.   Our Apprenticeship in prayer (On the Job Training).
        We overcome the Devil by the Word and Prayer.

6.   Our Authority on earth (Luke 10:19, Matthew 16:18).

THE WORD OF GOD: PREACHING CHRIST IN THE END DAYS

POWER OF THE GOSPEL

We seek to serve others and share the Gospel. We know from our experience in Israel that God loves both the Jews and the Arabs. He wants them to come to a knowledge of the Savior.   I experienced this firsthand during our service in Italy. During our second year, while living in Milan, we had a small Bible study in our home. We had a few believers and a Jewish lady named Adriana. She became a close friend.

One time she had to go to the hospital. At that time, we were hosting Dr. Louis Bahjat Hamada and his wife Hanan. I met Louis at Seminary. He was an Arab evangelist from Lebanon. He had just written a book *God loves the Arabs too.*   Billie and I brought Louis and Hanan to see Adriana in the hospital.

As we visited, Adriana said that there were some Palestinians in the next hospital room. They had been wounded in Lebanon and were flown to Milan to recover in the hospital. We decided to go visit them even though Louis was somewhat afraid because they were considered "terrorists." We went over and asked the security guard if we could enter. We entered the room and immediately saw a picture of Yasser Arafat. As we entered, Louis began to speak to them in Arabic. They began to cry and hug us. Louis then shared the Gospel and they prayed with us. As we left, they continued to cry and hug. We left in tears and in the joy of the Lord.

THE WORD OF GOD WHICH CONVICTS, COMFORTS, AND GUIDES: TERRIBLE TIMES IN THE END DAYS: WHAT SHOULD THE RIGHTEOUS DO?

II Timothy 3 and 4

Introduction:

A.   Condition of the World (3:1-9)

Here we find a description of the last days which are described as terrible. It will be filled with hatred, violence, disobedience, brutality, and general evil (including religious hypocrisy).

B.   Character and Conduct (3:10-17)

In the midst of this evil world we must be people of character and good conduct. We are to be full of faith, patience, love and faithfulness. We will suffer persecution because of our godly life style.

C.   Commission to Preach Jesus (4:1-5)

We are to live godly lives and preach Jesus when it is convenient and when it is not.

We preach sound doctrine and the good news of the Gospel.

The preaching of the Word is a powerful weapon.

D.   Cost of Following Christ (4:9-16). When we follow Christ there is a cost. Many will abandon us and betray us. Some will attack us viciously.

E.   Crown of Righteousness (4:8): God will reward us for our serve for Him and our fighting the good faith with perseverance.

F.   Conquest of the Gospel (4:17) Even though many will abandon us, God will always be with us and will give us strength to fully proclaim the message.

G.   Comforting Hand of God (4:17-18) The Lord will be with us and will protect us from all evil attacks. We will be delivered from the lion's mouth.

COMBATING TOGETHER

As believers in Jesus Christ we are all part of God's team and God's army. We have one Commander in Chief. Each one is called to duty and each one is equipped differently. We must all work together in unity. I came across a book a few years ago called *Principles of War, A Handbook on Strategic Evangelism* by Jim Wilson. (Christian Books in America 1964). In the Preface, the author quoted from Antoine Henri Jomini, saying,

> *"There exists a small number of fundamental principles of war which could not be deviated from without danger and the application of which on the contrary has been in almost all time crowned with success."*

The author affirmed the idea that warfare is not a metaphor but a reality. He shared 11 basic principles which are essential to victory in warfare. He applied these to spiritual warfare especially regarding evangelism. It is a warfare of the soul.

Principles of War by Jim Wilson

1.   Objective

Our goal as believers is victory through our Lord Jesus Christ (I Cor. 15). Matthew 28 and Colossians 1:24-29 share God's end game - it is to reach the world for Christ and make disciples of all nations. Some sow and some reap but we all work together for the goal. We all must be going in the same direction.

> **IN WAR, THEN, LET YOUR GREAT OBJECT BE VICTORY, NOT LENGTHY CAMPAIGNS**
>
> SUN TZU

We must have unity of purpose.

2.   Offensive

Bold and Aggressive. Prayer and Preaching. Jomini said,

"They want war too methodical, too measured; I would make it brisk, bold, impetuous, perhaps sometimes even audacious."

Our goal as Christians is to reach the world with the Gospel. We are on the attack as we preach Jesus to all nations beginning in Jerusalem. The one on the offensive has an advantage as he decides when to attack. He has more control over the situation. We may attack the whole front or just one segment of the enemy army. This should be the decisive point. Our offensive is against the devil. Jesus Christ dealt the devil the decisive blow at Calvary. Now we must occupy the land and proclaim the freedom of Satan's captives. We preach the Gospel.

Our two offensive weapons are **prayer** and **preaching**. We teach in the power of the Holy Spirit without quarrelling about it. Our battle is on the spiritual plane. 2 Timothy 2:23-26 says, *"Have nothing to do with stupid, senseless controversies, you know that they breed quarrels. And the Lord's servant must not be quarrelsome but kindly to everyone, an apt teacher, forbearing, correcting his opponents with gentleness. God may perhaps grant that they will repent and come to know the truth, and they may escape from the snare of the devil, after being captured by him to do his will."*

We must pray (1 Timothy 2:1-6).

We ask the Lord to send laborers into the harvest field (Matthew 9:37,38). We pray and preach in the Holy Spirit. Our objective is people, cities, and nations. The enemy holds them captive and we preach Christ, the Liberator.

3.   Concentration

Matthew 18, Luke 10:1. We have more power and success when we work together. When 2 or 3 come together in My name, there am I with them (Matthew 16).

I quote directly from this book, *Principles of War*. This was in regard the use of airplanes in WW I.

"It glamorized use of air aces and heroes. However, there was not much effect on the final outcome for one used it in concentration. Major General Claire Chennault, when a young Army Air Corps aviator, noted this lack of application of principle. In his Way of A Fighter he wrote, "For four months we flew and fought all over the Texas sky in the fashion of the Western Front, flying long patrols in formation, looking for a fight, and then scattering in a dive on the enemy into individual dogfights. As sport it was superb, but as war, even then, it seemed all wrong to me. There was too much of an air of medieval jousting in the dogfights, and not enough of the calculated massing of overwhelming force so necessary in the cold, cruel business of war. There were no sound military precepts that encouraged the dispersion of forces and firepower, that occurred in dogfighting."
Way of a Fighter, G.P. Putnam's Sons, New York; p. 11

We should always seek to team up with someone as we serve the Lord. One can pray and one can preach.

We can concentrate prayer at certain decisive points.
This failure to apply the principle of concentration continued through the Spanish Civil War and into World War II. Chennault himself put an end to these individual tactics with his American Volunteer Group, better known as the Flying Tigers.

The First American Volunteer Group (AVG) of the Republic of China Air Force in 1941–1942, nicknamed the Flying Tigers, was composed of pilots from the United States Army Air Corps (USAAC), Navy (USN), and Marine Corps (USMC), recruited under President Franklin Roosevelt's authority before Pearl Harbor and commanded by Claire Lee Chennault.

When he went to Burma and China, his pilots stuck together. Outnumbered in the air and on the ground in planes, pilots, and parts, they destroyed 217 enemy planes and probably 43 more with a maximum of 20 operational P-40's in 31 encounters. Chennault's losses were six pilots and sixteen planes. In order to accomplish this, Chennault used concentration. He was outnumbered in the air ten to one, However, Chennault's two always outnumbered the enemy's one. If each Flying Tiger had taken on ten of the enemy, probably we would not remember the Flying Tigers today.

Regarding spiritual warfare we have a great example in Luke 10:1,2. The Lord appointed 70 and sent them out by twos to all places. He encouraged them to pray the Lord of the harvest to send laborers into the harvest. We are also encouraged to pray together (Matthew 18:19,20).

In most cases Paul had a "wing man." When he was alone in Athens, he preached, but had little success. When Silas and Timothy joined him in Corinth there was more success (Acts 18:8-10).

We should go out in teams with some of us praying
and some preaching.

We can concentrate our praying and preaching at certain decisive points. When Jesus gave the Great Commission to go into the whole world and preach the Gospel, the apostles were told to first gather in Jerusalem to pray and await the Holy Spirit. They were together and prayed and  then preached (Acts 2:11). What was the result? Three thousand came to faith in Christ.

In the Billy Graham crusades, thousands pray for him, the team, and the city. Many help as counsellors and choir members. All work together and God blesses.

I close with an interesting illustration. In a town in the USA, a church got together to pray for the salvation of the worst sinner in the town. They focused their prayer and persevered. When he got saved, they began praying for the salvation of the second worst sinner in that town.   He got saved and they continued with the same pattern. Revival came to that church and the city.

4.   Mobility

Exodus 12:11 *"And thus shall you eat it; with you loins girded, your shoes on your feet, and your staff in your hand; and ye shall eat it in haste; it is the Lord's Passover."*

The children of Israel moved 600,000 men, women, and children out of Egypt in one night. In the battle at Dunkirk, the British were mobile as they crossed back and forth to England on the North Sea. They were mobile by sea, but the Germans were not.

We are told to go into the world and preach the Gospel. We can go everywhere. We can use cars, trucks, ships and airplanes. We can preach, use tracts or books, use the internet and TV.

Our weapon is the Word of God.

We can use it defensively or offensively. We can study the Word of God and be prepared to use it in various ways and in different opportunities. We can also pray anywhere for any person or church around the world. The power of God is not limited and prayer is not limited.

5.   Security

"The art of retrenchment.... shall serve the defender, not to defend himself more securely behind a rampart, but to attack the enemy more successfully." Clausewitz.

In Ephesians 6 Paul shares that we must be strong in the Lord and in the power of His might. We must put on the whole armor of God so we can stand against the evil one. We do not fight against flesh and blood. Our fight is against principalities and forces and rulers of darkness.

There are three parts to the subject of security.
I.   Intelligence of the enemy.
II.   Continual protection against the enemy.
III.   Final stand against the enemy.

We have the CIA, M14 and Mossad which carry on spy assignments to know about the enemy. In the spiritual realm, Satan is our enemy and we are not to be ignorant of his schemes (2 Corin. 2:11). Satan is not omniscient or omnipresent. He is limited. We put on the Armor of God to defend ourselves and to attack. We look for a fight.

> "The good fighters of old, first put themselves beyond the possibility of defeat and then waited for an opportunity of defeating the enemy." Sun Tzu

We must then take an aggressive stand against the enemy. It is risky but necessary.

6.   **Surprise**

> "One belligerent must surprise, the other must be surprised. Only and when the two Commanders play these respective roles will a battle lead to the annihilation of one Army." General Waldemar Erfurth

Acts 3:10 says: "And they were filled with wonder and amazement at what had happened to him."

We have the wonderful story of Gideon who learned this principle from the Lord. *"The amassed armies of the Midianites and Amalekites and all the children of the east lay along in the valley like grasshoppers."*
This force consisted of 135,000. Less than 15,000 got away. We can say that Gideon with 300 men surprised the enemy and won in a battle of annihilation. The surprise of Gideon was one time (night), method (lamps, torches, voices, trumpets), and place (3 sides of the camp).

There are two commanders in spiritual warfare: God and the devil. Only God can surprise because he is omniscient. The Devil is not. Nothing surprises God.
Surprise in warfare means more than "to cause wonder or astonishment or amazement because of something unexpected."
It means to "to attack or capture suddenly and without warning."

Christ came and died for the ungodly. He loved us even though we were sinners and died for us (Romans 5:6-8). People will be amazed at this message of grace. We must use the Word of God which is sharper than a 2-edged sword. It discerns the thoughts and intentions of the heart. All is laid bare to the eyes of him with whom we have to do (Hebrews 4:12.13). We surprise with the Word of God which reveals the sin in people's lives but also gives them the answer in Jesus.

7.   Cooperation

John 17, I John 1:5-7, Acts 4:32, Mark 9:38-40, Phil. 1:15-18

"Fellowship is the keynote of this belief; such a deep fellowship with God through Christ as shall inevitably lead to a deep fellowship with others of His children. The revival of the Christian Church will surely come only through the disciplined and creative fellowship of surrendered Christians; for such a fellowship in Christ is God's supreme weapon for the evangelization of the world (I John 1:5-7 and John 17:22,23). The isolated Christian is an anomaly."

(Howard Guinness in Total Christian War).

Acts 4:32 says, *"And the multitude of them that believed were of one heart and one soul: neither said any of them that any of the things which he possessed was his own: but they had all things common."*
Cooperation is important in warfare and in the church.
We must cooperate with our allies and not our enemies. The cooperating forces come under one commander. Cooperation with an enemy is treason. To not cooperate with an ally is a gross error. We must cooperate and communicate with our fellow believers. When two or three are gathered in His name, He is there (Matthew 18:20).
Pride can hinder cooperation. We must confess our faults one to another and pray for one another (James 5:16). In the military, pride is generated in order to encourage obedience and high quality in the performance of duties.   Rivalry and competition in training bring the units to the peak of readiness. Yet platoons should cease to compete when they act as a company.

As believers we must not be proud of our denomination, distinctives, or doctrines and methods. Our ultimate loyalty must be to the Lord Jesus Christ. Paul speaks about cooperating with those with wrong motives. He says that as long as they preach Christ, he will rejoice. We must spend more time with Him to know Him better. When we love Him, we will naturally love each other, and the world will see it (John 13).

8.   Communication

Jeremiah 15:16 says: *"When your words came, I ate them; they were my joy and my heart's delight, for I bear your name. O Lord God Almighty."*

When an army moves, it needs to have adequate supplies to keep up. Napoleon made the mistake of invading Russia and then finding out he did not have a line of supply to cope with the winter climate.   Probably the same thing happened to Hitler when he invaded Russia.

Those of us in the Lord's work must keep in communication with our Commander in Chief. He supplies all we need. He gives us spiritual food, ammunition, information, and orders.   We have two-way communication with the Lord. We speak to Him in prayer and He speaks to us through the Word. We must pray constantly (I Thess. 5:17). Everything we need to know to defeat the enemy, Satan, is in the Bible. We must maintain fellowship with the Lord for spiritual strength. In Luke 10:38-42 we have the story of Mary and Martha in Bethany.   Martha was distracted in her service. Mary was sitting at the feet of the Lord worshiping Him. Jesus rebuked Martha and commended Mary. In Worship we gain strength, refreshment, and anointing to serve the Lord. They that wait upon the Lord will renew their strength. They will mount up with wings as eagles. They will walk and not faint. They will run and not be weary (Isaiah 40).

9.   Economy of Force

"The more the concentration can be compressed into one act and one moment, the more perfect are its results." Clausewitz

Judges 7:20,21 tells us, *"And the three companies blew the trumpets, and brake the pitchers, and held the lamps in their left hands, and the trumpets in their right hands to blow withal: and they cried, The sword of the Lord, and of Gideon. And they stood every man in his place round about the camp: and all the host ran, and cried, and fled."*

Economy of force is efficiency in fighting, effectiveness in warfare. If our objective is the annihilation of the enemy army, we will take the offensive at the decisive point. To do this effectively, the combined application of all principles of war is necessary.

> *"To concentrate overwhelming superior members at the decisive points is impossible without strategic surprise. The assembly of the shock-group must be done as quickly as possible in such a way that all units can attack at the same time." General Erfurth*

This statement implies most of the principles of war.

Christians must come together to pray and evangelize at strategic points where there are many non-Christians (a decisive point).

We can concentrate in another place where we are just training and practicing. However, we must come together at the decisive place of need and opportunity (where non-Christians are). Jesus said to his disciples to stay in Jerusalem until they were filled with power from on high. He promised them the power of the Holy Spirit to enable them to be bold witnesses in Jerusalem and the rest of the world. They waited and prayed for 10 days. Jesus said the harvest is plentiful, but the workers are few. We need to pray for the Lord to send workers into the harvest.

10.   **Pursuit**

> *"Only pursuit of the beaten enemy gives the fruits of victory." Clausewitz*

Acts 5:42 says, *"Day after day, in the temple courts and from house to house, they never stopped teaching and proclaiming the good news that Jesus is the Christ."*

General Allenby, the British ruler during the Mandate period believed in this principle. He never gave up. Gideon continued to pursue the enemies of Israel even after they were defeated.

In the spiritual realm we do need to follow up converts, but since they are on our side now, only a few are needed to do this. Most of us should continue to pursue those without Christ. Revival begins with individual men, but then the rest of the saints continue the pursuit. We can give personal witness, or use tracts, radio, and other means. We should emphasize the message of judgment and mercy. Men need to know they are sinners. They need to turn to the Savior for mercy and salvation.

The church at Thessaloniki had heard the gospel for only three Sabbath days. Paul writes to them a few weeks later. *"For from you sounded out the word of the Lord not only in Macedonia and Achaia, but in every place your faith to God-ward is spread abroad, so that we need not to speak anything."* (I Thess. 1).

We must follow their example.

11.   Obedience

Jesus said, *"If you love me, keep my commandments."* Jesus told his disciples to follow him. They immediately obeyed. He did not ask for volunteers or challenge them. God calls all men to repentance (Acts 17:30).

MARINES, NAVY SEALS, AND ISRAEL DEFENSE FORCES

Even though I have never served in the military, I am interested in studying the philosophy and training techniques of the elite military corps. Some of my best friends are Marines. I remember that while I was attending the University of Maryland I was being recruited by some Marines. It would have been an interesting thing to pursue. It was during the time of the Vietnam War and so it was a scary proposition.

Marines are committed to certain principles which include integrity, excellence, and never leaving anyone behind. There is a great commitment to teamwork. They are also very loyal to God and country. This inspires me.

I wear a Marine hat most of the time to show my solidarity with them. Sometimes a man will say to me, "*Semper Fi!*" [2] (always faithful). He thinks I am a Marine. I say that I am not but I thank him for his service. Todd Greene is a pastor in North Carolina and a Marine. He actually considers me his mentor. I'm around 20 years older than he is. Actually, he is my mentor. He is a loyal, thoughtful, man of integrity. He has helped me so many times. He has been here to Israel on several occasions and God has used him to touch an Israeli family and others. We also work now together at a sports camp in Poland.

My friend Teddy Robbins is a Marine who served in Vietnam and fought in the Tet Offensive. He volunteered to be a Marine. He was given the opportunity to be a chaplain in the military but chose to be a warrior who wanted to fight. God preserved his life while many of his fellow Marines were killed.

Richard Ayling is a good friend and also a Marine vet in Vietnam. God preserved him and he serves the Lord now with his wife, Francine.

We need to think like Marines and be people of integrity and excellence.

Probably the most difficult military training is Seal training.

Mark Divine wrote a book called, *The Way of the Seal. Think like an Elite Warrior to Lead and Succeed.* He was a 24-year-old accountant in New York City who wanted to be warrior. He knew the best way was

to be seal. He prepared himself mentally and physically. He achieved his goal and became a seal commander. He then formed a training institute to help people think like an elite warrior. In the book he deals with goals, focus, and being mission oriented. He talks about the 3 D's - Discipline, Drive and Determination. He teaches total commitment and the importance of adapting.

---

2 *Semper fidelis* (Latin) means "always faithful" or "always loyal". It is the motto of the United States Marine Corps, usually shortened to *Semper Fi.*

Of course, as believers we are to follow Christ and give our lives for him.   It is a life of dedication and discipline. It involves rejection by the world and persecution.   There is a physical and a mental cost. There is a social cost because we can be rejected by our friends.

The Israeli Defense forces recruits all men and woman, except those who object for religious reasons.   Israel is constantly in military preparation and presence. It is good training for life. You must serve before going to college, so it is a good way to figure out what you want to do. It builds teamwork and even networking for future business partnerships. (see book *Start-up Nation*).

Israel also is benefited by a great air force, and a great intelligence agency, the Mossad (top in the world).

Why do they succeed? They are great learners, smart people, they work hard and are strong.

COLONEL ORDE WINGATE

In Israel there is a sports institute in Netanya named the Wingate Institute. It is where Olympic teams are trained and special forces for the IDF are prepared. It is named after Orde Wingate, a famous Christian Zionist. He was a Colonel with the British Army stationed in

Israel. His job was to train the early Israeli Defense Force. He even trained Moshe Dayan who was a great military leader. He trained them in the Biblical way of fighting - when the leader goes first and leads the troops. That is why Israel has many casualties among its high ranking officers. However, it does lead to great results and victory. Colonel Wingate did this because he loved Israel.

PRINCIPLE 9

CHEMISTRY
THE ART OF DEALING WITH PEOPLE

I will never forget my speech teacher in high school. His name was Eugene Kopacz, a former Roman Catholic priest, turned high school teacher. He taught Latin and Speech Communication. There are two things about him that stand out in my mind. First, he was always abreast of current events and would share them daily. He was the first one who told us about the 1967 Six-Day war.

The second thing was that he would always mention Dale Carnegie. Dale Carnegie was a former salesman from Missouri who gave lectures and wrote books on communication (*The Quick and Easy Way to Effective Speaking*) and human relations (*How to Win Friends and Influence People*). I never got around to reading them until I had finished my university studies.

When I arrived at Seminary, I discovered that two of the professors were also teachers at the Dale Carnegie Institutes. It made sense. In life, business, and ministry you must know how to communicate and get along with people. As I read *How to Win Friends and Influence People*, I was anxious to put into practice the principles I learned. Especially when I discovered that the principles are quite Biblical. We are told to speak the truth with love (Ephesians 4).

Here are just a few of the principles.

1.   Be interested in other people and their life situation.
2.   Remember and use their names in conversation.

3.   Be an active listener (this is actually in the chapter, "How to be a good conversationalist").
4.   Admit your faults.
5.   Avoid arguing with people.
6.   Appeal to a person's best interest.

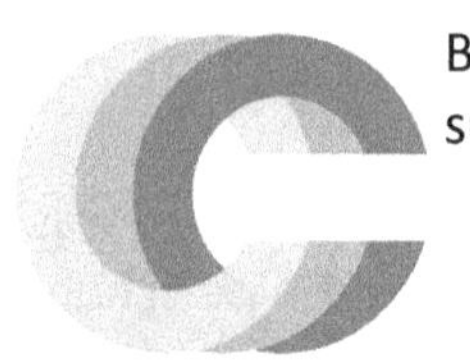

Bill Hybels often refers to the three C's regarding success in the ministry:

⇒   **Character**
⇒   **Competence**
⇒   **Chemistry**

The first two - Character and **Competence** are self-explanatory. **Chemistry** has to do with how we get along with people.

The Bible has much to say about friendships and human relationships. The Book of Proverbs gives many practical insights into effective human interaction. In Proverbs 17:17 we read that a friend loves at all times. He is loyal and faithful. Proverbs 18:24 says that a man with too many friends comes to ruin, but there is a friend who sticks closer than a brother. A few loyal and trustworthy friends can really help you in life. Proverbs 13:20 shares with us that he who walks with wise men will be wise and the companion of fools will suffer harm. We had better be careful about the friends that we chose. They can influence our lives positively or negatively. One of my favorite verses is Proverbs 27:17, which states, *"As iron sharpens iron so one man sharpens another."*

We need friends who will not only comfort us when we are down, but also rebuke us when we are going down the wrong path (Proverbs 27:5-6).

We love to sing the song, "What a Friend We have in Jesus."
It is true that Jesus is our best Friend if we know Him. He told his disciples in John 15 that they were his friends. He said a friend will lay down his life for others. They were qualified to be his friends by their obedience to Him.

True friendships are necessary for our wellbeing in this world. We read in Ecclesiastes 4:9-10 that two are better than one. One can lift the other up in time of need. The Lord created us for companionship.

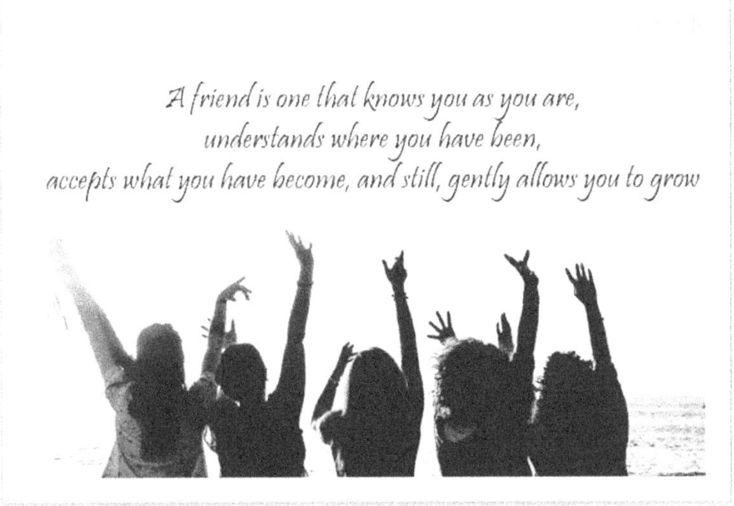

God has provided marriage for intimate relationships. The local church is a wonderful provision for fellowship and friendships which encourage and stimulate us to service (Hebrew 10:34,35).
Even our witness to the world can be enhanced as we seek to befriend those with whom we share the Gospel. People need to see how much we care for them. They need to experience our love and see Jesus in us. Our friendship along with our message can touch their lives and be used of God to bring them to a saving knowledge of Jesus.

FELLOWSHIP AMONG BELIEVERS

"As iron sharpens iron, so one man sharpens another", says a proverb. Of course, the key is to demonstrate true love. True love comforts and confronts. *"Rebuke a fool and he will hate you. Rebuke a wise man and he will love you."* I hope we are all wise.
How can we become true channels of God's love to others? That is the key for true friendship and dealing with people.

First of all, we need to understand the three types of love referred to in the Bible:

1.   *Eros* or sensual love.
2.   *Phileo* or friendship
3.   *Agape* or God's unconditional love demonstrated at Calvary.

How can we describe the love of God? He loves us unconditionally (John 3:16, John 15:13). The characteristics of true love are found in I Corinthians 13. Read them and be blessed and ask God to use you as an instrument of His love.

How does God want to love through us?

1.   We are commanded to love God (Matt. 22:37).
2.   We are commanded to love our neighbors (Matt. 22:39).
3.   We are commanded to love our enemies (Matthew 5:43-47).
4.   We must realize that we are accepted by God and accept ourselves (Matthew 22:39). This is key to loving others.
5.   We must realize we cannot love with our own strength. It is not our nature to love as we should. God must love through us with his love.
6.   We must love by faith. We must be filled with the Spirit (Gal. 5:22,23). The fruit of the Spirit is love, joy, peace, patience, kindness, goodness, self-control. He commands us to love (John 15:12), and He will give us the strength and power to do it.

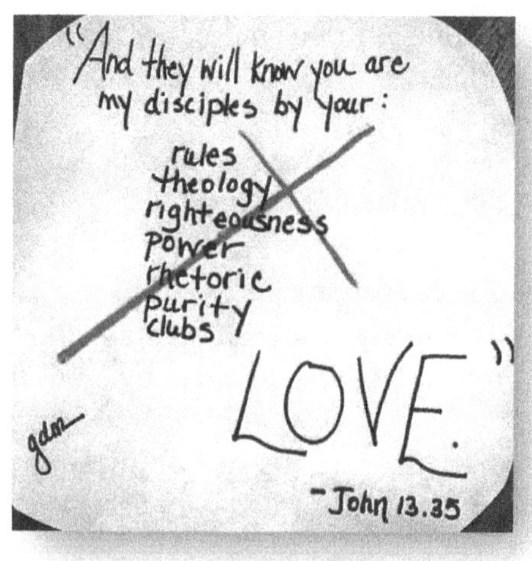

God has ordained certain institutions for the good of society. These include government, the church, the family, and work. They are necessary elements in the formation of a sane and stable society. Obviously, we see attacks on the family. There is infidelity, homosexuality, abortion, and the liberation of women.

The breakdown of the family has caused irreparable damage to the lives of countless people. There are labor problems. There are problems between employer and employee. God did not intend it to be this way. He has a plan that includes the well- being of His people and the well-being of society.

In Ephesians 5:21-6:9 we see God's principles for sane living in the domestic and working worlds. The Apostle Paul begins this section with a significant statement. We are to submit ourselves one to another in the fear of God (vs. 21.) Mutual submission and respect are essential for effective relationships. In verses 21-33 he presents the vital relationship between a husband and wife. He begins first with the wife and says that she is to submit to her husband as unto the Lord. This is not slavery. It is loving submission.

Husbands are to love their wives as Christ loved the church and gave Himself for her. He uses this illustration to show the mutual relationship between the two. Both are equal but both do not have the same functions. God meant it this way. He wants an orderly family. Obviously with two heads this would be impossible. The husband is the head. However, he must be a loving head. His love is to be a sacrificial giving of himself for his wife. Christ did the same for us.

Marriage produces children and God has something to say in this regard as well. Children are to obey their parents (v. 6,11). They are to honor them (v. 2). Fathers are not to irritate or provoke their children. They are to bring them up in the instruction of the Lord (6:4).

In the working world God also has declared His will. Slaves (or employees today) are to obey their masters as unto Christ. They are to serve them with enthusiasm and with a good attitude. Employers or their lords are to treat their employees with dignity.

GREAT TEAMWORK AND COOPERATION DISPLAYED BY GEESE[1]

Scripture: Amos 3:3, 1 Samuel 30:8

Do we understand how wonderful God's creation is? Study has revealed that geese fly in a V-shaped formation (skein) when they are migrating. This serves several purposes.

The V-formation improves the efficiency over long migratory routes. This formation conserves their energy. Each bird flies slightly higher than the bird that is in front of him resulting in a reduction of the wind resistance. Each bird flies in the up wash of wind from the bird in front. Each bird has a reduction of drag and they increase their range by 71%. The birds flying at the tips and front are rotated in a timely cycle way. The V-formation conserves on the energy and efficiency of energy consumption. As the bird flaps, the air rolls off the wing tip and creates a downwash and the air behind it pushes upward. If you observe the flight pattern almost always one side of the V is longer then the V-formation. The lead bird tires more quickly so it rotates to the back of the V-formation. If a goose falls out of position in the V-Formation, it suddenly feels the drag and resistance and the goose will quickly return to the proper formation.

GOOSE TALK

Gander:	Male goose
Goose:	Female
Gosling:	Baby goose
Gaggle:	Geese on land or in water
Skien:	Geese flying in a V-formation

---

[1] By Wade Martin Hughes, Sr , 2020. Assembly Of God

WHAT CAN WE LEARN ABOUT THE SKIEN? THE V-FORMATION...

1.   Geese can fly a great distance by teamwork.
2.   Geese stay together to protect and support each other. When geese grow tired and flying gets hard, their unity supports each other.
3.   Most migrating birds fly very quietly, but geese honk very loudly to encourage each other to keep up their speed and altitude. "Honk! Honk!" Geese are helpful to each other and the honk helps to keep the geese flying, gives a sense of direction and coordinates position changes.
4.   Geese are very loyal. They mate for life. Often, when a mate dies, they refuse to mate again. Geese are protective.
5.   Geese often fly at night because the night is cooler. On long distance flights, geese tend to overheat. They don't soar, but flap their wings to maintain distance, so the night helps geese to stay cooler.
6.   Geese teach us that we are stronger together than when alone.
7.   A sick or wounded goose descending is followed by two geese dropping out of the formation to help out. Those geese stay with the weak goose until it dies or gets better and is able to fly again. Then they catch up with the formation.
8.   The power of synergy: alone, we are weak. United we stand. We are stronger together. Scriptures: 1 Samuel 30:8, Amos 3:3.

FRIENDSHIP EVANGELISM

Probably the most effective way to reach people is through family and friend web evangelism. Cold-contact visitation and open-air preaching has its place but more people come to Christ as a result of a friend or relative who witnesses to them or invites them to a meeting. Lifestyle evangelism does not play down the need to communicate the Gospel. It just allows it to be communicated in a natural way that does not offend people. The Gospel itself offends. It takes advantage of natural contacts that we have through our work and play. Jesus Christ was a friend of sinners. He attracted people to His message because He showed concern for them. We win a hearing as we demonstrate love for people. Let us look at principles to keep in mind as we seek to make friendships and win people to Christ.

PRINCIPLES [2]

1.	Communicating the gospel involves identifying with people. We must be willing to share our weaknesses and failures.
2.	Jesus Christ identified Himself with others. He was willing to spend time with them.
3.	We must accept non-Christians as they are. We must be willing to build a friendship with them even if they don't accept Christ.
4.	Our responsibility is not to be "soul winners" but witnesses. God wins souls. It is His work to regenerate people. Of course, I still like the term and still use it. Our aim is souls and confrontational evangelism does have its place.
5.	We must look at the whole man, his body, personality, will, emotions, gifts and abilities.

---

[2] Excerpt article on "Friendship Evangelism" by Floyd McClung of Youth with a Mission. He is putting many of these principles to practice in the heart of Amsterdam, Holland.

6.   True identification will lead to involvement in the lives of people. This involves a sacrifice of time, money, lifestyle, pleasure, personal goals and ambitions.

7.   We must grapple for insight into the problems that people face, the frustrations they experience, the pressures they are going through, etc. We must seek to understand their particular culture.

8.   We must be honest with people and admit we don't have all the answers. If we don't know all the answers, we should read, pray and search.

9.   We must never pressure people to accept Christ. They must understand first the message and then the cost of discipleship.

10.   We must wait until the person wants to receive Christ and be available to help him.

11.   When he does make that decision, we must help him to grow in his new-found faith.

**"Friendship evangelism'
is the freedom to Agape
others without an
agenda (Young)."
R. Alan Woods**

**"Effective evangelism and discipleship are
most often the fruits of genuine
friendship."**

THE STORY OF MY JEWISH FRIENDS

In April, 2020 our friend Sybil Kaplan called me. "Can you please come over?" she asked. "Barry is not moving."
While she called for an ambulance, I rushed to their house. My friend Barry was in bed and I didn't feel a pulse. Guided by a medic, I tried CPR. The ambulance arrived ten minutes after I got there, and for another 20 minutes they tried to revive him, to no avail. Barry had passed into eternity.

He was buried the next day and after their Rabbi spoke, others shared and I also had an opportunity to tell about our relationship over the past 11 years.

I first met Barry while we studied at Ulpan here in Jerusalem. We often had coffee together during the break. Even though Jewish Barry came from Kansas City and I, a Christian, from the New York City area, we had a few things in common. Importantly, I am Italian, and the Jews are like Italians. We have good strong mothers and families and traditions. The Italian mother will always ask, "Have you eaten?" The Jewish mother will ask, "Have you studied?" We both enjoyed sports and discussing politics. We would sometimes get together for cappuccino and a croissant, pull out our *Jerusalem Post* and discuss current events and how we could solve the problems of this world. Occasionally I would insert a thought from the Bible. Our common good sense of humor also cemented our friendship.

Barry's wife Sybil became good friends with Billie. Billie takes her shopping a lot. We did many things together like going on outings, eating out, and in each other's homes.

One day, Barry said, "I will come to your church but don't try to convert me." Jokingly, I responded, "I will come to the synagogue, but don't try to convert me."

We did go to their synagogue for Purim and Chanukah celebrations and some Trivia night parties. Many times, he and Sybil came to the church, especially during our Christmas and Easter celebrations and for several concerts. At first, I tried to be sensitive in my preaching but then thought, *I must not be afraid to be bold and direct with my preaching of the Gospel.* During one of their visits, I prayed that God would help me to preach boldly and directly. "It was an amazing message," they told me afterwards. It was not me, but it was the Holy Spirit.

Barry was very eager to find out about Biblical sites that were related to Jesus so I took him to some on several occasions. "Barry, I'm giving you an education," I told him. Before cutting my hair, my Jewish barber in the States would say, "I am going to give you an education." I got a hair-cut and learned some new jokes and Jewish stories. Jews like being educated. They are a curious people.

One day I went to visit Barry when he was confined to his bed because of a back ailment. He appreciated that I prayed over him and Sybil even remarked that it helped him. On another occasion, I visited him with two Nigerian sisters in the Lord from my church in Vienna. I told sister Maria, to pray but maybe not to use the phrase, "In Jesus Name" for fear of offending him. She said, "Pastor, we must always pray in Jesus name." "OK, Let's go," I responded.

When we arrived, I told Barry that Maria wanted to pray for him in Jesus Name. "I guess it won't hurt," he responded.

Wow. She prayed and Barry was touched.

Barry and Sybil have met many of our friends from the church and from around the world. They have enjoyed it so much.

At one of our church thanksgiving gatherings we invited Barry and Sybil.

During our time of sharing words of thanksgiving, Barry and Sybil said, "We thank God for our Christian friends."

One time we brought them to see the Oklahoma Singing Men at the YMCA. After the group sang the Gospel Song, "The Midnight Cry," a song about the second coming of Jesus and the rapture, I began to cry. The first time I heard that song was in 1998, the year my father died. Barry leaned over to me and said," Al, Jesus is really your Savior." I knew God was working in Barry's life. We know that God enabled us to meet for a purpose. He loves the Jewish people and wants them to be saved. He uses each one of us. We share our lives and our testimonies. Only God knows if Barry accepted the Lord before he passed away. We leave this in the hands of God. In the meantime, we pray for Sybil and their family. We pray for members of their synagogue whom we have gotten to know. For all of us, pray that we too would be available to befriend and share with our Jewish folk.

 Let us ask the Lord to make us channels of his love for others and true friends to those who God brings our way.

PRINCIPLE 10

COMING TOGETHER
AS A TRUE BODY OF CHRIST

God created the church for a purpose. The Church is His body. It is people united under the Lordship of Jesus Christ. It is not a building or a denomination. In this section we will look at both the Universal Church comprised of all born-again true believers in Jesus Christ no matter where they live or what denomination they are a part of, and at the local church which can have both wheat and tares (believers and non-believers).

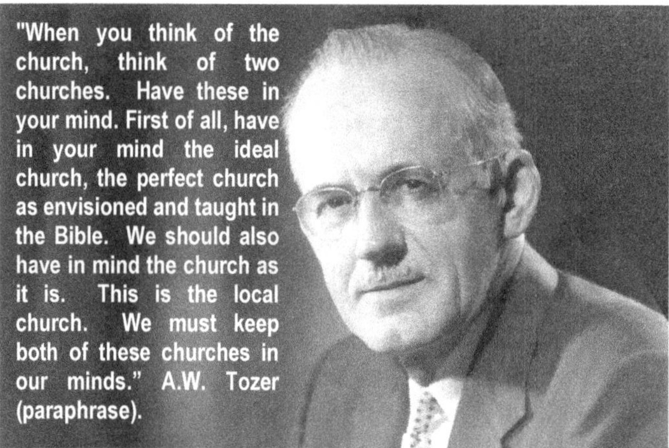

If we just think of the ideal church, we will be frustrated. If we just think of the real church, we will not strive to get better and improve it. We must always strive to build the church after God's design as described in the Bible. We must study and pray to that end. However, we must also show compassion and accept the church as it is.

As the father has pity on his son so God has pity on us because He knows we are but dust (Psalm 103:13, 14).

Let's look at all the components of a church as described in the Bible (our standard).

THE CHURCH OF JESUS CHRIST

1. What is the church?
   A. *EKKLESIA* = Those who are called out.
   B. The Universal Church (Matthew 16:18; Col. 1:18)
      1. Christ is the founder and builder of the church through the Holy Spirit.
      2. Images of the Church
      a. The Head and the Body (I Cor. 12). Christ is the head and we receive our direction from Him.
      b. The Bridegroom and the Bride (Ephesians 5). Christ gave Himself for us.
   c. Christ is the Vine and we are the branches (John 15). We depend on Him for our spiritual life.
      d. We are the spiritual temple of God (Ephesians 2:22,23). We are the stones and Christ is the cornerstone.
      e. The High Priest and a kingdom of priests (I Peter. 2). We are in a spiritual kingdom.
      f. The Family. We are all part of God's family. It is like an Italian family which is very close. It is said in I Timothy 3:15 that we are in God's household, which is the church of the living God, the pillar and foundation of the truth. Ephesians 2:18,19 shares that we all have access by one Spirit to the Father. We are fellow citizens with the saints and members of God's household.

2. What is the local church and what is its purpose?

A.   It is not just two or three who are gathered together.

B.   It is a visible expression of the universal church which has a certain organizational structure and is practicing certain ordinances.

C.   It has a three-fold purpose:
a. The first purpose is to worship the Lord.
b. The second is to edify the saints. This is done through the Word and through the stimulus of fellowship. The church is the pillar of truth (I Timothy 3:15).
c. The third purpose is to evangelize the world.

D.   I must add that the church should have a place to meet. In Acts 2:42 the church was together and gave themselves to the Word, prayer, fellowship, and the Lord's supper. With the present Corona virus, churches are meeting through the internet and zoom. It is OK for a while, but we must get back together. *"I was glad when they said unto me, let us go into the House of the Lord. "* (Psalm 122:1). Hebrews 10:24,25 tells us not to forsake the assembling of ourselves together.

During the Corona crisis we continued with our Sunday meetings, which were held either in the garden or inside with 'distanced' fellowship.

3. How is the church to be organized?

A. Organization is implicit in the following New Testament references:
a. Submission to church leaders (Heb. 13:7; 17;24)
b. The local church met together weekly to break bread (Acts 20:7).
c. Disciplinary action was to be done by a corporate decision (I Cor. 5).
B. Elders are to be the spiritual leaders of the church. There s should be a plurality of elders in each assembly. The churches in every city in the New Testament account, had this plurality (Acts 14:23). Paul addressed many of his letters to elders in general. Elders are not to be chosen based on popularity, wealth, or position. There are certain qualifications they must meet. These have to do with their character and gifts. (I Tim. 3:1-7, Titus 1:6-9). They are to teach, shepherd, govern, and protect the flock from false doctrine (Acts 20:17-28; I Tim. 3:1-5,17; Titus 1:9; I Peter 5:2).
C. Deacons are to serve the elders and take care of the physical needs of the assembly (Acts   6:1-6).
a. Deacons must have the right qualifications (I Tim. 3:1-10).
b. Deaconesses were also present in the early church (Romans 16:1, I Timothy 3:11).
D. Trustees may be necessary because of tax laws and the need to put church property under individual names.

4. What are the ordinances of the church?

The Lord's table was established to regularly remember the death of our Lord Jesus Christ (I Cor. 11:23-26).
Adult baptism of one who professes faith in Christ is to be done in obedience to our Lord. It is by immersion (the primary meaning of the word), and for the purpose of identifying oneself publicly with the Lord Jesus Christ.

5. What are the various types of church government.

a.   There is the national church type as seen in Sweden with the Lutheran church.

b. There is the no government type or at least a very loose government as practiced by the Plymouth Brethren.

c.   There is the hierarchical type as practiced by the Roman Catholic Church.

d.   There is the federal type with representatives. The reps are usually elders who rule the church. This is practiced by various Presbyterian churches.

e.   There is the congregational government in which the congregation itself decides most questions. This is found among Baptist churches.

6. What about Church discipline?

a. It is necessary to keep the church pure (I Cor. 5).

b. Principles for it are found in Matthew 18:16-17.

OLD TESTAMENT PICTURES OF THE CHURCH

There are many pictures of the Church in the Old Testament. The nation of Israel is a picture of the church. It was a group of people gathered under God to display His glory. God gave Israel patriarchs, kings and judges to rule His people. He also gave them prophets to be instruments to convey God's message. He ordained priests to intercede for the people. Exodus 18 shares about Moses who became overworked in leading and judging the people. His father-in-law, Jethro, advised him to distribute the workload. He advised him to

delegate his responsibility of judging the people while Moses was advised to give himself to teaching the people and to praying for them.

This is a picture of a church with people working together according to their gifts. Nehemiah also organized the people to build the wall. Ezra

was in charge of preparing the people spiritually, and Zerubbabel was to build the temple. Nehemiah assigned people to different gates of the wall. They were divided by family and prepared to work and to fight the enemy as needed.

JESUS CHRIST AND THE CHURCH

Christ said in Matthew 16:18 that He *"will build His church and the gates of hell will not prevail against it."* He predicted the church. He chose His disciples as a way of picturing the church. It was his choosing. He trained them and sent them out. He sends all of us out to make disciples of all nations.

THE EARLY CHURCH

In the first few chapters of the book of Acts we see the birth of the church. The apostles and others prayed for 10 days and then the Holy Spirit descended upon them.

Peter preached and 3000 people came to the Lord. This was the first church, the church at Jerusalem. In Acts 2:42 we read that the church gave themselves to the apostles' teaching, to fellowship, to prayer, and to the Lord's Table (to remember Christ). They also shared their faith. God continued to bless them. These are the basic functions of the church. In Acts 6 we see a problem in the church with the serving of the widows. It was solved as they divided up the work. Some took care of the widows and some gave themselves to prayer and the word. Both are needed.

Antioch was the first international church, as described in Acts 13. They worshiped the Lord and the Lord set apart Paul and Barnabas to go forth and preach the Gospel. These were components of a model church.

The **church at Thessalonica** was also a model church. All of its components are described in the first chapter. It was a unified church born of the Spirit of God. They were committed to faith, hope and love. They were outreach oriented. They put Christ first and were not idolaters, and, they were a second coming church.

The Corinthian church, on the other hand, was in the Lord, but had problems. Paul wrote to correct them so they could be better testimonies. They had division and moral problems as well as abuses of the Lord's table.

BIBLICAL IMAGES OF THE CHURCH:
NATURE AND GROWTH (IN DEPTH STUDY)

"No man is an island unto himself."
John Donne

Whether in business, sports, politics, or in life, it is important to work with other people. God created us to have fellowship with Him and with each other. We are to encourage one another as we do this (Hebrews 10:24,25). The modern term for this is teamwork. We work together as a team. God has provided the church as our team. Each team is called together for a purpose. We are given certain gifts and abilities to function as good members of the team. Unselfishness and comradery are two key elements needed to make a team work. The pictures of the church we saw above convey to us the concept of a team that works together to accomplish the purposes of God. Let us look at these beautiful pictures and be encouraged to work together for the glory of God.

"Individually, we are one drop.
Together, we are an ocean."
Ryunosuke Satoro

THE CHURCH DESCRIBED AS THE BODY OF CHRIST

The human body has many parts, but the many parts make up one whole body. So it is with the body of Christ.
(1 Corinthians 12:12 NLT)

The church is like a human body (I Cor. 12:12-31). It is one unit with many parts. Christ is the head of the body (Ephesians 1:22).

Each member must receive their directions from Christ.

As believers, we were baptized into this one body (v. 13). In a human body, every part is different, and every part has a function (Romans 12:6-8, Ephesians 4:11). God has made us different so that we can help each other. We have differing gifts. If one suffers, we all suffer. If one rejoices, we all rejoice. There is unity in diversity. Obviously, we must stick together and minister to each other as equal members of His body.

In Ephesians 4, the Apostle Paul speaks of unity in the body of Christ. Since we are one in Christ in our position, we should strive to be one in Christ in our experience. We are to be completely humble, gentle, patient, and loving. We are to keep the unity of the spirit in the bond of peace. Paul emphasizes our unity as he shares that we have one Lord, one faith, one baptism, and one God and Father of all.

We are one but we are also different. Paul shares that the Lord gave some to be apostles, some to be prophets, some to be evangelists and others to be pastors and teachers. God provided these gifted people to train and prepare the church for service. The body of Christ is to be built up and reach unity in the faith and in the knowledge of Jesus and become mature. We are to attain to the fullness of Christ. A healthy body will grow. As we remain unified in Christ and exercise our gifts to minister to one another, we will remain healthy. This is true qualitative growth and becomes an attractive element of the Gospel.

THE BUILDING OF GOD

I had the unique privilege of growing up in a builder's home. My father worked for the Prudential Insurance company as a project manager for various building projects including malls and stadiums. My grandfather also lived with our family after the death of my grandmother. He was an Italian architect who was still designing homes and churches at the age of 95. He was also a carpenter and craftsman. He believed in building on a strong foundation and doing things the right way.

Now, I have been called to the ministry of helping to build the church of Jesus Christ. The church is a spiritual building. The New Testament portrays the church as a building in the form of a holy temple. In Ephesians 2:19-21 we read, *"So then you are no longer foreigners and strangers, but fellow citizens with the saints, and members of God's household, built on the foundation of the apostles and prophets, with Christ Jesus Himself as the cornerstone. The whole building is being fitted together in Him and is growing into a holy sanctuary in the Lord, in whom you also are being built together for God's dwelling in the Spirit."*

The Apostles and Prophets are the foundation of this building. This refers to their teachings and instructions. Jesus Christ is the cornerstone. He is the one holding the building together. The Holy Spirit is the cement that also keeps the bricks and pieces together. We are the living stones that God uses to build His temple. We read in I Peter 2:4-8, *"Coming to Him, a living stone - rejected by men but chosen and valuable to God - you yourselves as living stones, are being built into a spiritual house, for a holy priesthood to offer spiritual sacrifices acceptable to God through Jesus Christ. For it says in Scripture: 'Look I lay a stone in Zion, a chosen and valuable cornerstone, and the one who believes in Him will never be put to shame.' So, the stone will come to you who believe, but for the unbelieving, the stone that the builders rejected; this One has become the cornerstone, and a stone that causes men to stumble, and a rock that trips them up. They stumble by disobeying the message; and were destined for this."*

THE BRIDE OF CHRIST

Everyone loves a wedding. It's a time of celebration as two people commit themselves to one another. The believer is in a love relationship with His Lord and Savior Jesus Christ. It is actually a royal love relationship since He is the King of Kings. The Bible tells us that

Christ is the Bridegroom of the church and that the church is the bride of Christ (Ephesians 5:23-32, II Cor. 11:2, Rev. 21:9). As the church grows in its love relationship to Christ it becomes a beautiful trophy of the grace of God. It is this love which motivates a believer to serve the Lord. We love because He first loved us (I John 4:19). Paul prayed that the Ephesian believers would grow and experience the love of God in a very profound way (Eph. 3:14-21). He prayed that the Thessalonians would grow in their love for each other (I Thess. 3:12).

FAMILY OF GOD

Coming from an Italian family, I understand the true meaning of "family." Jews are often compared to Italians with their emphasis on the family. The mother is the focal point who cooks great meals and encourages her children to succeed in life. Of course, the children respect and love their parents. This concept of family extends beyond the immediate family. In my family, I felt very close to my aunts, uncles, and cousins.

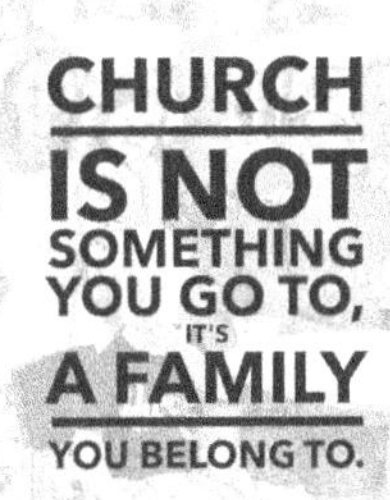

The church is also a family. We have God as our father. We also have brothers and sisters. In 1 Timothy 3:15, we read, *"But if I should be delayed, I have written so that you should know how people ought to act in God's household, which is the church of the living God, the pillar and foundation of the truth."*

Jews and Gentiles alike make up the spiritual household. Ephesians 2:18,19 states: *"For through Him we both have access by one Spirit to the Father. So, then, you are no longer foreigners and strangers, but fellow citizens with the saints, and members of God's household."*
We become a child of God by receiving Christ (John 1:12). God wants to develop the family into a unified body that attracts other people to the family.

THE FLOCK OF GOD

In John 10, Christ is described as the good shepherd. As a good shepherd, He lays down his life for His sheep. He knows His own and they know Him. His desire is to find lost sheep so that there will be one flock. The sheep follow Him because they know His voice. He goes ahead of them and leads them. According to I Peter 5:4, Christ is the chief shepherd. He protects his sheep and provides the proper diet so that they can be healthy and attractive. The writer to the Hebrews closes the epistle with this benediction: *"Now may the God of peace, who brought up from the dead, our Lord Jesus-the great Shepherd of the sheep-with the blood of the everlasting covenant, equip you with all that is good to do His will, working in us what is pleasing in His sight, through Jesus Christ, to whom be glory forever and ever. Amen."*
Of course, before providing for His sheep, the Lord must find sheep. A well-known teacher stated *"God wants countable lost persons found. The Shepherd with ninety-nine lost sheep who finds one and stays at home feeding and caring for it should not expect commendation. God will not be pleased by the excuse that His servant is doing something "more spiritual" than searching for strayed sheep. Nothing is more spiritual than the actual reconciliation of the lost to God."*
This is the main teaching of John 10 and Luke 15.

THE GARDEN OF GOD

The Bible uses many images from nature and agriculture to describe the growth of the church. As one theologian said,

"The teaching of the New Testament was charged with the expectation of growth."

We see this in the way the Lord described the world as white for harvest (John 4:35) and the Kingdom of God as being like a mustard

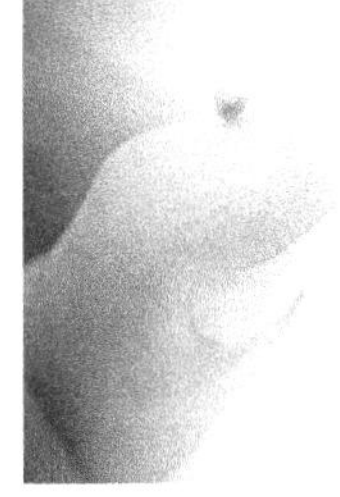

seed (Matthew 13:31,32). In particular, the mustard seed parable speaks about the growth of the Kingdom.

The growth of the Kingdom of God is both a qualitative and quantitative growth. It is qualitative because the Kingdom is in each believer in a spiritual sense (Luke 17:21). It is quantitative in that people are brought into the Kingdom from darkness (Colossians 1:13) and are added to the church.

The Bible also speaks of the church as the vine, with Christ as the vine dresser (John 15). God prunes the vine so it will bear more fruit. This fruit is the fruit of the Spirit (Galatians 5:22,23) and the winning of souls to Christ.

CHURCH PLANTING

My wife, Billie, and I had a wonderful visit recently with the great Evangelist Luis Palau. He preached on Matthew 6:33 at Dallas Seminary when I was there. It spoke to my life and led me to commit my self to go overseas as a missionary. This verse speaks of seeking first the kingdom of God and His righteousness. Then all things will be given to us.

For me, this meant that my priority should be reaching others with the Gospel. I stepped out by faith and God blessed me with a wife and a church planting ministry in Italy, a church ministry in Austria, and a church ministry in Israel. All these ministries were fueled by evangelism.

Church planting is the heart of God. Luis Palau's mother shared with her children to go and preach the Gospel and plant churches. That became Luis' mantra. He loved evangelism, but he also loved the church. While in Italy I attended a seminar on church planting given by a Dutchman, Richard Haverkamp. He planted six churches in seven years in Roman Catholic Belgium. He was part of the Plymouth Brethren. This is a very effective group in Europe and around the world. I worked with them in Italy and found them to be doctrinally sound, and evangelism oriented. They believe in a plurality of elders and the importance of the Lord's table.

I am going to share the notes I took at this seminar with you. They are so instructive and encouraging. Even for a pastor in a church, the principles can be very helpful. Sometimes we need to plant a church within a church.

LET'S START CHURCHES[1]

As we approach the subject of church planting, we need to consider the words of the prophet Haggai who said, *"Consider your ways..."* (1:2) Our goal, as church planters, should be to keep Christ as the center, use the Bible as our authority, and allow the Holy Spirit to control. We can think of all kinds of excuses for not seeing fruit today. Some say we are living in "Noah's day." It was a day when most people did not listen to God.

MAN, MESSAGE, AND METHODS

As we begin, we first need to consider three things:

1.   Consider the messenger, or the man
2.   Consider the message
3.   Consider the method

---

[1] Notes from seminar on church planting by Richard Haverkamp.

1. Consider the messenger.

Are we surrendered to the Lord, obedient to Him, and in relationship with the Holy Spirit? We need to be balanced in our lives and ministries. In Europe, the two largest evangelical groups are the Pentecostals and the Brethren. The Brethren put emphasis on the Word. Many of their churches, however, seem stuffy and rather dead. The Pentecostals put the emphasis on the Spirit. There is, however, a tendency towards fanaticism. We need to have the emphasis of both. The messenger must have vision. This vision must be born of prayer. It says in the Bible, *"According to your faith be it done to you"* and *"As you think in your heart, so you are."* Read Hebrews 11 and find out about men of faith.

2. Consider the message.

We must not make the Gospel too cheap. Jeremiah 48:10 says, *"Cursed be he who keeps his sword from bloodshed."* In Acts 17:30 Paul say that God commands all men to repent.

3. Consider the methods.

We must become more businesslike in our approach. Many businessmen take 2 hours a week to consider the quality and quantity of their work. We should do the same.

BASIC STUDY OUTLINE [2]

I. The Goal: What are we aiming at?
II. The Strategy: What is our plan?
III. The Weapons: What are our resources?

"Strategy is a pattern in a stream of decisions"

– Henry Mintzberg

---

[2] From One Hundred Bible Lessons by Alban Douglas, OMF Publishers 1966

I. THE GOAL - A LIVING, ACTIVE INDEPENDENT CHURCH

A. Old Testament figures:
1. The tabernacle (Exodus 25:1-7; 40:34) - Moses the builder.
2. The temple (I Chron. 28:9-11: II Chron. 6,7) - Solomon the builder
3. In building both of these, God gave the command to do it, ordered the design, and took care of providing for their needs.

B. New Testament:
Christ's goal was given in Matthew 16:18, *"I will build My church, and the gates of hell shall not prevail against it."*

Let us examine this statement in detail:
1. **"I"** - He will do it. All power has been given to Him (Matt. 28:18-20).
2. **"will"** - In the future tense. There is no doubt here.
3. **"build"** - From start to finish He will do it. There are four things he uses:
    1) Christ and the Word are the foundation.
    2) The stones are believers.
    3) The beams are the elders (Acts 20).
    4) The cement is love (I Cor. 13).
4. **"My"** - He owns it.
5. **"Church"** - This can be the universal church or a local expression of it. We are to make disciples, not just press for decisions. We are to teach and baptize. Christ loved the church and gave Himself for it (Eph. 5). It is better to have 50 people in a church than 100. With 50, everyone has to be active.
6. **"the gates of hell"** - We are on the offensive against these gates. Church planting is difficult in every place in the world.
7. **"shall not prevail against it"** - If you move out for God, you will get opposition.

C. The New Testament Local Church

1. Why is it so important?
   a. It is the dwelling place for God on earth.
   b. It is God's testimony on earth (Tim. 3:15).
   c. It is the place of development for the believer here on earth.
2. It has three purposes:
   a. Upwards - Adoration and Worship
   b. Inwards - Edification
   c Outward – Evangelization
3. It should be involved in disciple-making, baptizing, and teaching.

II. THE PLAN - OVERVIEW

A. Make contacts - use different means to get 30 contacts
B. Salvation - Personal work and home Bible studies.
C. Baptism - as a way of commitment to God and the church.
D. Teaching - to ground them in the faith.
E. Church Meeting - to remember the Lord's death
F. Training - for future elders
G. Get out - let the Holy Spirit work
H. Return for help - be available
I. Appointment of elders - to continue the work

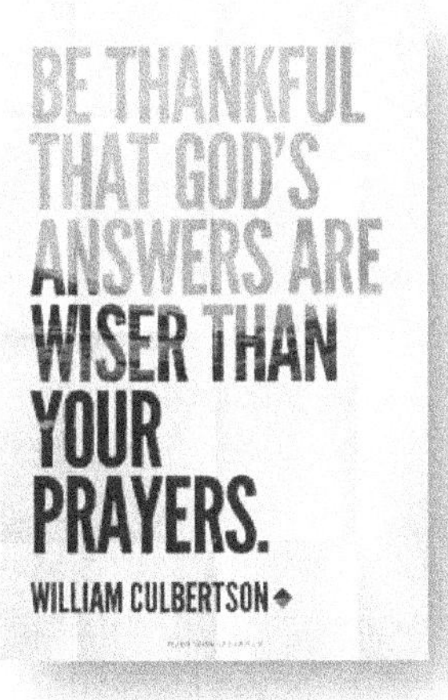

II. THE PLAN - THE DETAILS

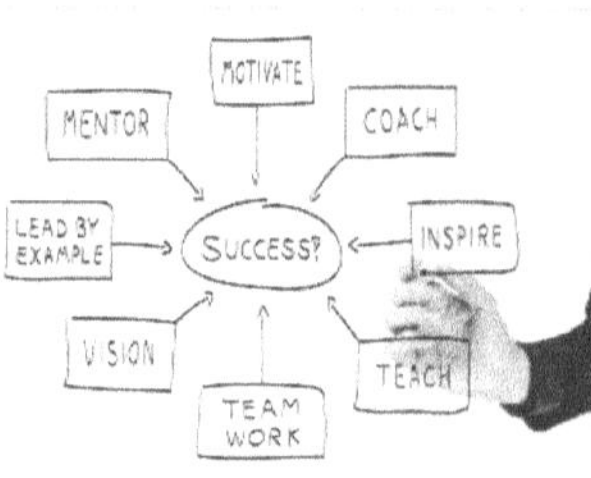

II - A. Make contacts:

1. The means:
    a. The natural way - e.g. with the milkman
    b. Survey
    c. Colportage
    d. Open air meetings - it also helps Christians
    e. Tent campaigns
    f. Film evenings
    g. Market stand
    h. Ladies', or children's meetings
    i. Bible Exposition or Home Bible Study
    j. The Andrew Way - Tell Your Brother.
2. Verses in dealing with contacts include Mt. 9:35, Deut. 29:29, Rom. 11:33. They should be encouraged to get converted or get out.
3. You should ask them if they have a Bible. If not, you should give them one.
4. Let them read the Gospel of John or the Gospel of Mark.
5. Give them books to read like *More Than a Carpenter* by Josh McDowell, *Know Why You Believe* by Paul Little, and *The Late Great Planet Earth* by Hal Lindsey.
6. Go back and answer their questions.
7. After you have made 30 contacts, stop. Begin to really work on those contacts. Get into their homes.

II- B. Salvation

1. Personal work

There are three types of people to deal with:

1) Indifferent - We must awaken them and create an interest. This can be through the use of apologetics such as reasons why the Bible is the Word of God, fulfilled prophecies (about the return of the Jews for example). We can also deal with arguments for the existence of God and proofs for the resurrection of Christ. You may need to shock them and deal with the ever-present possibility of death.

2). Self righteous people who think they're fine. They need to be awakened. You need to create a need in them. They need to see their need. They must see that they fall short of God's standard. Verses to share include Deut. 7 and Exodus 20 (The Ten Commandments), Matt. 5; 22:36-38, Rom. 3, Gal. 3:10, James 2:10, Prov. 28:9, John 8:47.

3) Interested ones - These are the open ones. With them you can use the back door approach and give them as much as they can take and no more. It takes the weapon of love. You can shock and insult people, but it must be done in love. The message we use - Man is body, soul, and spirit. Because of sin, there is a barrier between God and man. This is his first problem.   His second problem is that he is dead. That is, he is separated from God (Ephesian 2:1-3). Body and soul have been separated from the Spirit. The first problem was solved by Christ's death and payment for sin. The barrier is removed but man is still dead. The second problem was solved by His resurrection. The living Christ can come into us if we receive Him. If we do, He will give us life again. Conversion is making Christ Lord of our lives. We make ourselves God and decide what we want to believe, but we must let God be God in our lives. That's conversion!

C. HELPFUL ILLUSTRATIONS

1) **Radio waves:** I Cor. 2:8,9 says that the natural man does not understand the things of God. Only the Spiritual man can. A room is always full of voices even though we can't hear them. You can't receive radio waves with your 5 senses. You need something outside yourself to receive them. The same is true with God. The problem isn't that there is no God.  We just can't hear Him because of our sin. We are on two different wave lengths. We need the 6th sense which is the Holy Spirit.

2) **Blind flying:** When you fly a plane, you cannot go by your own feelings. You must trust the instruments. In the clouds, a pilot can lose his sense of direction. This is why he needs to rely on his instruments which give an accurate reading. The instruments have proven themselves over and over. They are trustworthy. God also is trustworthy and so we can trust His Word.

3) **A book with instructions;** God made man with a book of instructions, the Bible. A washing machine, for example, always comes with a book of instructions.

4) **Speed limit** - The limits of sin.

5) **Ant Hill** - How can I warn ants of a coming destruction, like a tractor coming. The only way would be for me to become an ant. They wouldn't be able to understand a trumpet. They wouldn't understand if I spoke to them in English. But if I became like them I would be able to warn them. That is what God did when He became a man.

D. DO YOUR PERSONAL WORK WITH ENTHUSIASM

I Thessalonians 1:5 says that the Gospel comes in Word, in power, in the Holy Spirit, and with ENTHUSIASM (full conviction). Why not be enthusiastic? We have the most powerful message, the most reasonable message, and the most beautiful message. People are impressed by enthusiasm.

A. Home Bible studies - Matthew 9:35 illustrates Jesus' method of preaching and teaching everywhere. When conducting a home Bible study, it is best to study the Gospel of John (with a couple, the Gospel of Mark may be better).

Here is sample of a Gospel of John study (based on chapters 1-3.)

1. John 1:18 - Here we see the need for revelation. No man has seen God. God has given us the Word which reveals Himself. In this study it would be useful to talk about the reasonableness of the existence of God. Who is this God? Is He loving? What is the message of the Bible (John 3:16)?
2. John 1:1 - Christ the Word 1) Why was He called the Word (Heb. 1:1-3)? 2) Christ and the Word (Matt. 4:4). His whole life and ministry were based on the Word.
3. I John 1:1-18 - Verse by verse
4. John 1:19-29 - Verse by verse. Verse 29 talks about sin. This is man's problem (the Ten Commandments), Rom. 3, Gal. 3, James 3.
5. John 1:29 - Christ is the Lamb of God (Ex. 12). He died once for all (Hebrews 10:14).
6. John 1:29-34: The work of the Holy Spirit.
7. John 1:35-51 - The four testimonies of Christ. John the Baptist - The Lamb of God. Andrew - the Messiah. Phillip- We have found Him. Nathaniel - Here is a true Israelite in whom there is nothing false.
8. John 2:1-25 - Wine, happiness, Holy Spirit, cleansing.
9. John 3 - The new birth.

II- C Baptism

It means obedience and surrender. It doesn't say in the bible that one has to prove himself. Baptism is an open declaration, the first step of obedience.

II - D Teaching

In Acts 2:37-47 we notice 7 things:

1. Conversion - This involves the recognition of sin, repentance, the recognition of the Savior, and the work of the Holy Spirit.

2. Baptism - This involves obedience.

3. The Word

4. Fellowship - this is the church. The believer needs the church for teaching, fellowship (building up one another), for correction, for worship, and for service. The church needs the believer because the body needs her members. The church isn't an option. It also needs them just as the temple needs her priests. We must believe and practice the priesthood of the believer.   They are to come to church to bring something. The church also needs the gifts of each believer. What does God expect of each believer? He expects every believer to have a part in the worship. He expects every saint to share in the edification. He expects every   member to be active in evangelization.

5. The Lord's Table

6. Prayer

7. Sharing through good works and witnessing.

II - E The Church Meeting (Matt. 18:20)

1. What was it? (Luke 22:19, 20; Acts 20:7; I Cor. 11:17-20).

2. What was the purpose?

 a. Look up to Christ (Heb. 12:1-3).

 b. Look back to Calvary "Remember Me."

 c. To give Christ the central place (Rev. 5:6; Luke 24:27, 44-46). He must have first place. The Holy Spirit came to reveal Christ. Paul preached Christ and Him crucified.

3. Result: Motivation for serving (II Cor. 5:14).

4. How was it done? (I Cor. 14:26-32) There is to be worship and the exercise of the priesthood of the believer.

5. Seven reasons for the Lord's table.
   a. Christ's wish and command.
   b. The Apostle's example.
   c. The central and only regular meeting in the New
   Testament.
   d. Best way to worship (priesthood of every believer).
   e. Best way to get believers active.
   f. Best way to recognize gifts.
   g. Best preparation for times of persecution.

II - F Training

   1. We need to train others and work ourselves out of a job
   (II Tim. 2:1,2; Eph. 4:11,12).
   2. What are we to train them to do?
      a. to teach Sunday School
      b. to give Bible studies
      c. to witness and evangelize
      d. to shepherd
         1. How to train elders
         a. Teach qualifications (1 Tim. 3, Titus 1).
         b. Teach work of an elder (Acts 20; I Peter 5; Ezek. 34).
         c. Allow time for the person to develop and prove
            himself.
         d. Pray both on an individual and group level.
   3. The recognition of elders - 4 factors necessary
      a. The Holy Spirit
      b. The man himself
      c. The church planter or associate
      d. The church itself

II - G. Move out - Allow the Holy Spirit to work.

II - H. Return to help - be available.

II - I Appoint elders - to continue the work

III. The Weapons (Our resources) II Cor. 10:3-5.
A. The Word of God.
   1. Promises for us (Matt. 16:18; 28: 18-2-; Haggai 1:8; 2:4).
   2. A sword to use (Heb. 4:12:12; Eph. 6:17).
B. Prayer
C. The Holy Spirit
D. Love (I Cor. 12:31; I Cor. 13).

CONCLUSION:

**A successful church planting ministry
involves five things:**

1. **Enthusiasm,**
2. **Simplicity**
3. **Boldness**
4. **Persistence**
5. **Hard work**

DESPISING THE CHURCH

What does it mean to despise the church? It is when we hurt the church through our bad beliefs and behavior. In the Old Testament God dealt with a nation. In the New Testament He deals with a Church. After Pentecost, when the Spirit descended, they were all baptized into His body. The church is more than an earthly organization. It is Christ's Body. At conversion each one of us is baptized into this body. Some have prominent positions like eyes, tongue, hands, etc. but most Christians occupy a minor, insignificant, hidden place inside the body, probably a minute cell. But if that hidden cell is damaged the whole body suffers.

The Church is the invisible body of believers. The visible Church is an earthly organization that includes good and bad, wheat and tares, saved and hypocrites. The earthly Church is unfortunately divided into sects, denominations and isolated ones. Jesus' present occupation is building the Church. Matt. 16:18 says, *"upon this rock I will build My Church."* This is not an edifice of stone but a living Body. Do we despise this Church? To despise means to treat with contempt, to loathe, abhor.

HOW MAY THE CHURCH BE DESPISED?

The unbeliever ridicules the Church as a useless organization. The Christian might not despise the church this way, but could in subtle ways.
How?

> 1. By forsaking church attendance. Heb. 10:25, *"Not forsaking the assembling of ourselves together, as the manner of some is."* People come up with all kinds of excuses.
> 2. By accepting the benefits of the church without accepting responsibilities.
>   a. We take our children there to be dedicated but not to Sunday School.
>   b. We use it for our children's weddings, but never have a family altar.
>   c. We have our names on the roster, but never go to church.
>   d. We have communion once a month, but never win souls.
>   e. We enjoy Christmas and Easter but never learn the truth of God's Word.
>   f. We take our dead there to be buried but continue to live wickedly and not prepare for death.

*"Jesus didn't die so that
we would come to church.
He died so that we would become the church."*

g. We reduce the church to a social club for business, entertainment or matrimonial purposes.
3. By failing to make preparation for the service.
4. By failing to listen during the sermon.
5. By permitting lax religious beliefs, views, and convictions regarding doctrine.
6. By living inconsistent lives.
7. By not giving or giving little to the church.
8. By using our talents poorly.
9. By being detached from the church. The Church is not holy enough some say.
10. By slandering others and judging people unfairly. Proverbs 17:15 says, *"To condemn the innocent or acquit the guilty, it is an abomination to the Lord."* I have seen for myself those who were judged by God for doing these things. It is scary.

RESULTS OF DESPISING THE CHURCH OF GOD

1. The Lord Jesus is hurt.
2. The Church is weakened.
3. Sinners are repulsed.
4. Christians are weakened.
5. The non-attender is the loser. Spiritually, Economically, Morally, Physically.

HINDRANCES TO THE UNITY OF THE BODY

It is vitally important that the church be unified. How can we win the world if we lose each other? Paul deals with this in I Corinthians 1. He exhorts the believers to be of one mind and spirit. There was a problem of disunity and division. One was saying he was of Paul, another Apollos, another of Peter, and some of Christ. He said, "Is Christ divided?" He was telling them to be united in Christ.

Even though they were a gifted assembly they needed to be reminded that they are nothing without *Agape* love (I Corinthians 13).

In Ephesians Paul shares with the believers their common calling (Eph. 1), their shared participation in the death of Christ, and the unity they have in the Holy Spirit. He prays that they may be united together by the Spirit in love (Eph. 3). He then says that because they have one Lord, one faith, one baptism and one Spirit, they should endeavor to maintain the unity they have and be of one mind.

Romans also urges believers to love each other (Romans 12) as members of the same Body. They must act as a team and use their gifts to help and complement each other.

In John 14-16, Jesus promises His disciples that they will not be left alone. He will send them the Holy Spirit who will teach them, guide them, and always be with them to comfort and encourage. Even though God uses people to teach, the Holy spirit is ultimately our teacher using the Word, other people, and the circumstances of life to teach and instruct us.

We need to be careful not to promote our particular doctrine or belief. I am not talking about the basic doctrinal foundation or belief system.

We should all be united on the inerrancy of Scripture, the existence of God, the person of Christ as God Himself, salvation by grace through faith. We also must believe in the second coming of Jesus the Messiah. But, there are some who say that only when we speak in tongues and have the baptism of the Spirit are we truly believers.

There are others who believe that we should use only one version of the Bible. Others hold a doctrinal position on the sovereignty of God which appears to make us seem like robots with no choice. Let us be careful not to go to extremes but be Biblically balanced.

THE CULT OF THE TEACHER

I heard a message by Jim Cymbala, pastor of the Brooklyn Tabernacle Church in New York City. He spoke of the cult of the teacher. He shared from Scripture that God wants each church to be a house of prayer. That is the foremost calling. We also learn from the Scripture that God uses gifted men to unfold the Word of God. However, many times we look to these men instead of to the Lord and His Word. It happens to Jews who look to their Rabbis for guidance. It can happen in churches as people view Scripture and events through the lens of their priests or pastors. We must be like the Bereans who checked out everything they heard (Acts 17,18).

"For the wisdom of this world is foolishness with God, for it is written "He catches the wise in their own cunning" (1 Corinthians 3:19)

Now concerning food offered to idols We know we all have knowledge. Knowledge puffs up, but love builds up (1 Corinthians 8:1)

Sometimes a pastor will think of himself as a great authority on Biblical things. He will put a great emphasis on the Word of God which can lead to extremism if he neglects prayer and evangelism. He can become very proud.

Remember: knowledge puffs up but love edifies.

A few years ago, we had a sport camp in Poland, and, as was our custom, we had a number of coaches and teachers. In this camp we do sport activities and have Biblical teaching and preaching. I was the organizer of our teaching and preaching. I was also the water boy and whistle blower to start the activities. We had five teachers and I divided up the responsibilities according to the theme. For example, our camp emphasized the **four principles or values of FCA.**

1.	Integrity,
2.	Pursuit of excellence,
3.	Servanthood
4.	Teamwork.

Each of the teachers spoke on one of the topics. I just did the introduction. Team teaching is wonderful.

It was interesting however, that before we had the camp we were at the church and a pastor was concluding his teaching with the young people. His wife made the comment that her husband had such great things to share with the group. She exalted his teaching. I am sure if was great teaching because it was from the Word of God. However, I was glad that we took a team approach. The focus was not on us but on the Holy Spirit teaching us.

GRACE AWAKENING

This is the name of a great book by Chuck Swindoll. It is a message that we need to hear in the church. Too often legalism infects the church. We judge each other on minor things. We divide over stupid controversies. We need to learn grace again. We need to learn to accept one another. Yes, we must admonish each other if we fail, but we must also learn to forgive and accept one another.

BALANCED CHURCH GROWTH

When we speak of balanced church growth, we mean a church must grow quantitatively, qualitatively, and organically. This means the church must grow in numbers (quantitatively). It must reach out and win souls for Christ and bring them into the fellowship. It must also grow spiritually or in holiness (qualitatively). It should help converts to grow in the Lord. This is discipleship. It also must grow in leadership (organically). It must develop leaders who can lead others. All three aspects are important.

CHURCH GROWTH PRINCIPLES

I conclude this section with principles which were shared by two pastors as to how their churches grew.

Principles from Pastor John MacArthur

1. A plurality of godly leaders
2. Functional goals and objectives
3. A strong emphasis on discipleship
4. A strong emphasis on community penetration
5. An aggressive, active, ministering people
6. An intense "caring" spirit
7. A genuine, high devotion to the family
8. Strong biblical teaching and preaching
9. Willingness to change and innovate
10. A constant effort to stretch the people's faith
11. A spirit of sacrifice
12. The primary thrust must be on worshipping God.

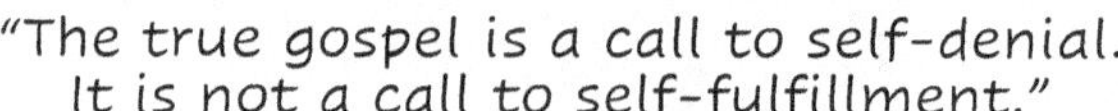

"The true gospel is a call to self-denial.
It is not a call to self-fulfillment."

John MacArthur

Principles from Pastor David Hocking

1. A continual desire and challenge to reach as many people as possible with the Gospel until Jesus comes again
2. A constant dependency upon God's power and direction through much prayer and careful study of biblical principles.
3. Emphasis on the body of Christ and the unity and fellowship of God's people rather than denominational affiliation and distinctives.
4. A simplicity of organization and operation
5. A dedication of pastors to do what God tells them to do and to refuse to do what the people should do and must be trained to do.
6. A desire to grow
7. A continual learning spirit
8. A resistance to and exposure of sin as the one thing hindering true growth.

Addenda

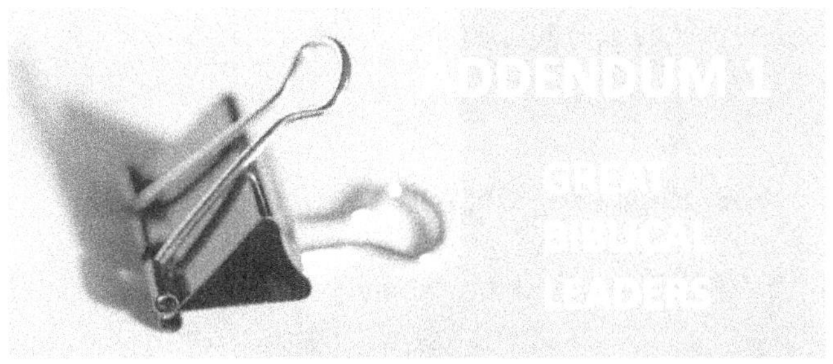

God has given us the Bible as a book which reveals His will and His plan for mankind. The Word contains law, prophecy, and history. History is the account of people and events. The Bible shares the stories of great men and women whom God used as His spokesmen and women and as His leaders. These people were great, not because they had a high position or were successful in human endeavors. They were sinners, saved by the grace of God, who lived lives of faith (Hebrews 11).

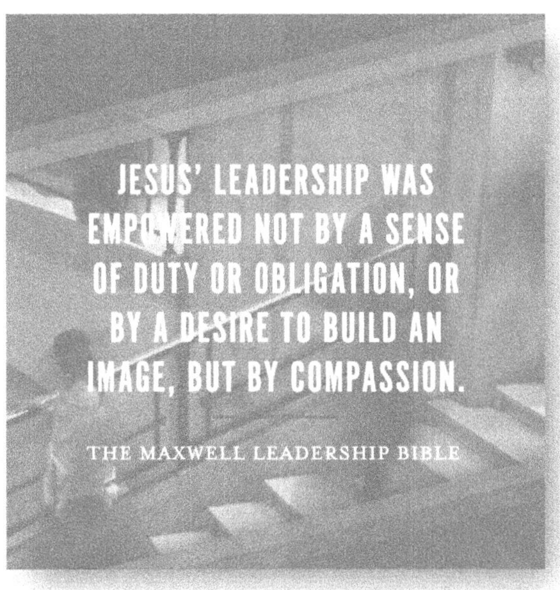

OLD TESTAMENT LEADERS

ABRAHAM - THE GREAT FATHER OF THE FAITH

Abraham is revered by Jews, Christians, and Muslims as the father of faith. His family were idolaters from Ur of the Chaldees. They were moon worshippers. However, God in His sovereignty chose Abraham to be the father of His chosen nation. He was called in the city of Haran to go to the land of the Canaanites. He was to leave all things and follow the Lord. He was promised a land and progeny. He would be the father of many nations. He obeyed God and went out from his home. He was promised a son with his wife, Sarah.

"Yet with respect to the promise of God, he did not waiver in unbelief but grew strong in the faith, being fully assured that what he had promised he was also able to perform." (Romans 4:20, 21). He believed the promise of God regarding a son but, had times of doubt. He let Hagar his maidservant bare Ishmael. He lied about his wife before the king of Egypt.

Principles of Leadership from Abraham

1. God uses our faith no matter how weak it may be. God can use imperfect people.
2. Faith is demonstrated as we step out and do something. Abraham left his land and went to the land God had promised.
3. The importance of faith and obedience.

Joseph, one of Jacob's sons, was a man God used to save a nation. But before that, he was betrayed by his brothers who were jealous of him. Then he was falsely accused by the wife of Potiphar and unjustly put into prison.

God worked all things out and he miraculously was delivered.

This reminds us of what happened to Jesus Christ. He was betrayed and falsely accused. Basically, he was rejected. But God had a plan for Joseph. He became the prime minister of Egypt. We know that in the providence of God he was able to help his family during a great famine and brought Israel into Egypt. He knew that all that happened to him happened for the good of the nation (Romans 8:28).

Principles of Leadership from Joseph

1. Trust God in all circumstances.
2. Live a pure life and God will use you.
3. All things work together for good to those who love God.

MOSES

As the Jewish people multiplied in Egypt, they became a threat to the leaders of Egypt. They were enslaved and commanded to the build the pyramids. They were treated harshly. The cried out to God for deliverance. God raised up Moses, who was one of them, but who had been miraculously saved by Pharaoh's daughter and put into the position of prince of Egypt. He escaped into the wilderness because he had killed an Egyptian soldier for beating a Hebrew. It was in the wilderness that God prepared him to be the instrument of deliverance for the Jewish people. He was a herder of sheep and learned how to deal with them. People are like sheep. Good experience. He was also divinely called by God through the burning bush. He felt unqualified but God encouraged him. God gave him divine signs to demonstrate his delegated authority. He also received help in communicating since he had a speech defect. God gave him the rod and staff and the power to send plagues. Aaron became his spokesman. God used him to speak to Pharaoh. God said, *"Let my people go."* God sent the last plague which killed all the firstborn of the Egyptians. The Jewish people were saved as they put the blood on the doorposts of their homes. This represents the blood of Jesus for us. We are saved from death. As Moses led people out, he demonstrated his leadership through prayer and meekness. However, he did get angry and struck the rock to get water. This was disobedience. Yes, God can use flawed men.

> *"God uses flawed people*
> *To share hope to a flawed world."*

Principles of Leadership from Moses

1. Moses was chosen of God.
2. He made a commitment to serve God.
3. He demonstrated great faith - see Hebrews 11: 23- 29.

Hebrews 11: 23- 29 says: *"By faith Moses, when he had grown up, refused to be called the son of Pharaoh's daughter but chose to suffer with the people of God rather than to enjoy the short-lived pleasure of sin. For he considered reproach for the sake of the Messiah to be greater wealth than the treasures of Egypt, since his attention was on the reward. By faith he left Egypt behind, not being afraid of the king's anger, for he persevered, as one who sees Him who is invisible. By faith he instituted the Passover and the sprinkling of the blood, so that the destroyer of the first born might not touch them. By faith they crossed the Red Sea as though they were on dry land. When the Egyptians attempted to do this, they were drowned."*

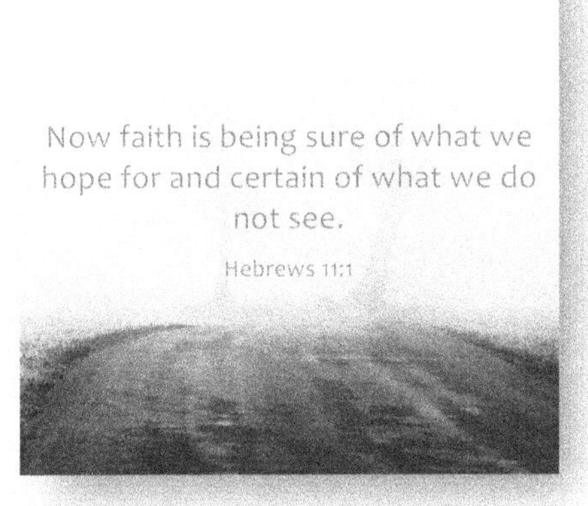

JOSHUA THE GREAT LEADER
WHO GUIDED THE PEOPLE INTO THE PROMISED LAND

Joshua was Moses' understudy. He took over for Moses when Moses died on Mt. Nebo. Joshua led the people over the Jordan River. Before he started to conquer the promised land, God gave him a promise. Joshua 1:8 says,

"This book of the law shall not depart from your mouth, but you shall meditate on it day and night so that you may be careful to do all that is written in it. Then you will have success and prosperity." If they trusted and obeyed, they would conquer. It happened with Joshua as God had promised, but there were some defeats along the way, like Ai. In Joshua 24, Joshua gathered all the people. He spoke about all that God had done to help them conquer the land. He gathered them between Mt. Gerizim and Mr. Ebal near Shechem. Remember that Moses had called some people to proclaim the blessings and some to proclaim the curses from these two mountains. He asked the people who they wanted to serve. Will it be the gods of Baal or the God of Abraham, Isaac, and Jacob? Joshua said, *"As for me and my house, we will serve the Lord."* The people responded, *"We will also serve the Lord."* Then they made a covenant before the Lord and put down a stone of remembrance. You can still see that stone today. From a high point on Mt. Gerizim you can see three things:

1.   Mt. Gerizim and Mt. Ebal,
2.   The stone of remembrance
3.   The land that God promised Abraham he would possess.

Principles of Leadership from Joshua

1. The key is to trust and obey
2. He showed leadership in judging Aachan.
3. He showed courage.
4. He showed faith as he obeyed God in marching around Jericho as the Lord told him. The walls came down by faith.

SAMUEL

God raised up Samuel for a purpose. He was a judge and a prophet. He was born to Hannah who prayed for years for a child. He received a great calling from God. He set up his center in Shiloh. He was to judge the family of Eli. He was a great prayer warrior who encouraged Israel to return to the Lord with all their hearts. He told them to get rid of their foreign gods and commit to the Lord and serve Him. If they did this, God would deliver them from the hand of the Philistines. He interceded for the people. He did not want to sin by not praying for the  people. He also anointed Saul as King. Even when Saul was King, Samuel was used of God to remind the people to fear the Lord and serve Him faithfully. He rebuked Saul. He became a true leader.

Principles of Leadership from Samuel

1. Obey God when He calls you.
2. Be a man or woman of prayer
3. Be courageous

DAVID

David was called a "man after God's own heart". This is surprising because after his calling and assumption of the kingship, he sinned against the Lord with Bathsheba and basically killed her husband. His sin found him out and he confessed it before the Lord (Psalm 51). As a young man he demonstrated his faith as he killed Goliath with s sling shot. He did it in the name of the Lord. He sinned by taking a census but repented of it. He wrote many psalms relating his trust in God when he faced foes like Saul and others.

Principles of Leadership from David

1. Fight the good fight of faith in the name of Jesus.
2. Be careful not to fall into sin. Deal with temptation (I Cor. 10:13).
3. If we sin, we can confess our sins and repent of them.
4. We must trust God in every situation.

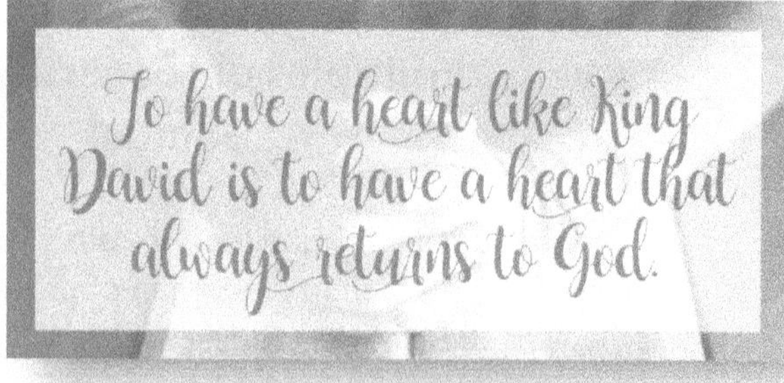

Elijah was raised up as a prophet to confront Israel with their sins. He preached and rebuked King Ahab and Jezebel, his evil wife. He had the famous battle between God and Baal's prophets in I Kings 18. God came through and sent fire to burn up the sacrifice on the altar Elijah had built. He was a man like us, but he prayed fervently and received an answer from God. He had great faith. When he prayed for drought, it came. When he prayed for rain, it came.

He exercised great authority as a believer. He also was a man who got discouraged and became afraid of Jezebel. He wanted to die. God encouraged him. He told him to eat. God spoke to him directly. He gave him a team of prophets. We all need people around us. Then he gave him an assignment to anoint Elisha and Hazael.

Elisha receives Elijah's mantle

Principles of Leadership from Elijah

1. Have faith in God to defeat the enemy.
2. Don't be afraid to rebuke even a king.
3. Let God encourage you through supernatural provision and a good team.

NEW TESTAMENT LEADERS

JESUS CHRIST

Our greatest example of leadership is the Lord Jesus Christ. He is God who became man. He came to die for our sins. During His earthly ministry he trained disciples to carry on His work. He taught them, modelled His teachings, and then sent them out to preach and perform miracles. He also demonstrated true servant leadership when he washed his disciple's feet (John 13). He was a servant.

Mark 10:45 tells us, *"For even the Son of Man did not come to be served but to serve and give his life as a ransom for many."*

He was very God but became a man who would serve others and give his life for all (Phil. 2).

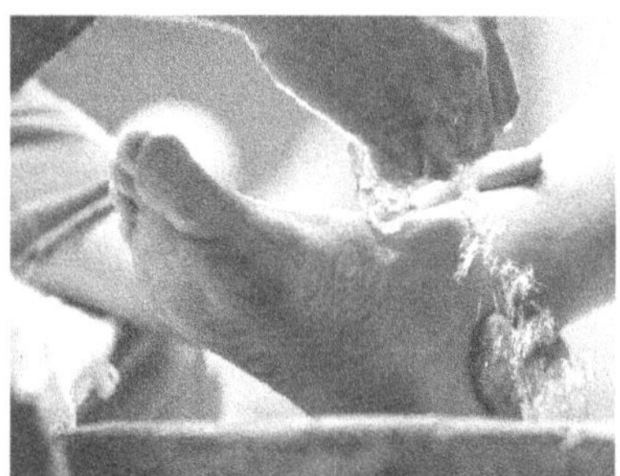 

Principles of Leadership from Jesus

1. Be a true servant.
2. Exercise authority.
3. Pour your life into other's lives.

Peter was a flawed follower of Jesus Christ. Yes, he was called of God and left his fishing job to follow Christ. He said he would never deny Christ, but when the pressure came, he did. He denied Christ three times before the cock crowed. After his rejection, he was remorseful. He confessed to God and repented of his sin. Then He was restored to ministry by the Lord. After Christ was raised from the dead, he met with Peter. He said, *"Peter do you love me?"* Peter said, *"Yes Lord, you know that I love you."* Christ then said, *"Feed my sheep."* When the Holy Spirit came upon Peter, he preached with boldness about Christ and the need to repent. He testified openly before men who previously had heard Peter deny Christ.

Simon Peter answered, 'You are the Christ, the Messiah,
the Son of the living God.'

Principles of Leadership from Peter

1. Be bold for Christ
2. When you sin, confess it, repent of it and carry on.
3. Be an example (I Peter). Follow Christ and be a model.

PAUL

The Apostle Paul had a dramatic conversion. He went from being a persecutor of the church to a preacher of the Gospel. He was there at the stoning of Stephen, giving his approval. He went out in pursuit of Christians to bring them to jail but was arrested by the Lord on the road to Damascus.

The Lord saved him and transformed his life.

He then went on to preach Christ without stop throughout the known world. He also helped to start churches. In Acts 20, he shared with the Ephesian elders about his commitment to live for Jesus and die for Him if necessary.

Principles of Leadership from Paul

1. Be a bold witness for Jesus
2. Pour your life into your Timothy's.
3. Learn to forgive.
4. Have a balanced ministry of evangelism, church planting, and leadership development.

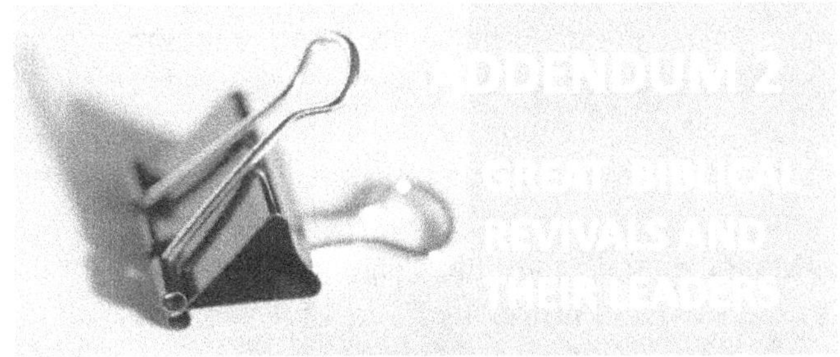

The Bible shares some great stories about revivals which God sent to bring His people back to Himself. Usually these revivals would come after people had fallen into sin. When judgement came, they called on the Lord. God used Kings and leaders to bring the people back. Here are some great revivals and their leaders.

JEHOSHAPHAT

Jehoshaphat, the son of Asa, became King and he walked in the ways of his father David. He did not consult the Baals but sought the Lord and kept His commandments. He got rid of idols and false worship. The fear of the Lord came upon all the other nations. He built cities and fortresses and he built up the military. He had great wealth and prosperity.

In 2 Chronicles 18, Ahab, King of Israel, asked Jehoshaphat to go with him to fight against the King of Aram. Jehoshaphat agreed, and in the heat of the battle when he was about to be killed, Jehoshaphat called on the Lord and the Lord helped him. This was not true of King Arab of Israel. He was with Jehoshaphat, and even though he did not go into battle wearing his royal robes but was disguised as a regular soldier, King Arab was killed by a random arrow.

Jehoshaphat was a good administrator and appointed judges. He encouraged them to follow the Lord and fear Him.

He also appointed Levites, priests and heads of Israelite families to administer the law of the Lord and to settle disputes. He told them to act with courage.

When the Moabites and Ammonites came to make war, Jehoshaphat inquired of the Lord and proclaimed a fast for all Judah. All began to seek the Lord. Jehoshaphat stood up before everyone and prayed and blessed the Lord. He acknowledged the sovereignty of God. He reminded the people that they had said if disaster or plague or famine came, they would stand before the Lord and cry out in prayer. He rehearsed before the Lord what their enemies had done and were now doing- -trying to destroy them. He ends with these words, *"O our God, will you not judge them? For we have no power to face this vast army that is attacking us. We do not know what to do, but our eyes upon you."* The prophets told the people to go against the enemy saying, *"Do not be afraid or discouraged because of this vast army. For the battle is not yours, but the Lord's."* Jehoshaphat told the people to listen to the prophets and appointed men to sing to the Lord. When they sang the Lord sent ambushes against the enemy. At the end of the battle, everyone returned to Jerusalem joyfully. They rejoiced over the defeat of their enemies. They entered the temple with harps and lutes and trumpets. Fear came upon all the other kingdoms when they heard how the Lord had helped Jehoshaphat and the people. They then had peace and the Lord gave them rest. This was revival.

Leadership Principles

1. Get rid of sin.
2. Call on the Lord.
3. Delegate responsibility.
4. Start singing and praise the Lord.

HEZEKIAH

Hezekiah was one of the greatest kings of Israel. He came from a wicked family. His father was the wicked King Ahaz. Ahaz was involved with Canaanite worship with the sacrificing of children. Hezekiah became king at the age of 25. By the grace of God, he did what was right in the eyes of the Lord. I believe it was the prophet Isaiah who led him to the Lord and mentored him. Isaiah's conversion and call by God are described in Isaiah 6. I believe Hezekiah had a similar experience. Isaiah saw the Holy God (Isaiah 6). He saw himself as a sinner (woe to me), was touched by a burning coal (touched by grace) and said, *"Here I am Lord, send me."*

II Kings 18 tells the story about what Hezekiah did in obedience to God and how God brought revival. 1. Hezekiah had a passion for God. God put His fire in Him. 2. He purged sin, getting rid of idols. 3. He put into practice the whole word of God, holding fast to the Lord. 4. He restored temple worship and reconstituted the Passover providing the provision of God for the atonement for sin. 5. He sent couriers around the country to tell the people to return to God and to return to Jerusalem to celebrate the Passover. 6. He praised and worshipped God. 7. He prayed with Isaiah against Senacherib. We can apply each of these things used by God to bring revival in Hezekiah's time to our own lives.

Leadership Principles

1. Get the fire of God.
2. Get rid of sin.
3. Be committed to the Word of God.
4. Preach Jesus Christ and Him crucified.
5. Praise the Lord.
6. Pray against your enemies.

Josiah was 8 years old when he became king and he reigned for 31 years. He did what was right before the Lord. He sought the Lord and began to purge Judah and Jerusalem of high places, Asherah poles, carved idols and cast images. He repaired the temple of God. He delegated the work to his Levites and laborers. As they were repairing the Temple, they found the Book of the Law. Hilkiah, the priest was the one who found it. King Josiah tore his robe and inquired about what was written in the book.

God said that he would bring disaster if they did not obey the word of God. Josiah read the Bible before the people. He renewed the covenant before them... He had all the people pledge their allegiance to the covenant, and he removed all the idols from Israel.

He also brought back the celebration of the Passover which not been celebrated since the time of Samuel. He died in battle and all Judah mourned his death. While he reigned, there was peace and success.

Leadership Principles

1. Be devoted to God.
2. Get rid of idols.
3. Build for the glory of God and delegate responsibility.
4. Dedicate your life to know and obey the Word.

NEHEMIAH

Many pastors have studied and preached on the book of Nehemiah especially when they were in the midst of a big project like a building a building or a campaign. The principles are good ones for all who want to be better managers or administrators. Nehemiah was a true leader.

When he heard that the city of Jerusalem was in ruins, he sat down and wept. He heard that the walls were down, the temple was destroyed, and the people were discouraged. Nehemiah prayed and fasted. Then, when he took wine to the king (he was the king's cupbearer), the king saw that he looked sad and asked what was wrong. Nehemiah told him about Jerusalem and asked if he could go to Jerusalem and rebuild it.

He got the permission and started to organize the people to rebuild all the walls. Of course, he had to deal with opposition and ridicule. We can all expect this as we attempt to do a great work of God. Expect Satanic attack and keep praying.

The people got to work and persevered. They worked with swords beside them so they would be ready to fight if attacked. They also contributed to the material needs to build the wall. The wall was completed in 52 days.

Nehemiah then assembled everyone to register them by families. Later, all the people assembled and asked Ezra to read the Law of Moses before them.   The people stood for the reading of the Law then bowed down and worshiped the Lord with their faces to the ground. There was weeping as they heard the Word. The Word brought conviction and people began to weep for their sins. This is the beginning of revival. Nehemiah told them to not weep but to eat and rejoice in the Lord. He said the joy of the Lord was their strength. So, there was a great celebration.

They celebrated the feast of Tabernacles. There was joy all over. In Nehemiah 9 we see national confession of sin. They spent a quarter of the day reading the Word of God, and another quarter of the day confessing and worshiping. This is the fruit of a true revival. God uses prayer and the Word. In this chapter they prayed and reviewed all that God had done for them. After praying this they made a vow of faithfulness to the Lord.. The book continues with accounts of more thanksgiving, singing, joy and reforms.

Leadership Principles

1. Observe the situation and pray.
2. Be bold to approach authorities.
3. Ask God for a vision.
4. We need passion to persevere.
5. Read the Word, confess sins, repent, and rejoice.

Another great revival took place in the book of Acts in the church at Jerusalem. Christ said that his disciples would be filled with the Holy Spirit and that they would be witnesses in Jerusalem, Judea, Samaria, and the uttermost parts of the earth. The apostles and others joined together constantly in prayer. The Holy Spirit descended on the believers on the Day of Pentecost.

Peter preached and 3000 came to the Lord. This was a great revival. They continued to be in the Word, to be in prayer, to fellowship and to celebrate the Lord's supper.
God continued to add to the church. There was great preaching with boldness and a wonderful spirit of love and unity in the church.

Leadership Principles

1. Be filled with the Spirit.
2. Persevere in prayer.
3. Preach boldly.
4. Go back to the basics—the Word, prayer, fellowship, and witness.

Revival has been defined in many ways. It is God awakening His people from spiritual slumber. It is a people saturated with God. It is restoration to normality from an abnormal spiritual condition. In the previous section we have looked at revivals in the Bible and their leaders. I have been fascinated by the study of revivals in church history. II Chronicles 7:14 says this, *"If My people who are called by My Name shall humble themselves and pray and turn from their wicked way, then I will hear their prayer and heal their land."*

Here are some significant movements of God.

JOHN AND CHARLES WESLEY AND GEORGE WHITEFIELD

John & Charles Wesley

In a time of great spiritual and moral decline in the 18th century in England, there was also a laxity in the clergy. God raised up three great men. It was part of the Wesleyan Revival or "Great Awakening" with John and Charles Wesley and George Whitefield.

The revival spread through the British Isles and America. In the 1730's the Wesley brothers gathered students together to pray and study the Word. They wanted to live a life of holiness. They fasted and prayed. They also spent time in America preaching the Gospel. They joined up with George Whitefield. They preached the doctrine of immediate salvation.

They began to preach outside the church both in big meetings and as they travelled around by horse.

Whitefield was the great evangelist and John Wesley the great organizer. Whitefield had one goal and that was to win souls. He was called the "Awakener" and the "The Fire-Bringer." He preached with fervor in London and Bristol. I have seen the fields and churches where he preached.

He preached with great anointing and thousands came to faith but he also had much opposition. This is normal. When you preach Christ you will suffer persecution (II Timothy 3:12). His message was about being born again. He revealed his view of salvation when asked how many people had come to the Lord during a campaign.

He said, "I do not know, we will see next year." He wanted to see fruit in their lives. One time he was told, "Mr. Whitefield, you talk about being born again all the time."

He then asked, "Are you born again?"

They said, "No."

Mr. Whitefield said, "I will continue to talk about being born again until you are born again."

Mr. Whitefield also had a great burden for children and set up orphanages in America.

Leadership Principles

1. Be born again and preach about the new birth.
2. Have a vision to reach the world.
3. Be bold and be clear in the presentation

JONATHAN EDWARDS

Another great instrument of revival in America was Jonathan Edwards, a great pastor during the 18th century in New England. He was a great man of God who spent time in prayer and preached the truth about God's justice and compassion. He was a Calvinist.

Sometimes he would come to preach and people would weep in the seats before the preaching even began. This was the result of prayer. He also preached a great sermon called, "Sinners in the Hands of an Angry God." He described us as hanging over a fire like a spider. We are on the verge of hell and must confess sin and repent.

Leadership Principles

1. Be much in prayer.
2. Be bold in preaching the truth about sin, hell, and the redemption we have in Christ.

"How can you expect to dwell with God forever,
if you so neglect and forsake Him here?"
Jonathan Edwards

"Being sensible that I am unable to do anything without God's help, I do humbly entreat Him by His grace to enable me to keep these resolutions so far as they are agreeable to His will, for Christ's sake."
Jonathan Edwards

CHARLES FINNEY

In the mid 1880's God raised up a lawyer turned evangelist. He came to Christ and then began to preach Jesus. He was bold and had a lawyer's directness. He prayed much and had people praying for him. Father Nash, who was a pastor, and Abel Clary, a layman, followed Finney and when the evangelist spoke, they were in a room praying for him. As a preacher he was all over the place and God moved in the hearts of people.

As he preached, he was known to invite people to the alter or mourning room to examine their lives before a holy God. He also founded Oberlin college. This became a base for him.

In summary, some people object to Finney because he was an Arminian as opposed to a Calvinist. Arminians place emphasis on the need to repent of sins and turn to Jesus. He was often criticized by a Calvinistic preacher named Ashatel Nettleton.

Leadership Principles

1. Be much in prayer.
2. Have a vision to reach people.

"There can be no revival when Mr. Amen and Mr. Wet-Eyes are not found in the audience."
Charles Grandison Finney

"A state of mind that sees God in everything is evidence of growth in grace and a thankful heart."
Charles Grandison Finney

FOURTH GREAT AWAKENING

From 1857-59 God began a movement of revival harvest in the United States that spread throughout the British Isles. Dr. J. Edwin Orr named this the Fourth Great Awakening (*Revival Fire* by Wesley Duewel). It was all started by prayer. God used Charles Finney as an instrument for this revival. His book, Lectures on Revival, sparked the flame. Revival broke out throughout America.

In New York city God raised up a simple businessman named Jeremiah Lamphier to ignite a flame of revival. He felt led to begin a weekly noon-time prayer meeting at a Dutch Reformed Church. During the first meeting he was alone at first but later six others joined him.

The next week there were twenty people there to pray. A week after that the number reached 40. They decided to meet every day.

A week later there were 100 people present. One month later, other pastors began similar meetings in their churches. Within 3 months all America had prayer meetings for revival. By the end of March six thousand were meeting in prayer just in New York City. Revival broke out where there was the sovereign work of the Holy Spirit and the obedience of God's people. It was a revival of prayer, not preaching. Fifty-thousand people were converted. Later on, there were 100,000 people converted.

The fruit of this revival was unity. People did not think of their denominations. It was only Jesus. How we need this today. We need to be humble and come to the Lord in brokenness. There was revival during the Civil War. General Robert E. Lee and General Stonewall Jackson, devout Christians, encouraged the revival. Over 150,000 soldiers were converted, both Unionists and Confederates.

Leadership Principles

1. Start with prayer.
2. Persevere in prayer.
3. Expect God to work.

WELSH REVIVAL

The Welsh Revival of the early 1900's was not a revival of preaching or evangelism. It was ignited by brokenness and prayer. In February 1904 a young girl in New Quay, Wales stood up and said, " I love Jesus Christ with all of my heart." The believers asked the Lord to raise up someone to usher in the revival.

That man was Evan Roberts. He was a young man of prayer. At first, he was a coal miner but then was filled with the Holy Spirit and began to pray and encourage others to do likewise. His prayer was, "Bend us Lord." He began to pray for 100,000 soul to be saved. God began to work.

Roberts emphasized 4 things:
1. Confess openly and fully any unconfessed sin;
2. Put away from your life anything doubtful;
3. Obey promptly anything the Spirit tells you to say and do;
4. Confess Christ openly.

At his meeting there was a sense of the presence and holiness of God. Bars were emptied. Mules did not know what to do because their owners did not curse them anymore. People began to sing all over. The jails were empty. It was a revival of prayer and singing, verse sharing and exhortation. Revival spread. Evans emphasized, "Bend the church and save the world."

In Oct. 1932 Roberts wrote: *"My work is confined to prayer, and it is to such that I have devoted myself for the last 25 years... I work as hard at prayer as if I had undertaken any other form of religious work. By preaching I would reach the limited few-- by and through prayer I can reach the whole of mankind for God."* He knew the challenge of spiritual warfare and coauthored a book with Mrs. Penn-Lewis, *War on the Saints.* The emphasis was on being filled with the Spirit.

Together with my wife Billie and my daughter we visited the Moriah Chapel where Evan Roberts ministered and where he is buried. We even stayed at a bed and breakfast which was the home of Evan Roberts. What a delight. We took a tour of the chapel and sang with some of the local folk the main song of the revival - *Here is Love.* Here are the words.

Here is love, vast as the ocean,
Lovingkindness as the flood,
When the Prince of life, our
Ransom, Shed for us His
precious blood. Who His love will
not remember? Who can cease
to sing His praise?
He can never be forgotten
Throughout Heav'n's eternal
days.

On the mount of crucifixion,
Fountains opened deep and
wide; Through the floodgates of
God's mercy Flowed a vast and
gracious tide. Grace and love,
like mighty rivers, Poured
incessant from above. And
Heav'n's peace and perfect
justice Kissed a guilty world in
love.

Leadership Principles

1. Confess sins and pray.
2. Sing for joy.
3. Be obedient to the Holy Spirit.
4. Be aware of Spiritual Warfare and fight the good fight of faith.

In II Timothy 2:19-22, Paul shares with Timothy two pictures of the life of a true disciple. They are pictures of a vessel and of a servant. As a vessel we are to be pure and holy, prepared by God to do His work. God wants to use us as clean vessels. God can also use us as we are gentle servants faithfully praying and teaching the Word. God can use this to grant repentance and deliver people from the snare of the devil.

I am reminded of what God did in the revival in the Hebrides off of Scotland. Many Christians were praying for revival. One pastor, Rev. James Murray, prayed for a great outpouring of the Holy Spirit. In a small cottage lived two elderly sisters. Peggy Smith was 84 and blind, and her 82 year old sister Christine was afflicted with arthritis. They were unable to attend worship but spent time praying for revival in Barvas, their little village in the Hebrides. They prayed for their neighbors and their church.

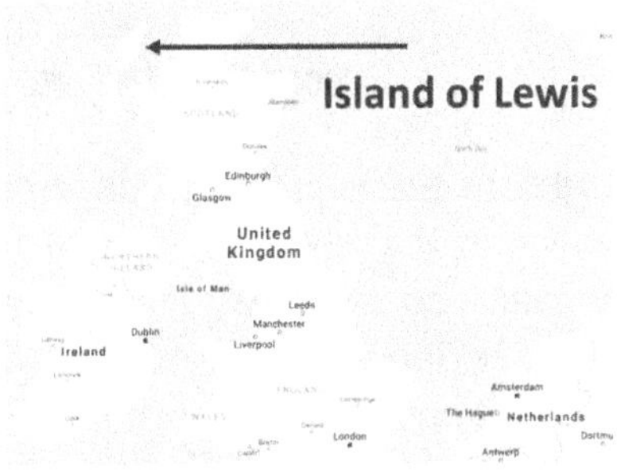

Another group of young men from another side of Barvas, were also praying for revival. They took encouragement from the verse in Isaiah 62:6-7, *"I have posted watchmen on your walls, O Jerusalem; they will never be silent day or night, You who call on the Lord, give yourselves no rest, and give him no rest till he establishes Jerusalem and makes her the praise of the earth."* They continued to persist in prayer.

One night a young deacon shared this verse with the group, *"Who may ascend the hill of the Lord? Who may stand in his holy place? He who has clean hands and a pure heart... He will receive blessings from the Lord."* (Psalm 24). The deacon examined his own life and asked the Lord if his hands and heart were pure. He encouraged the group to get right with God and cleanse their own hearts.

Duncan Campbell with Peggy and Christine Smith

God sent the evangelist Duncan Campbell and used him to spark the revival in the Hebrides. One of his assistants was a teenager named Donald who came to the Lord and helped Campbell in his work. The whole region became saturated with the presence of God.

I have known about this revival and the two elderly sisters who prayed. However, I discovered something that blew my mind and greatly encouraged by soul. These two elderly sisters had a niece named Mary. Mary emigrated to the USA and met a man named Fred. They married and had children. Do you know who one of their sons was? Yes, President Donald Trump. In fact, the young man in the revival, Donald, was the cousin of Mary. Could it be that she named Donald after her cousin?

What can I say? Certainly, God has a purpose for this and these prayers for revival had an effect years later.

Leadership Principles

1. Be in prayer at all times.
2. Expect God to do a great thing.

As Christian leaders we can learn much from the business world, the sport world, and the military world. In fact, the Bible uses illustrations from these worlds. I remember when Howard Hendricks spoke at a leadership conference in the Philadelphia area. He spoke of Biblical principles of leadership as well as principles we can learn from others and mentioned companies like Disney. He also said the Christian Ministry, Focus on the Family, was a good example of a well-run organization. He then spoke of Willow Creek Church under the leadership of Bill Hybels as a good example of an innovative, growing church. I had a chance to visit all of these and note the principles that were behind their success. I would like to mention some great men who were examples in different areas of human enterprise that we can learn from.

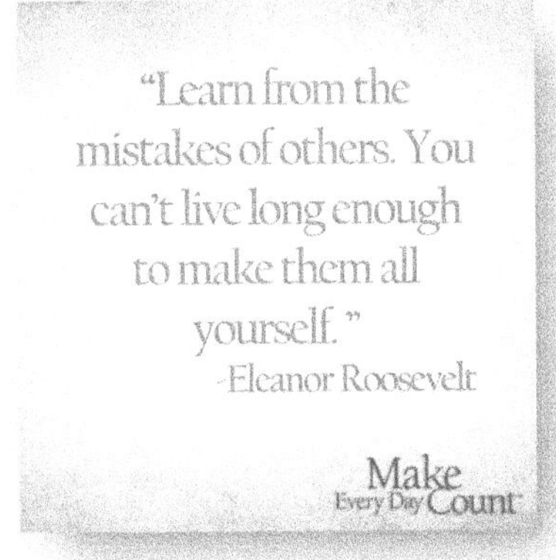

MODELS FROM THE BUSINESS WORLD

The (Walt Disney Company

I have been to Disney Land and Disney World on several occasions. It has been a memorable occasion and of course, reminded me of my life as a child watching the Mickey Mouse Club - it was so wonderful. Kids and parents are brought back into a fantasy world that is beyond imagination. Even the Epcot Center educates us about other countries around the world. This was the fulfillment of the dream of Walt Disney, a true innovator and entrepreneur.

Principles of Leadership and Success from Disney

1. It is extremely well organized.
2. The staff are very friendly and ask you where you are from, etc..
3. They keep the place very clean.
4. They are innovative and utilize the quality of imagination.

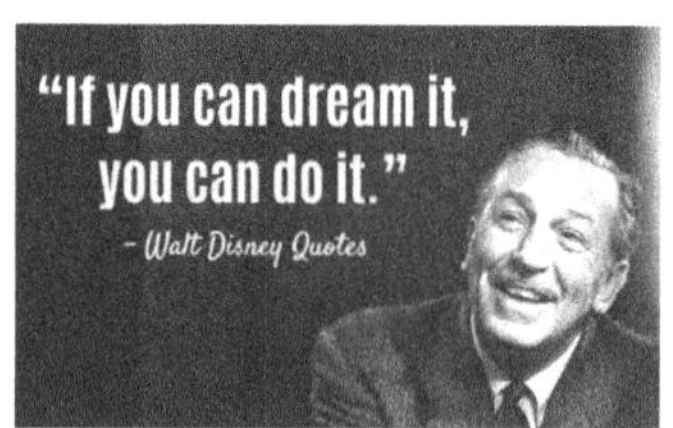

"We keep moving forward, opening new doors and doing new things, because we're curious and curiosity keeps leading us down new paths." Walt Disney

 COOPERATION

This company was cofounded by the DeVos family who are believers. The cooperation is built on Christian principles. Of course, they sell excellent products for the household and other things. They are built on personal contacts selling and recruiting people to be on your team. They also have weekly sales meetings with worship and Bible preaching. Even non-believers are ministered to. I met a Jewish man in my hometown who was an Amway salesman who spoke very highly about the enthusiasm of the Christians he met at their sales meetings.

Principles of Leadership and Success from Amway

1. Sell great products.
2. Build great teams.
3. Enthusiasm for the whole company.

"It is impossible to win the race unless you venture to run, impossible to win the victory unless you dare to battle."

"If you wait until you know everything, you'll never know anything."

Everyone in America knows about Chick-fil-A. They are known to be a company whose founder - S. Truett Cathy (1921-2014) was a Christian. Their board prays before every meeting. They keep the restaurants closed on Sunday. They often are public about their Biblical stands and sometimes get boycotted. In spite of the boycotts they continue to thrive. Just go to a food court in a mall and you will see that the longest line is at Chick Fil-A. It is good food and the service is great. The staff will greet you and help you and serve you at the table if you want. Even during the Corona crisis, they had home delivery with great service and a friendly smile.

Principles of Leadership and Success from Chick Fillet

1. Stick to Biblical principles.
2. Commit to an excellent product. Their chicken sandwiches are scrumptious.
3. They are servants to all. Totally client oriented.
4. They donate to charities around the world.

HOBBY LOBBY

Hobby Lobby is a home goods and craft store. It was begun by the Green family. They are born again believers who, like Chick Fil-A, seek to build their company on Biblical principles. They are also closed on Sundays.   They have excellent products and service. And also contribute to worthy causes like the building of the Museum of the Bible in Washington, D.C.

Principles of Leadership and Success from Hobby Lobby

1. Base the company on Christian Principles.
2. Sell a great needy product of proven quality.
3. Be client oriented.
4. Contribute to worthy charities and causes.

I'M PRETTY POSITIVE THAT HOBBY LOBBY PUTS SOME KIND OF POTION IN THEIR AIR VENTS THAT MAKES YOU LOSE TRACK OF TIME AND PURCHASE A RIDICULOUS AMOUNT OF THINGS I DIDN'T INTEND ON BUYING.

Today I saved $189.98 because Hobby Lobby is closed on Sunday.

"There is a God, and he's not averse to business. He's not just a "Sunday deity." He understands margin and spreadsheets, competition and profits."

David Green, Hobby Lobby founder.

GREAT SPORT LEADERS

The Apostle Paul, I am sure, was interested in sports. He used many analogies from the sporting world. We are to run the race of faith. We are to fight the good fight of faith. We wrestle against spiritual forces in the heavenly places. We can learn from sport leaders both Christian and non-Christian. Here are some spiritual role models.

JOHNNY WOODEN

Johnny Wooden was the coach of the college basketball team, the UCLA Bruins. His team holds the record for the most championships in university basketball in the USA. Mr. Wooden was a committed Christian who taught great principles. He felt that we win when we do our best using our full potential. He believed in setting the example. If the team stayed in a three star hotel, he stayed in one. I had a chance to meet him in March of 1970 as his team was playing in the final four at my university. I went away very inspired.

TIM TEBOW

Tim Tebow is the son of missionaries to the Philippines. He dedicated his life to Christ as a young man. He played American football at the University of Florida and became a Heisman Trophy winner. He went on to play professional American football. He was known to put Bible verses under his eyes to reduce the glare from the sun as he played. He spoke openly about his faith and also went on various mission trips.

TONY DUNGY

Tony Dungy was a former player and coach in the American football league. He coached the Indianapolis Colts to a championship in the Super Bowl. He is an outstanding Christian leader who speaks often of his faith.

GREAT SECULAR SPORT LEADERS

MIKE DITKA

Mike Ditka, a former Defensive End who won the Super Bowl three times, was the legendary coach of the Chicago Bears. He was tough and he emphasized the basics. He was once interviewing for the coach's position at Chicago. George Halas was the owner. Mr. Halas asked him, "What is your philosophy of football?"
Mike responded, "Mr. Halas, it is the same as yours. Just kick the other guys rear-end!" (euphemism).   He got the job.

TONY VERDUCCI

Tony Verducci was the legendary coach at Seton Hall Prep in New Jersey. He was the coach of the decade from 1960-1970. My two cousins played for him. He was tough and inspirational. His favorite slogan was, "*You gotta move. If you don't move, you lose.*"

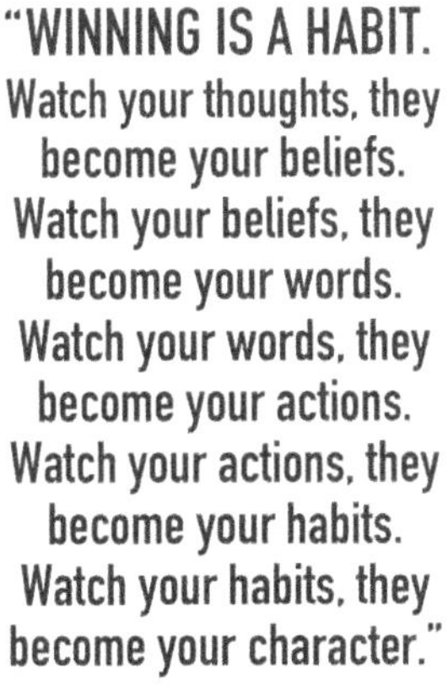

VINCE LOMBARDI

Vince Lombardi is the legendary American football coach of the Green Bay Packers. He was a tough disciplinarian having been in a Jesuit School and coaching at West Point. He emphasized the basics. One time after a bad game he told his players, "Let us go back to the basics. This is a football. Gentlemen, we will now learn again how to pass, run, and tackle."
He is quoted often, especially this phrase,

"Winning isn't everything, it is the only thing."

Lessons on leadership from the sport world

1. Keep you eye on the goal.
2. Be disciplined.
3. Get back to the basics.
4. Be a servant.
5. Work for the team.

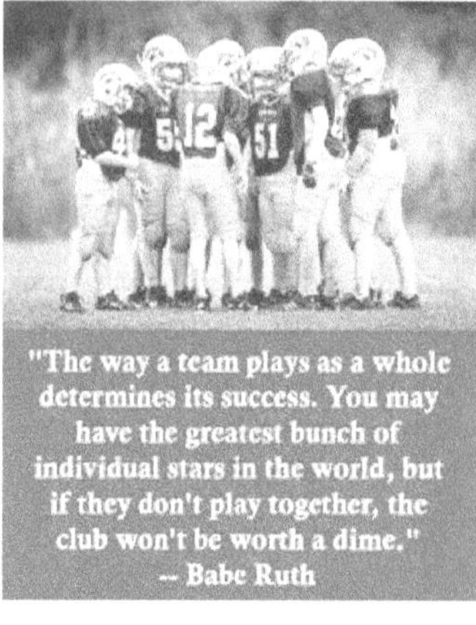

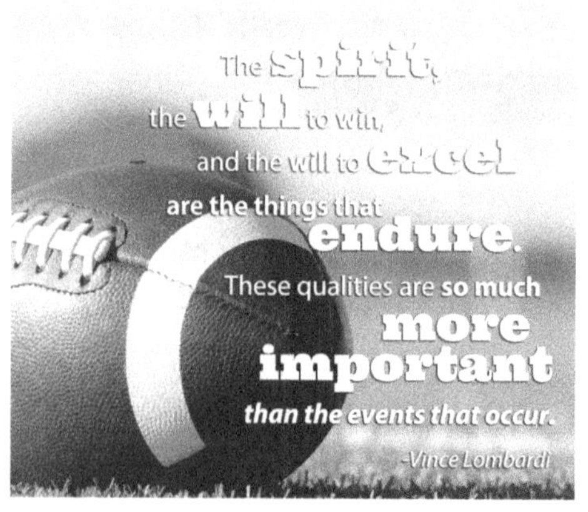

GREAT MILITARY LEADERS

The Bible gives us various illustrations from the military. We are in spiritual warfare. We are fighting not against flesh and blood, but against forces of darkness (Eph. 6:10). We are to be good soldiers of Jesus Christ (II Timothy 2). We can learn from some great military leaders.

GIUSEPPE GARIBALDI

General Garibaldi was an Italian general who united Italy and fought against Austria.   At one time he was a mercenary soldier and even Abraham Lincoln wanted to hire him to lead the Union Army. He was famous for challenging men with these words, "If you want to follow me, I offer you blood, sweat, tears, and death. Who will come?" Men volunteered and became known as the red shirts.   My great grandfather was one of them.

GENERAL DOUGLAS MCARTHUR

General McArthur was a Christian man who led the US forces in Asia during World War 11.   He is known for his declaration to the Philippine People, "I shall return."   When he came back, he said, "Philippine people, I have returned."   At the end of the war he suggested that 1000 missionaries should be sent to Japan.   He saw there was only one solution for man's problem, the message of Jesus Christ.

GENERAL GEORGE PATTON

George Patton is a well-known general who was feared by all during World War 11. His nickname was 'Old Blood and Guts'.   He is well known for his pearl-handled revolver.   He is also known for rallying the troops to defeat the Germans in several campaigns, especially the Battle of the Bulge.   He was known to lead from the front and was able to inspire his troops with his colorful speeches.   His rapid and aggressive offensive action proved very effective.   He is known for this quote when he was in battle, "I love it."   He was born for battle.

GENERAL SOBIESKI

General Sobieski was a Polish General who came down to Vienna Austria to push back the Turkish Muslims from invading Europe. Instead of saying like Caesar, *Vieni, vedi, vinci* (I came, I saw, I conquered). He said instead, *veni, vedi, deo vinci* (I came, I saw, but God won). He believed in the power of God. He went on to become the King of Poland.

WINSTON CHURCHILL

I call Churchill a military man. He was in the military and wore a military uniform during his time as prime minister. He rallied England as they were attacked by the Germans. He said, we will fight on the beaches, in the cites, in the country. We will never, never, never quit.

Lessons from these Military Leaders

1. Commit to be a good soldier in Christ.
2. Fight the good fight of faith with prayer and preaching.
3. Do not be afraid of the enemy.

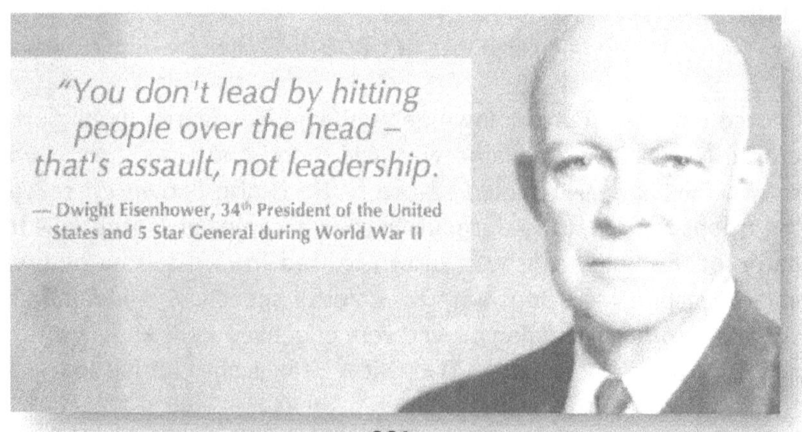

BROADCASTING EXCELLENCE

I include this section because certain broadcasters have inspired me to be a better communicator.

RUSH LIMBAUGH

Rush Limbaugh is perhaps the number one talk show host and radio commentator in the world. His views are conservative and very forth right. He is also very entertaining. He just won the American Freedom Award for his contribution to American patriotism. Just a side note: we share the same birthday and year - January 12, 1951.

SEAN HANNITY

Sean Hannity is a favorite talk show host on radio and on Fox News TV. He, like Rush Limbaugh, is conservative and to the point. He also is very friendly and engaging. Both Sean and Rush do their homework and are super prepared for any encounter.

OPRAH WINFREY

Oprah Winfrey is the quintessential TV talk show host. She is an Afro American and came from a poor and abused background. She worked hard and climbed up the broadcasting ladder of success. Her appeal is in her empathetic personality. You really see she feels for people. She is so friendly and authentic. You may not agree with her political positions, but you can agree she has appeal.

Lessons from the Broadcasting World

1. Be totally prepared. Study the material and work at your presentation.
2. Be yourself.
3. Identify with your audience.

One of the greatest lessons we can learn is the importance of following good examples. Jesus taught His disciples to follow Him. Paul said, *"Follow Me as I follow Christ."* Today we can study church history and learn about men of God who were used by God to influence people Godward. I would like to share some examples of these great men who have become mentors to me even though I do not know them well personally. Their lives, ministries, and books have impacted my life for good. Here they are and what we can learn from each one of them.

Dr. Graham has probably reached more people for Christ than any man in history. He is my spiritual father since I came to Christ at a Billy Graham Crusade in 1970. He is known to be a very humble man. He is bold and focused on the task of preaching the Gospel. He has been the adviser to many US Presidents. He had a great team surrounding him for fellowship and accountability.

Leadership Principles

1. Be humble.
2. Keep focused on God's purpose of reaching people with the Gospel.
3. Work with a team.

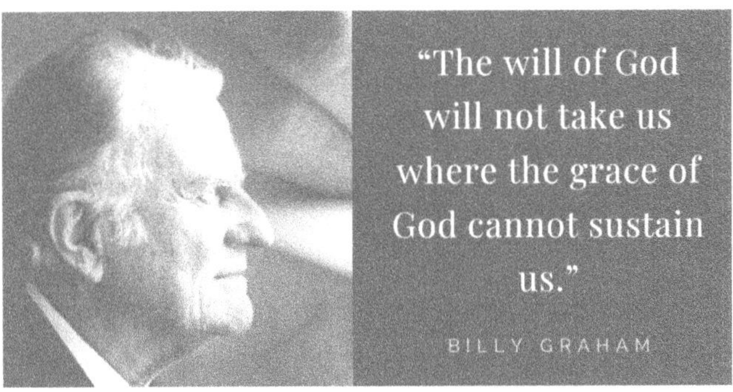

"We are not cisterns made for hoarding,
we are channels made for sharing."
Billy Graham

GEORGE VERWER

George Verwer is the founder and former head of Operation Mobilization, a mission organization with a thousand members scattered around the world serving the Lord. He comes from northern New Jersey and was a troublemaker in high school. An old lady in his town heard about George and prayed for him. She prayed for the whole high school, that God would save students and send them around the world to preach the Gospel. Verwer went to a Billy Graham Crusade in 1957 at Madison Square Garden and trusted Christ as his Savior. He went back to his high school and started a spiritual revolution. He went on to Moody Bible Institute and founded OM. I worked with OM for several years in Europe. We had OM teams stay with us in Italy. We also attended the Love Europe Conferences in the 1980's and were challenged to pray for the cities of Europe, outreach in Eastern Europe, and Muslims who came to Europe. These were the key targets of Love Europe. God did a great work.

Leadership Principles

1. Pray for the Lord of the Harvest to send forth laborers in the harvest field.
2. Be absolutely committed to Christ.
3. Have a vision for the world.

JOSH MCDOWELL

I met Josh McDowell at a retreat sponsored by Campus Crusade for Christ. He spoke about Jesus meeting the woman at the well and his message greatly impacted by life. His messages on the second coming gave me an urgency to preach the Gospel. He is a national speaker for CRU (the new name for Campus Crusade for Christ). He formerly ministered in South America where he boldly spoke for Christ to crowds of committed Communists. He has written books on apologetics. His books, Evidence that Demands a Verdict, and, More than a Carpenter, are classics. I also heard him speak on forgiveness in Iraq before thousands of people who needed this message. He shared his own experience of forgiving a man who took advantage of him.

Leadership Principles

1. Be committed to reaching the world for Christ.
2. Know what you believe and defend your belief.
3. Be bold in your witness.

"True love is spelled G-I-V-E. It is not based on what you can get, but rooted in what you can give to the other person."

"It is more rewarding to resolve a conflict than to dissolve a relationship."

Josh McDowell

AL MARTIN

Dr. Albert Martin is a reformed Baptist preacher who has greatly influenced many men of God around the world. He went to Columbia Bible College with my parents-in-law. Through his studies he came to a Calvinistic point of view.

I first came into contact with him in 1973. He had a great tape ministry. His series on the Sovereignty of God had a great impact on my life. His series on Pastoral Ministry based on I Timothy 4:16, has helped me so much. This verse says, *"Pay close attention to yourself and to your teaching, persevere in these things, for as you do this you will ensure salvation both for yourself and for those who hear you."*

As we work on our character and our teaching, we will be used by God to reach others. His booklet, What's Wrong with Preaching Today. has helped me understand my basic priorities. The problem with preaching today is either with the man or with his message. We need to work on ourselves and our message. We need pure lives and we must have pure doctrines. He has held several pastors' conferences to impart these principles and has also established the Trinity Ministerial Academy.

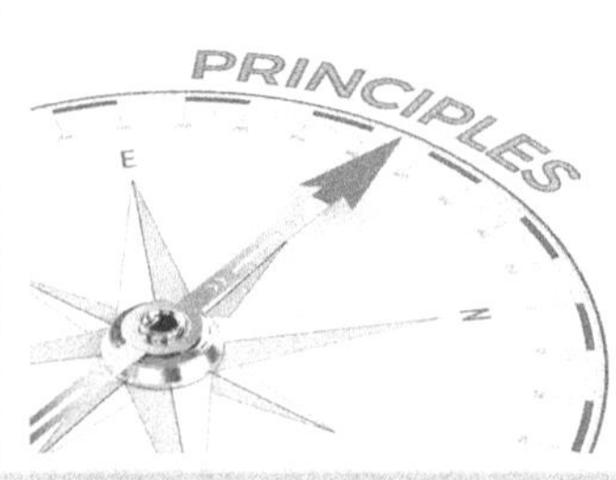

Leadership Principles

1. Be strong in your devotional life- Prayer and the Word.
2. Be bold in your preaching.
3. Seek holiness in your life.

JOHN MCARTHUR

Dr. John McArthur is known as the Charles Spurgeon of this generation. He is a godly, gifted, Bible teacher.
I have met him on several occasions and have attended two of his Shepherd's Conferences. His philosophy has guided my life. It is, "Be concerned with the depth of your ministry and God will take care of the breadth of your ministry." His basic concern is to understand God's Word, to live it, and to preach it. His series on the Anatomy of a Church has helped me in my church planting and church ministry in Europe and the Middle East. (In the section on coming together of the church, I have included his teaching on the Anatomy of a Church).
God has given him a wonderful expository ministry at his church and around the world. He also started The Master's College and Seminary to prepare young people for the ministry.

Leadership Principles

1. Give yourself to the Word.
2. Our ministry should be the overflow of our walk with God.
3. Preach boldly the Message of Christ

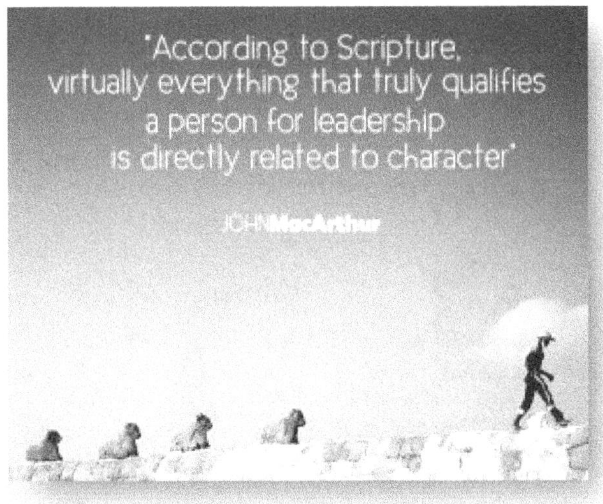

Billy Graham considers Stephen Olford to be his pastor. He is a man of God who has preached the Word and reached out to people with the Gospel. He pastored Calvary Baptist Church in New York City. While he was pastoring, he also spent the weekends doing open air preaching in the parks. He said that when Paul wrote to Timothy to preach in season and out of season (II Timothy 4), he meant preach inside the church and outside the church. He has done much preaching about revival and was the catalyst for a revival starting at Wheaton College.

Leadership Principles

1. Spend much time with God in prayer and meditating on His Word.
2. Be bold in your preaching,
3. Do open air preaching to enhance your ministry and to give fire to your proclamation.

"What God expects us to attempt, He also enables us to achieve."

Stephen F. Olford

John Maxwell is the number one authority in the world on leadership. He was also a pastor for many years and has helped pastors and leaders become more effective and successful. His books deal with subjects like motivation, teamwork, and having good attitudes. His seminars have helped both Christians and non-Christians.

Leadership Principles

1. Put a priority on relationships.
2. Work on your attitudes.
3. Improve your communication skills.
4. Study everything you can on leadership
5. Put an emphasis on personal development.

"The measure of a leader is not the number of people who serve him but the number of people he serves."

"A successful person finds the right place for himself. But a successful leader finds the right place for others."

John Maxwell

Howard Hendricks known as "Prof," was a professor at Dallas Seminary. I studied under him and took a minor in Christian Education just to take his courses. He taught Bible Study Methods, the Family, Discipleship, and other practical courses. He encouraged his students to go back to the basics. His series on communication and management are outstanding. The Leadership Institute at Dallas Seminary is named after him.

Leadership Principles

1. Be a contagious communicator.
2. Go back to the basics.
3. Be authentic

"The key to successful leadership today is influence, not authority."

"A good leader has a compass in their head and a magnet in their heart."

Howard G. Hendricks

LUIS PALAU

Luis Palau, from Argentina, is known as the Billy Graham of South America. His family were believers. His father died when Luis was a young man, so his mother took over. She encouraged her children to, *"seek first the Kingdom of God."* To her, that meant to go out and preach the Gospel and start churches. My wife and I had the opportunity to meet Dr. Palau at his headquarters in the summer of 2019 and were able to pray and share with him. I had met him while I was a student at Dallas Seminary when he spoke at our missions conference there. He met with a group of six students (I was one of them) and prayed with us four hours. What a privilege! God spoke to my heart to go to the mission field at that conference, so it was a wonderful experience to meet him again so many years later. I also met him at an evangelistic meeting in Turin, Italy. He has preached all over the world and has a great burden for the big cities of the world.

Leadership Principles

1.	Seek first the Kingdom of God.
2.	Have a vision to reach the world.
3.	Go and preach the Gospel and plant churches.

"When you face the perils of weariness, carelessness, and confusion, don't pray for an easier life. Pray instead to be a stronger man or woman of God."

"God is not disillusioned with us. He never had any illusions to begin with. "

Luis Palau

Jim Cymbala is the pastor of the Brooklyn Tabernacle Church in Brooklyn NY. When he first arrived at the church, he was discouraged about how slowly the church was growing. God spoke to his heart. He felt God was telling him to give himself to prayer and to lead his church to do the same. He started a Tuesday night prayer meeting. Today, it is attended by thousands of people. He considers the prayer meeting to be the most important meeting of the church. Explosive growth resulted from this prayer emphasis.

Leadership Principles

1. Give yourself to prayer.
2. Be open to the Holy Spirit.
3. Honor the Lord.

"I discovered an astonishing truth. God is attracted to weakness. He can't resist those who humbly and honestly admit how desperately they need Him. Our weakness in fact makes room for His power."

"God nowhere asks anyone to have a large church. He only calls us to do His work, proclaiming His Word to people He loves under anointing power of the Holy Spirit to produce results that only He can bring about. "

Jim Cymbala

It is said that behind every great man is a great woman. Women are great influencers in this world. They raise children and they greatly influence their husbands. My wife shares this joke:

A mayor was walking around the town with his wife and as they passed a construction site, his wife said, "You know, I almost married that construction worker over there."
"Then you would have been married to a construction worker," the mayor quipped, to which his wife remarked, "No, if I had married him, he would have been the mayor."

Yes, women can make us or break us. I am thankful for the following women in my life who have greatly influenced me:

My mother, Mae Nucciarone

I thank God for my mother who taught me so much about life. She was faithful and diligent and a great cook. She built us up and was always proud of my sister and me. She had a good heart for people and had emotions which she could not hide. Sort of like me. She believed in God and decided to attend a Bible Study Fellowship class at a Baptist Church near our home. One day she called and said she had been born again. Praise God! I was able to share that testimony of her at her funeral.

My wife, Billie Nucciarone

I met Billie while we were summer missionaries in Rome, Italy in 1975. We were on the same music team. I played the mandolin and she played the ukulele. We came together as a couple three years later, got married, and headed off to Italy as missionaries. We had both prayed that God would give us believing spouses who loved Jesus and who wanted to serve the Lord overseas. Billie's parents were missionaries in Quito, Ecuador. I felt that I needed to marry a girl who came from a stable Christian home and God answered that prayer. My friends tell me that my wife keeps me in line. She is beautiful, tender, a great cook, wife, and homemaker and an outstanding mother.

My Daughters Libby, Emily and Allison

I thank God for my three daughters. Libby is married to Brandon and is the mother of four (Clare, Savannah, Ella Mae, and Beau). They live in Wheaton, Illinois. Emily is married to Seth and they have a son, Levi. They both serve here in Jerusalem. Allison, our third daughter, is living and working in Ghana, West Africa. All of them love Jesus. They all have musical gifts and were all good students and have tremendous leadership qualities.

Petra Van der Zande

Petra is a talented Dutch sister who is the Media Director at our church, the Jerusalem Baptist Church. She has written or edited and published over 40 books. She is an amazing lady who is a great servant of God. She encourages us all.

Irene Levi

In my opinion, Irene is the greatest saint in Jerusalem, and we are blessed to have her as a member of our church. She is 101 years old and still serving the Lord. She has been in Israel for over 70 years and is a great Bible teacher and Hebrew scholar. Psalm 92 says that "the righteous will bear fruit even in their old age." This is Irene. May her tribe increase. I pray we may all be like her and live long to serve Jesus.

The Bible teaches us much about our responsibility to teach and train others, especially for leaders. In the Old Testament, in Exodus 18, we have the story of Moses and his father-in-law, Jethro. Moses was overwhelmed with the work of teaching and judging the people. Jethro told Moses that he was doing too much. He would burn out. He told him to delegate the task of judging people to others and that Moses should be their representative before God. He should pray to God for them and teach them the Word. These men would be trained about how to do the judging.

Samuel, the prophet, began a school for prophets in Shiloh. Jesus Christ chose twelve disciples. His purpose was to be with them, teaching them and then to send them out to preach (Mark 3). He also modeled what He taught. After sending them out to preach, he gathered them again for review and evaluation (Matthew 10, Luke 9,10). Here are some good examples of pastors who have started training schools for future pastors and leaders.

CHARLES SPURGEON

Charles Spurgeon is known as the Prince of Preachers who preached in London in the 19th century. He was a prolific author. He also was concerned for training pastors. He developed Spurgeon's College. His book, *Lectures to My Students*, is a classic for those seeking to train others. In his book he deals with many subjects. It is summed up by emphasizing the minister's self-watch and his ministry.

When asked about studying German, Robert Murray McCheyne responded, *"It is good you want to study German, but what is more important is that you study yourself and keep yourself. Keep the sword sharp. A holy man is an awful instrument in the hands of the Lord."*

He also had an excellent section on soul winning and open-air preaching. Yes, a pastor must do the work of an evangelist. This gives fire to our ministry. In Southern Baptist Seminaries the evangelism department is called the "Chair of Fire." Very appropriate.

JERRY FALWELL SR.

Jerry Falwell Sr. is known for founding Thomas Roads Baptist Church and Liberty University. He was a great evangelist and sought to reach a city for Christ. He wrote the book, *Capture a Town for Christ*. It is quite inspiring. It comes from the book of Acts where the Apostles filled Jerusalem with their doctrine (Acts 2-5). It is also called saturation evangelism.

Liberty University has become the largest evangelical university in the United States. It also has a very sound theological seminary. At the beginning of the seminary the graduates would follow the example of the founder, Rev. Falwell, and go out and plant churches by faith.

JOHN MCARTHUR

John McArthur, the Spurgeon of today, has one passion. It is to know God through His Word and preach that Word so people will know God. His desire and focus is to know the truth and preach it. When a member wanted to start a tape ministry or radio ministry, he told them to do it. He just pursued the truth. When asked to take over a college, he did with the help of others and renamed it Master's College. On the campus of the church he began the Master's Seminary to train pastors.

Annually he has the Shepherd's Conference to inspire and train pastors around the world where 5000 gather. When I attended in 1985, there were 500 participants. Thirty years later it has reached 5000.

AL MARTIN

Al Martin can be called the spokesman for the Reformed Baptist. He is a godly man who developed an extensive tape ministry. His themes include the Sovereignty of God and Pastoral Ministry. God led him to start the Trinity Ministerial Academy out of his church Trinity Baptist Church in Montville, New Jersey. It was started to train men for the Gospel ministry. The academy taught all the normal courses a seminary would teach but with a Calvinistic, Reformed Baptist perspective. At the retirement of Rev. Martin, the academy came to a close. He now is writing a three-book series on Pastoral Ministry. Two are out already and one is coming. Very deep and convicting.

TEE: Theological Education by Extension

This is very popular, especially in the third world, where there are few opportunities for resident Bible College training. TEE brings the Bible and Theology training right to the pastors. The teacher travels to a site and teaches a course or courses for a limited time period like two weeks. I

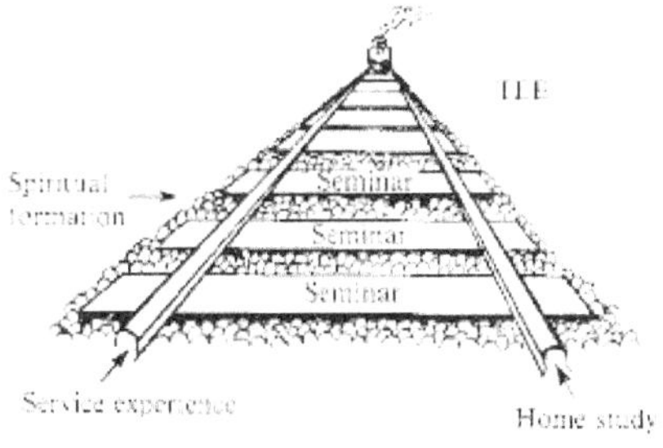

have personal experience with Biblical Education by Extension Eastern Europe. It began in Vienna, Austria where teachers would travel to Eastern Europe to teach pastors and leaders. Since the coming down of the Berlin Wall and the opening of Eastern Europe this type of training is less needed.

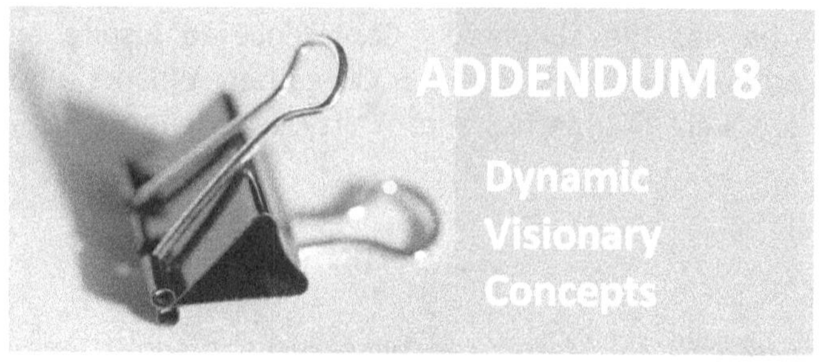

People like concepts put into simple terms that help them to focus and get them motivated. There have been a few concepts that have helped me understand God's purposes and our part in it.

BIBLICAL PERSPECTIVE

Jesus said that the law could be summarized like this: Love God and love your neighbor as yourself. This should be our goal.

CONVERSION, CONGREGATION, AND CONSOLIDATION

Dr. Charles Piepgrass, former associate director of Cross World, my former mission society, developed these definitions to help us understand our task in missions. Conversion has to do with our outreach and evangelistic efforts. Congregation means the planting of churches. Consolidation means the training of leaders to take over churches or institutes.

REACH UP, REACH IN, REACH OUT

Ray and Ann Ortland were speakers at an annual Christian workers conference in Italy that we attended every year. God used them greatly and revival resulted.   Dr. Ortland introduced us to a revolutionary but simple concept. He was a frustrated pastor and one time prayed to God slamming his pulpit and saying, "God make my life a miracle."

God gave him these concepts which are to be the main concern for the church:

1. We are to Reach Up to God
2. Reach into each other in love
3. Reach out to the world with love.

These are our priorities:

A. We must first worship God. We must get our lives in alignment with the Lord. Worship does that. Before we can reach men, we must reach God.

B. The second priority is to love each other (Reach In). He would state: "How can we reach the world if we lose each other?"

C. The third priority is to love the world by sharing the Gospel.

LOVE EUROPE

This concept was developed by Operation Mobilization in Europe. They had Love Europe conferences in Germany in 1986 through 1990. We attended while we were working in Italy. It gave me a burden for the whole continent of Europe.

The three emphases of Love Europe wereL

1. Reach the cities
2. Reach Eastern Europe
3. Reach Muslims in Europe.

We prayed during the conference that God would help us do these three things. The next year God had opened Eastern Europe and we were sending teams there, including Albania.

The Berlin Wall came down in 1991 (something we prayed for). As it worked out, God used this in my life and moved us to Vienna which became the centre of Europe as Eastern Europe became part of Europe.

We began week-long evangelistic campaigns called Reach the City, in Vienna. Then, we began to do the same in Poland, Slovakia, and Hungary. We ministered to Eastern Europeans in Vienna. We also had a ministry to Muslims. Iranians came to our church and wanted to know Christ. We baptized over 80 Iranian Muslims. We thank God for answering our prayers and using us to "Love Europe."

REACH THE CITY

This concept was popularized by Jerry Falwell who wrote the book, *Capturing a Town for Christ.* His desire was to reach a city with all means possible. This is called saturation evangelism. The Apostles were accused of filling Jerusalem with their doctrine (Acts 5:28). We began a 'Reach the City' campaign in the city of Vienna with the cooperation of Open Air Campaigners. It was Stephan Hoefler who came up with the name. It was an annual evangelism training seminar with time for practice during the week in the streets of Vienna.

WINNING, BUILDING, SENDING

This is the basic philosophy of Campus Crusade for Christ now called CRU. We first seek to win people to Christ.   Then we train and educate them (Discipleship). We then send them out to preach as Jesus did with His disciples.

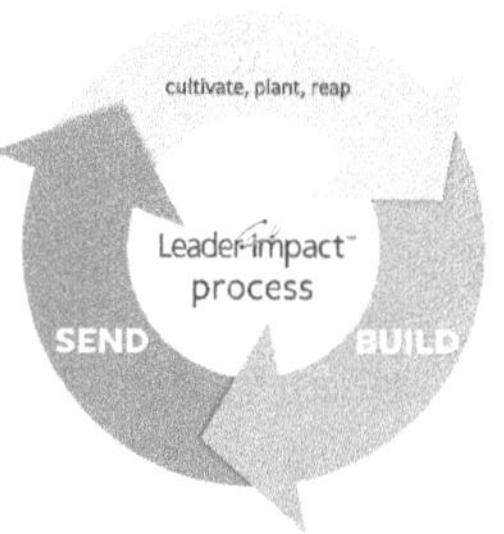

ENGAGE, EQUIP, EMPOWER

This is a concept that the Fellowship of Christian Athletes developed for their ministry. We engage people. We meet them and share the Gospel and our vision with them. Then we equip those who are willing. We also empower them by encouraging them and teaching them about the power of the Holy Spirit within them.

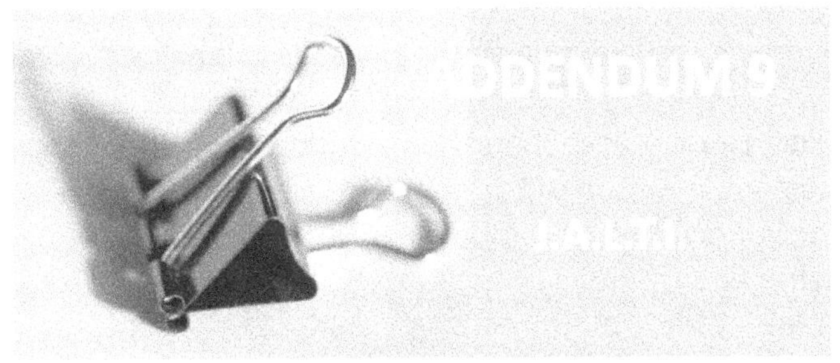

JERUSALEM ACADEMY for LEADERSHIP TRAINING INTERNATIONAL

My dream and vision is:

- To train international participants from the business, political, educational, military, sports and church world.
- To teach them to love the Land of the Bible
- To let them fall in love with Jerusalem
- To instruct them about the Bible and Theology
- To coach them on how to become better leaders

Each word in the institute's name stands for a concept:

- **Jerusalem** is our base.
- **Academy** is more than a school. It is an educational institute with a specific purpose.
- **Leadership** is our theme. We want to train leaders from all areas: business, sport, military, and churches.
- **Training** means more than teaching. It is teaching with practical application.
- **International** is our domain. We want to reach leaders from all over the world.

The Academy's curriculum encompasses the following subjects:

⇒ Mind, Heart, Hands (Knowledge, Attitudes, Skills)
⇒ Bible
⇒ Study, Pray, Preach
⇒ Hebrew
⇒ Greek
⇒ Theology Concepts
⇒ Church History
⇒ Attitudes: Love, Holiness, Patience
⇒ Skills: Preaching, Shepherding, Counseling, Evangelism

Pastors will act as regional coordinators for:

- USA
- Europe
- Africa
- India
- Philippines
- Spanish speaking nations
- Russian speaking nations
- Korea
- Middle East
- Australia and New Zealand
- Pacific Region: Micronesia, Polynesia and Melanesia

**For more information, please write
to email:**

jaltiorg@gmail.com

**Or go to website:
www. jalti.org**

SELECTED BIBLIOGRAPHY
And FURTHER READING

Principles of War: A Handbook on Strategic Evangelism by Jim Wilson
Publisher : Canon Press;
ISBN 0-912737-00-X

Lead on! Leadership that endures in a changing world by John Edmund Haggai
Publisher: Word Books
ISBN 0-8488-0544-3

One Hundred Bible Lessons by Alban Douglas by OMF Publishers 1966

A Handbook for Church Growth in Urban Italy by Al Nucciarone Doctor of Ministry Project.

Revival Fire by Wesley L. Duewel
Publisher: Zondervan.
ISBN 0-310-49661-6

The Soul Winner's Fire by John R. Rice
Copyright 1941 Moody Press
&Kessinger Publishing, LLC ISBN-10 : 1163165565

Good to Great: Why Some Companies Make the Leap and Others Don't by Jim Collins Publisher: Harper Business
ISBN 0-06-662099-6

One Hundred Bible Lessons by Alban Douglas by OMF Publishers Copyright 1966 (no ISBN)

Sermon Writer - Richard Donovan
https://sermonwriter.com/richard-niell-donovan/

Supernatural or just remarkable (medabrim.org)

The Indestructible Jews - By Max I. Dimont https://www.amazon.com/Indestructible-Jews-Max-I-Dimont-ebook/dp/B00KFU6S0G

What is wrong with preaching today – dr. Albert N. Martin
https://www.gracegems.org/29/whats_wrong_with_preaching_today.htm

Lord, make my life a miracle. Ray Ortland. Publisher : iUniverse (March 15, 2010) ISBN-10 : 1440197172

The golden path to successful personal soul winning. Dr. John R. Rice Sword of the Lord publishers 1961.
ISBN: 0873983068

The High Cost of Revival. Dr. John R. Rice - Publisher : Sword of the Lord (January 1, 1946) https://www.amazon.com/HIGH-COST-REVIVAL-John-Rice/dp/B000Z3QAY2

The Prayer of Jabez. Bruce Wilkerson. Multnomah; ISBN-10: 1590524756

Principles of war, thoughts of strategic Evangelism. Jim Wilson. Publisher: Canon Press. ISBN 1591280656

Way of a fighter – major general Claire Chennault. GP Putnam's sons. New York https://www.amazon.com/Way-Fighter-Memoirs-Claire-Chennault/dp/B001G8O5BK

Total Christian War –Howard Wyndham Guinness -S. John Bacon for Inter-Varsity Christian Fellowship, 1945

The way of the seal. Think like an elite warrior to lead and succeed – by Mark Divine. Reader's Digest; Updated, Expanded ed. edition (May 22, 2018) ISBN: 1621454037

Start-up Nation: The Story of Israel's Economic Miracle by Dan Senor and Saul Singer   Publisher : Twelve; ISBN: 0446541478

The Quick and Easy Way to Effective Speaking – Dale Carnegie. General Press (January 1, 2018) ISBN: 9387669033

How to Win Friends & Influence People - Dale Carnegie. Pocket Books (October 1, 1998) ISBN: 0671027034

Friendship evangelism by Floyd McClung YWAM

More Than a Carpenter by Josh D. McDowell & Sean McDowell- Tyndale Momentum; Revised edition (June 1, 2009) ISBN: 1414326270

Know Why you Believe – Paul Little – Inter Varsity Press; ISBN: 0830834222

The Late Great Planet Earth – Hal Lindsey - Publisher : Zondervan Academic (May 23, 1970) ASIN : 031027771X

The Grace Awakening: Believing in Grace Is One Thing. Living it Is Another. by Charles R. Swindoll Publisher : Thomas Nelson (February 3, 2012) ISBN: 0849911885

Lectures on Revival of Religion – Charles Grandison Finney - Bethany House Publishers, 1988 Publisher : CreateSpace Independent Publishing Platform (January 27, 2014) ISBN: 1495341763

Capturing a Town for Christ by Elmer L Towns (Author), Jerry Falwel (introduction) Publisher: Revell; ISBN: 0800706064

Great Soul-Winning Churches– by Elmer Towns. Publisher : Destiny Image Publishers (May 14, 2014) ISBN: 076840617X

The Middle East is in crisis. There is the threat of ISIS and other terrorist groups who have one objective: to dominate the world and get rid of Christians, Jews, and Muslims who do not believe exactly as they do.

In the twentieth century, Communism was the biggest challenge for the church. Today, it is Islam. How do we deal with this challenge? How can we have real peace in the Middle East? There is only one solution: the Gospel of Jesus Christ and a revived church that demonstrates the love of Christ. This book explores the revival and reformation principles that are exemplified in the life and ministry of King Hezekiah and encouraged by the prophet Isaiah. Today, more than ever, we need men and woman who have a passion for God and communicate that passion to others.

That is what revival is all about. And it starts at home.

ISBN: 9789657542040   Published June 2015
Paperback, 120 pages. Publisher: TsurTsina Publications

This book by Dr. Albert Nucciarone is a call to world revolution. We live in a decadent society that is on a collision course with God. The answer is the Gospel of Jesus Christ, Who was the greatest revolutionary of all time. Only He can change people, who, in turn, can influence society. More than ever, this world needs people with a revolutionary way of thinking and doing. Because we are involved in a spiritual conflict, believers must declare war against the forces of evil.

This Biblically based, biographical, and illustrative publication is a compilation of sermons I preached, articles I wrote and inspiring thoughts from others. The book can help leaders who are God's influencers in business, government, military, sports and the church. Because believers are called to a world revolution – God's Path to Total Victory – we all need a spark to inflame our hearts and souls.

ISBN: 978-965-7542-52-1   Published May 2017
Paperback, 232 pages Publisher: TsurTsina Publications

Many volumes on end time Biblical prophecies have been written by theologians and scholars. In his third book, Albert Nucciarone does not claim to be a theologian or a scholar. His interest in Biblical prophecy and seeing the signs of His coming, he is passionate to reach people with the good news of the Gospel of Jesus Christ.

Living and working in the Biblical Lands confirms the authenticity of the Bible and helps to understand its message. The living reality of Israel and the Jewish people are a sign of His soon coming. Pastor Al's study of the Bible, his interest in historical and current events, the prophecies being fulfilled before his eyes, prompts him to write this book. As a warning and encouragement to believers and non-believers alike:

Get ready for the soon return of Jesus the Messiah!

ISBN: 9789657542651   Published: May 2019
Paperback, 212 pages; Publisher: TsurTsina Publications